OTHER BOOKS BY CRAIG HAVIGHURST

Air Castle of the South:
WSM and the Making of Music City

MORE BOOKS FROM THE SAGER GROUP

*Meeting Mozart: A Novel Drawn from
the Secret Diaries of Lorenzo Da Ponte*
by Howard Jay Smith

*The Swamp: Deceit and Corruption in the CIA
An Elizabeth Petrov Thriller (Book 1)*
by Jeff Grant

Chains of Nobility: Brotherhood of the Mamluks (Book 1-3)
by Brad Graft

Death Came Swiftly: Novel About the Tay Bridge Disaster of 1879
by Bill Abrams

A Boy and His Dog in Hell: And Other Stories
by Mike Sager

Eat Wheaties: A Novel
by Michael Kun

Goodbye, Sweetberry Park: A Novel
by Josh Green

Lifeboat No. 8: Surviving the Titanic
by Elizabeth Kaye

Hunting Marlon Brando: A True Story
by Mike Sager

The Sing Sing Follies (A Maximum-Security Comedy): And Other True Stories
by John H. Richardson

Who She Was: My Search for my Mother's Life
By Samuel G. Freedman

See our entire library at TheSagerGroup.net

MUSICALITY
FOR MODERN HUMANS

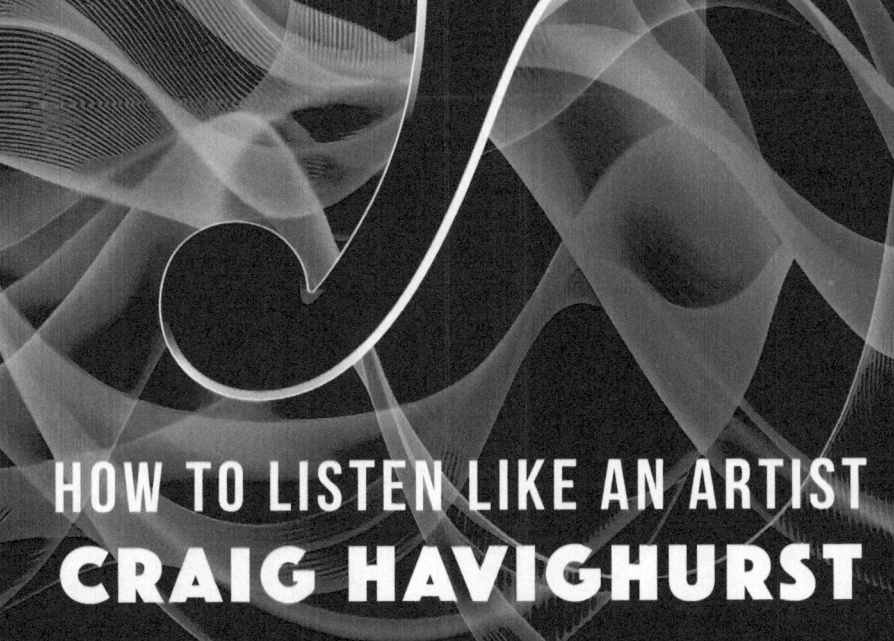

HOW TO LISTEN LIKE AN ARTIST
CRAIG HAVIGHURST

Musicality For Modern Humans: How to Listen Like an Artist

© 2025 Craig Havighurst

Cover and interior design by Siori Kitajima, PatternBased.com

Cataloging-in-Publication data for this book
is available from the Library of Congress.
ISBN-13:
eBook: 978-1-958861-82-0
Paperback: 978-1-958861-83-7
Hardcover: 978-1-958861-84-4

Published by The Sager Group LLC
(TheSagerGroup.net)

MUSICALITY
FOR MODERN HUMANS

HOW TO LISTEN LIKE AN ARTIST
CRAIG HAVIGHURST

THE SAGER GROUP

Artifex Te Adiuva

"If it sounds good and feels good, then it IS good!"
- attributed to Duke Ellington

" You've got to dig it to dig it, you dig?"
- Thelonious Monk

Dedicated to the Havighursts and the Kitchens, the families who showed me a musical path.

The author has created playlists of works mentioned in or inspired by this book at the major streaming services. To find them, search *Musicality For Humans* at your streaming service of choice, or visit CraigHavighurst.com for links to the lists at Tidal, Apple Music, and Spotify.

To keep in touch with news and commentary about *Musicality For Modern Humans* and its themes, please follow Craig's *String Theories* journal at: stringtheories.substack.com

CONTENTS

MOVEMENT

I don't remember much about what happened before or after, but I remember the chords and the goose bumps. I believe the year was 1982, making me about 16. Few were the rewards for a late-blooming violin student in a private school. But I'd suddenly found one.

I had auditioned for and been selected by the North Carolina All-State Youth Orchestra. And here we were, in Greensboro, rehearsing in a school auditorium. I remember riding there from Durham in a bus with my fellow string nerds.

The piece on the music stands was the orchestral suite from *Der Rosenkavalier*, Opus 59, by Richard Strauss. The open is dominated by brassy fanfares that are answered by the strings (that was us). Then we took over, leading a lush and sweeping theme, setting up punchy, dramatic blasts from, of all people, the typically introverted French horns.

Then it hits me. About two and a half minutes in, the music turns delicate and swanlike, and we violinists are doing our best to not stand out or be too loud or, heaven forbid, make an errant squeak at a time like this. And my body changed. I tingled, neck to knees, and my hair stood up with a thrilling frisson. When I listen to this passage now, I can still tear up. It's as beautiful as the Grand Canyon or Vermeer's *Girl With A Pearl Earring*, yet it's made of nothing but sound. Just chords! Shifting stacks of notes became more than ephemeral, somehow tactile, and they ignited a fire in my core.

I'd been in my local youth orchestra for a few years—good clean fun on Saturday mornings. I'd played concerts, with Mom and Dad rooting me on out there among the other parents. And the music? Well, sometimes it barely held together. There were 12-year-olds in the orchestra after all. It could be discordant and wobbly, but we were heading somewhere. Our conductor/director was a model of compassion and tenacity.

But on this day, playing with the elite of the North Carolina Piedmont's school systems, the music was just ... better. It was richer, more accurate, more lively, more exciting. And I was surrounded by it, lending my voice to a literal symphonic effort, feeling sound with an attention and awe that I had not experienced before.

I've been chasing that beautiful vibration ever since.

PART I

∫

RESET

1

MAKING OVERTURES
Listening for > Listening to

Music begins as an impulse and an imagining. Humans hear sound in their mind's ear, model it into something that excites them, and then conjure it out loud. They revise, iterate, and labor with tools—instruments, microphones, voice memos, pencil and paper, audio tape, and digital workstations. They seek out collaborators, artistic and strategic. They commit the work to an arrangement and a setting and ultimately a recording. They meticulously mix and master it. The recording is "released," as if into the wild. Other people, strangers from other places and times, happen upon this work. Some make an effort to hear it more than once. Some will pay for their own copy in some form. They'll drop a needle or press play on a system of decoders, amplifiers, and speakers. And for the briefest instant, the music becomes sound again, as it must.

Now, made of molecular pressure waves, the music travels fast, more than 700 miles per hour, jumping the air gap between speaker and listener. For this nanosecond, the music is fixed and finished, beyond the reach of the countless decisions and calculations that determined what it would sound like to waiting ears—from conception to instrumentation to the design of the amplifier and the loudspeakers that propagate the art into space. Only the receiving remains.

The listener has chosen, deliberately or passively, the music being played and the setting where the music will meet them—be it roaring along a highway or in a noisy kitchen full of family or in an immaculately quiet media library. The listener—a human being, with enthusiasms, passions, knowledge, concerns, and limited time—receives the work with some degree of attention, from very little to almost total, but probably somewhere in between. Only within and among the listeners is the music truly realized.

The energy in the air changes state from acoustic pressure to the motion of tiny bones, then to receptor cells to neural impulses. The listener's mind subdivides and dispatches the sonic river of input, sending the objective information in one set of directions to be processed as pitch, timing, texture, volume, and lyric, while other signals hit the limbic system, triggering emotions and rewarding needy neurons with dopamine and oxytocin. The motor cortex dances, implicitly or explicitly. The frontal lobes orient the listener with a cohesive idea of the music's structure and with memories of previous hearings or with passages and phrases generating predictions about what is about to happen. And then these many elements are unified again into a work of art, an aural sculpture that's far more than the sum of its parts. We are transported somewhere personal and connected with the composer, the performers, and others sharing the experience. We tune our bodies like an antenna that resonates with incoming signals, while filtering out the noise.

But do we filter out the noise?

How often do we give ourselves over to this remarkable chain of events, this entrancing mix of inspiration, passion, dedication, environment, even history and science, with something close to our full attention? In this noisy, visual, ultra-stimulated twenty-first century, how often do you listen to music actively and exclusively? Recorded music, the most common form of listening and sharing, is the focus of my opening scenario. But of course, music pulls with even greater gravity in live performance, whether in a club, a city square, a concert hall, or a pulsing arena. What was the last concert you saw? What was the last show you saw by an artist you only knew a little bit about, and how was that experience? Generally, how hungry are you to hear new ideas, especially from genres you don't intimately know? Do you let algorithms decide what's on your playlist, or do you seek your own path, building relationships with musicians from beyond the comfort zones of yourself and your social group? How ready are you to pause the world and truly be with and inside a cathedral of human-dreamed, hand-made sound?

When I was that 16-year-old getting my first taste of rapturous chords, magnificent melodies, and orchestral energy, I had no idea how involved in the art form I'd wind up being and how it would shape and color my life. I wasn't driven or destined to become a master musician or performer, but I was drawn to fascinating sounds, rhythms, and the thrill of discovery. I was, it must be said, privileged to have a family that took music seriously and that gave me access to instruments and lessons. Still, I had the bug, and I pursued the bug. I just kept asking the next question and seeking out the next musical experience.

I took up a sequence of instruments—violin, drums, bass, and guitar—in search of my voice and as a way of learning different aspects of music. I read about music on record jackets and in press reviews, magazines, and biographies. And I came to see that music felt more transparent and inviting as I learned more about its creators, its sense of place, and its story. I became aware that musicians and informed music fans listened with more tools and more expectations than most other people. While I know people far more obsessed and single-minded about music than I am, I know that it feeds me emotionally, intellectually, and spiritually, and I ultimately was drawn into making my life and living telling its story.

I didn't turn in this direction until about a decade into my journalism career, but now I've been documenting and writing about music for twenty-five years, and I've come to some conclusions that inspired this book. Music in America, even in our troubled and chaotic 2020s society, is remarkably rich and diverse. We're living in golden times for just about every genre I can think of, especially in the areas I follow most closely: Americana music, bluegrass/string band, and jazz. We have unprecedented tools for exposing, discovering, and sharing the best of our varied music scenes. At the same time and on the other hand, Americans aren't really buying it, not because they have a deliberate dislike of formal concert music or creative modern composing or experimental improvising, but because musical literacy is weak, and we don't know about its intricacies. Nobody tells us. Our schools and media haven't told the story of what music can be and how it works for decades. Most of the great music of today and yesterday is one click away, yet most of us aren't clicking.

Did you know that jazz, which was first created in America by African Americans, and classical music, which was imported from Europe and enhanced with new harmonic and rhythmic vocabularies, account for less than 4 percent of all music sold physically and less than 2 percent of what we stream? I'll talk about this more in Chapter 2, because it ought to concern us. It suggests our musical diet as a people is skewed and unbalanced. Popular music, from rock to rap to country, has been privileged in the media and marketplace for so long that many don't think about instrumental music or formal concert music at all. Composer-driven, ensemble-based music and collective improvisational music are healthy and robust on the supply side, at least in certain pockets of the country, but demand is anemic. Too many brilliant young and midlife professional artists are off the radar of 95 percent of us. Orchestras are struggling with an aging audience nationwide, and opening a jazz club today would, in most cities or towns, be either an act of philanthropy or a suicide mission. The American people don't dislike good and varied modern music. We have been separated, even estranged from it, and it's not our fault.

***

This book manifests my hope and belief that most anybody can build or rebuild a personal approach to listening and that a lifelong discovery mindset is possible, through a set of non-scary tools and concepts. I hope to activate and cultivate your relationship with the concept you saw prominently displayed on the cover: *Musicality*. And just what is that? Webster tells us that musicality means "sensitivity to, knowledge of, or talent for music," while others add important refinements, including "tastefulness" and "awareness." That's a lot of soul compressed into one word. Yet we're rarely invited to ponder it, and enrich it in our lives. Insider knowledge about music is often framed as something exclusive and out of reach, and that may be true of a full course in music theory, but musicality is part of everyone, to varying degrees, and it can be nurtured.

The cover also promises to help you "listen like an artist," which requires a little explanation, because that word is loaded. Don't think only of the music industry term, where "artist" means the featured performer, the star singer/rapper, the band that tours and makes albums. They are part of who I mean, and it's a term I use liberally. But let's agree to mean all musicians who take their art and craft seriously in every genre, as well as every songwriter and composer, every producer and conductor, every instrument maker, teacher, and sound engineer. As people who advance musical artistry, they count. And I'll go even wider, to include astute listeners, people with artistic outlooks, whether they're active, focused creators or not. Musicians and music people listen differently than most people, with an ear to motion, layers, nuance, novelty, skills, and surprise. When attending a good show, musicians may sit more still than the civilians, but they'll be the ones with their eyes closed, or an arched eyebrow, or a wry smile tugging at the corner of their lips. And I know many nonmusicians (and non-practicing musicians) who regard music with this artist's ear, and I hope these pages steer you in that direction.

Musicality is not the same thing as music theory or musicology, though it draws on both of those deep and distinguished fields. It's more like a form of mindfulness, an active engagement with sound, even a spiritual practice, that connects musicians with listeners with community. In the listener, musicality is an expanding sensitivity to musical expression and ideas based on knowledge and experience. In the musician, it's a multifaceted expertise that starts with technique and extends into emotional maturity and energetic expression. And if people can be "musical," then so can a performance, a recording, or even a place or environment, if the intent is pure and the elements work together to cultivate attention on sonic richness.

Musicality grows intrinsically in players and listeners, but it is also extrinsic—a set of timeless concepts and physical facts. I'll talk about these aspects in the pages ahead, because I'm convinced that our culture, in elevating the performer, performance, and recorded product above the visceral pleasures and endless possibilities of sound, has distracted us from harmony, rhythm, and resonance. Composers and musicians work extremely hard organizing sounds into densely packed passages of time, yet we may or may not be equipped to grasp the results. It's a complicated game with layers, and a game's not much fun if you don't know the rules.

I'll be describing concepts that play out across all genres of music. I'll draw examples from funk, country, bebop, chamber music, stadium rock, big band swing, experimental rock, Broadway show tunes, soul jazz, symphonic, African, jam band, bluegrass and newgrass, hip-hop, gospel, New Orleans brass band, and I'm sure a few more. What I lean away from is the star system or star mindset. Arena-scale pop and rock and mega-festivals are cool as far as they go, but a lot of that world draws people for the spectacle and lights, as well as feeling part of a group and having a great time. The music there tends to be more like a soundtrack to a bigger experience, while my hopes are to elevate the professionals who make music that stands on its own—music that does best in clubs and concert halls, with a focus on the sonics and the vibe in the room. A musicality mindset is about pulling such elements into the foreground—melody, harmony, rhythm, and more—and forming a deep and dynamic picture of what's happening.

"The ideal listener is both inside and outside the music at the same moment," composer Aaron Copland wrote in 1939's *What to Listen for in Music*, a breakthrough music appreciation book. The listener is "judging it and enjoying it, wishing it would go one way and watching it go another, almost like the composer at the moment he composes . . . .You can deepen your understanding of music only by being a more conscious and aware listener— not someone who is just listening but someone who is listening *for* something."

When I was young, I was lucky to know a lot of people who lived this ethos. While I'm always grateful to friends or reviewers for urging me to listen *to* this or that, my lasting musical knowledge came from those who urged me to listen *for*. They revealed nonobvious features of the music, such as a well-placed passing chord, selective use of dissonance, syncopated rhythm, subtle dynamics, and other concepts that will fill the pages ahead. Once I was urged to hear such features, they opened up the music and were impossible to un-hear. These insights arrived through one musical work and then transferred to other works as well. Think of it this way. You perhaps remember an art lecture where a teacher or docent pointed to some hidden visual code in a painting's composition, and it unlocked a bigger story about the work. Similarly in music, layers of intrigue and inspiration are right there in plain hearing, yet perhaps imperceptible to the less experienced or less engaged listener.

None of this exists in a vacuum either; musicality is a far bigger deal than the tapping of toes or even the coaxing of chills and tears. Music became a cherished fine art and a great popular art for some pretty heavy reasons—a matrix of some of humanity's most noble and vital values: cooperation, commitment, discipline, open-mindedness, humility, grace, assertiveness, intellect, narrative, curiosity, mentorship, stewardship, tenacity, faith, awe, expression, courage, vigor, humor, generosity. Even love. All of these virtues have direct reflections in music, and our greatest music couldn't have happened without at least some of them working in concert, as it were. Between the composition of a major musical work and its performance decades later and thousands of miles away, every one of these characteristics plays a part. Music can also lure us more deeply into our faith and encourage us in our fights for justice and progress. I even found scientific validation for my broadly humanistic view of the word in the work of Vanderbilt professor Reyna Gordon, who wrote in a 2022 paper that: "Musicality (broadly encompassing musical behaviour, music engagement and musical skill) impacts society by supporting pro-social behaviour and well-being." That's quite a finding, and I can offer anecdotal evidence to back it up.

I'm not saying that musicians are uniformly virtuous; they are as flawed as anybody. But in my experience, music of every genre I've worked around has been a magnet for caring, engaged people who value community. And I believe with my whole heart that music cultivates our humanity and our mental health. I even have a theory as to why—that no principle is more central to music than empathy.

By virtue of its collective effort in the making and the transmission of ideas and emotions to others, music might be empathy in audible form. Intuition and psychological research both tell us that musical training and musical expression build social bonds. Musicians have to humble themselves before others to make a complete picture, and listeners must avail themselves to the listening. Time and again through history, music countervails against the forces tearing our world apart: fear, paranoia, propaganda, enmity, and xenophobia. I was born during the hippie era, when music was culturally and chemically bonded to ideals of reconciliation, hope, and love. And while some of that was naive, I look at the turbulent years of the early twenty-first century with the rise of authoritarianism and populism worldwide, and I maintain my faith that music, like empathy, is nothing less than the polar opposite of authoritarian control.

In this pursuit, there's no entry exam, no right or wrong amount of knowledge, and no "too late" for the lifelong learning musical citizen. Indeed, taking on a new relationship with music, like a new language, is as blessed and rewarding a way to spend the latter decades of life as the early ones. Yet people get intimidated by music's inner workings when they need not. It's not as if the rules of music, theoretical and conceptual, are meant to be memorized, called up or looked up during the experience of music. For the attentive listener, the elements of music settle into the subconscious and assist from the background.

The book contains six parts that organize the building blocks of a music-first outlook. Part One is a pause to refresh and rethink our habits of mind around music. Part Two celebrates sound and its most fundamental musical elements. Then we move on to the heart of harmony in Part Three, about the way notes and chords flow and work together. Part Four consists of three interlocking chapters about rhythm, perhaps my favorite aspect of music. Part Five proposes ways to integrate harmony and rhythm into a satisfying overall experience with macro lessons about music's deeper aspects. And in the closing Part Six, something music appreciation books hardly ever address—how to practically take your curiosity about music into the world, with chapters about curating a musical diet, music journalism, listening environments, and the considerations in taking up and playing an instrument.

One more feature awaits you. Through the book, you'll encounter short profiles of artists who serve as sentinels or exemplars of this book's principles. Because I focus on musical concepts, theories, ideas, and history, with select examples scattered throughout the text, I thought it would be helpful for me to point you to a limited number of contemporary artists for pure enjoyment and exploration, a handpicked playlist of what I'm calling "Highly Musical Humans." My criteria: They are under 55 years old at the time of publication, because I want to encourage you to know more about and support mid-career musicians from our contemporary scene. They are American, or in one case a Canadian playing an American tradition, not because America corners the market on great music, but because American music is my field of expertise and because I want us Americans to know and be proud of our multifaceted musical heritage. Finally, they are personal favorites, artists I listen to frequently who I wish were better known, even while some of them are certainly famous in their field. I have published playlists of my cited examples (and music cited in the text) on the major streaming services. If they lead some of you to new favorites or down new pathways, then I've done my job.

No book could tell you everything you could or should know about music, and I believe most "music appreciation" books fail because they try to be too comprehensive, chronological and classically focused. Instead, this book explores and explains the elements of music mingled with memories of my own breakthrough moments. I hope to inspire you with my (relative) musical omnivorousness. I hope to help you discern whether music you encounter is good or not so good, even in genres you don't especially like. And because I can't help myself, it's also a manifesto of sorts. I'm opinionated, and I think that's a good way to be in life and in music as long as it's tempered with good information and humility. I have concerns with some aspects of our musical economy and cultural dialogue that you'll hear about, because I want you to join me in pushing back against efforts to devalue music or to distract us from music's essence and its unique powers. But mostly, I'm here to celebrate the forces and resources that lead us toward a richer relationship with art made of sound.

Now, what shall we listen for?

2

SOUND, NOT SONGS
For the time being . . .

Are you a lyrics person or a music person? It's a kind of parlor game—a provocative little inquiry into the musical personality of your friends or yourself. When you hear songs, new songs especially, what do you focus on intuitively? A lyrics person (LP) relates chiefly to the words and the voice and aura of the singer. A music person (MP) experiences a musical foreground dominated by a blend of instruments (one of which may well be a human voice), making melody, harmony, texture, and groove. An LP is drawn to a solo songwriter with only a guitar or piano, where an MP like myself probably craves a fuller arrangement. Even with lyric-forward genres like folk and country, I can get so transfixed by the *music* that I have to remind myself to focus on the words. Often I need printed lyrics and a little extra concentration to truly process a song as a *song*. Some singers seem to be trying *not* to be understood (I'm looking at you, Thom Yorke of Radiohead). Yet we MPs won't be put off if we like the music. Foreign language singers can move us as much as English speakers. We're there for the overall effect.

I raise this to push you to investigate some biases in our musical culture that may inhibit our feeling for music's immensity. We seem to be a country of LPs. Since the 1980s, our national conversation about music has been overwhelmingly focused on song-based music and even more so on singers and rappers themselves, with their personalities and charisma and celebrity. Songs dominate sound-based music in the marketplace by a ratio of almost 20-to-1. Singing and songwriting are held up by the music business and reality shows as the most realistic and legitimate path to chase a musical "dream." And all this conditions us to conflate "song" with "music," when song is but one form in a wide musical universe. So it's important, I believe, to reflect on how these forces affect your relationship with sound-based music.

If all the pop and rock and rap and country and folk—all the popular song-based music we stream into our headphones and hear in restaurants, cars, and music venues—was spirited away and we were left with only instrumental music, how would you feel? Would you still love music? What would you listen to and what would you relate to? Even if you're already deeply into instrumental music, this thought experiment is meant to invoke the spirit of the material that awaits you in these pages. For MPs, some of this will be comfortable terrain, though I hope you find insights ahead that help you grow your musical awareness. If you're an LP, I respect and honor that, but perhaps you have wondered how to deepen your feeling for the high-ambition, high-attention genres and styles that don't have words. This chapter invites you to set song aside, temporarily to be sure, to reboot your musical mind around sound and the nonverbal elements of music, to listen like an MP at least for a while.

To be clear, I cherish song, and I couldn't live happily without it. I work in the world of song, and the majority of my record collection is song. I've written songs and committed scores of country, folk, and blues songs to memory. Because obviously, vocal music can be great art. Twentieth-century America proved that, building the widest, richest culture of song in human history. Song is our sustenance and our first social medium. We need it as a means of self-expression, communal understanding, mass entertainment and social cohesion. Give me Bob Dylan and Paul Simon and Cindy Walker and Joni Mitchell. Give me Allison Russell and Jason Isbell and the other young masters of the art form. Songs truly matter. I'm merely saying there's so much more.

Our love of song has powerful roots. We're born with a vocal instrument, one with more variation, nuance, and possibility than any physical instrument ever invented. Those made of wood, brass, or bone are crude machines indeed, compared to larynx, lungs, muscle, and skull. Our aural experience in life probably began with the sound of our mother's voice, the foundation of our psycho-emotional world (if we're not unlucky). Voices and vocal styles tie us to our state and regional cultures and draw us in with their intimacy. Moreover, song is inherently accessible, a form that is all around us and simple to understand. Where many of us have been disoriented by tricky instrumental music, not knowing where we are or how to follow along, songs keep us guided and grounded, phrase to phrase, section to section. A song leads the listener by the hand as a matter of design.

So we are innately, psychologically, and intellectually drawn toward song-based music. The entertainment business, structured to serve you more of what you want and less of what might require learning and change, has reinforced these tendencies, juicing up song with star power, volume, spectacle, and an ecosystem of marketing. And this has had the unfortunate effect of devaluing and denaturing music broadly, by which I mean human-organized sound for esthetic, emotional, spiritual, and intellectual effect. Our greatest instrumental music has for years been marginalized as niche tastes for specialists, not a beautiful art form for everyone.

If this had always been true, we could maybe conclude that nonvocal music is simply limited in its appeal. Instead, we look back fifty years and see a robust instrumental and art music scene. When I was born, in 1966, jazz was widely heard and appreciated. It was covered in mainstream magazines and newspapers as an aspect of the good life. Thelonious Monk was on the cover of *Time*, and Dave Brubeck was a star. Leading classical musicians like conductor/composer Leonard Bernstein and violinist Jascha Heifetz were virtually household names. Pop radio played hit instrumentals by Duane Eddy, The Ventures, and Booker T. & the M.G.'s.

Then, as popular music grew into a global industry in the late twentieth century, songs and singers became the most bankable focal points. Pop instrumentals dwindled at radio, dying at last in the 1980s with some movie score themes. Instrumental music, as a percentage of music sold and promoted and acquired, eroded steadily from the 1960s onward to today's anemic numbers. Young musicians seeking a career path in classical or jazz face unprecedented odds against a sustainable career and few role models whom they can point to as mainstream stars. The next Bernstein or Monk will have to get there on YouTube, without the support of the major labels that supported their heroes.

That's not to say that great new instrumental music isn't being made. The talent and inspiration is there, perhaps more than ever before. What's lacking is demand. Art music for active listening isn't so much unpopular as unknown. It's a cultural orphan and strange territory for most listeners. Today's American audience for new sound-based music is small, educated, White, upscale, and old. I'll certainly cop to being some of those things, but nothing I've learned suggests to me in any way that instrumental music and a music-first mindset is a demographically or culturally specific thing. Music is for everyone, and while that means we all sing and dance together, it should also mean we might listen together and talk about music in terms other than the song and the singer and their popularity. We might well have conversations about tonality, concept, structure, dynamics, inspiration, story, and context. But our media, fixated on the star singer, has left many of my passions behind as too niche to be relevant to the audience at large. And that becomes self-fulfilling prophecy. We lose exactly what's necessary in any healthy musical ecosystem: a virtuous cycle of exhibition, information, promotion, education, participation, fascination, and consumption.

***

The first time I remember being overwhelmed by sound-only music, I was 10 years old, with my family on the one and only overseas trip we took while I was growing up. We were in London—I'm pretty sure the British Museum—where an exhibit was commemorating the centenary of Wagner's famous *Ring of the Nibelung*, the fifteen-hour epic cycle of four operas that has fascinated and intimidated audiences since its premiere in 1876. There were costumes and set designs and ephemera on display. And there were listening booths— little cocoons in which you could curl up comfortably and listen to Wagner's music on high quality sound systems (British audio designers of the '70s were not messing around). I remember feeling enthralled and surrounded by something truly new, a cascade of emotions brought on by thundering brass, sweeping strings, and ecstatic voices singing in German. It's not like I decided there and then to become a composer or conductor, but I was changed. The event sticks in my mind as a gateway to the explosive pleasures of complex concert music. Because in truth, I was high, in a dopamine state brought on by a visionary composer and a world-class ensemble. In coming chapters, I'll discuss the vital role of the musical epiphany, and this was one of my earliest.

Today, I don't enjoy Wagner because he's too bombastic for my taste, and anyway it turns out he was kind of cozy with the Nazis. But this isn't about him. My point is that this and other experiences in concert halls, with records and music lessons, revealed models of music that guided me to an expansive, wide-ranging musical diet. Moreover, every sound insight I gained fed back and helped make me a more active and excitable listener to song-based music. Without knowing why, I always favored the musically imaginative and innovative song-based artists—The Beatles, Earth, Wind & Fire, Joni Mitchell, The Grateful Dead, Stevie Wonder, and Steely Dan among them. Because I'm an MP, born and raised.

Sound-based music has another advantage—its embrace of subjective thought, limitless emotion, and freedom of mind. Words and lyrics specify where the communicative relationship is going, moment by moment. With sound-based music, every piece and every passage and every gesture can be packed with meaning and broad in its implications. I like to quote David Byrne of Talking Heads on this subject: "Words can be a dangerous addition to music—they can pin it down," he wrote in his 2012 book *How Music Works*. "Words imply that the music is about 'that' and nothing else. They can destroy the pleasant ambiguity that is a lot of the reason we love music so much. That inherent ambiguity means that we can psychologically tailor music to our own needs, sensibilities and situations—but words limit that, or they can." That's quite a thing for a highly influential songwriter to say! The saxophone genius John Coltrane said it more economically: "If the music doesn't say it, how can words say it *for* the music?"

Before moving on, I want to point out that shifting our focus from song to sound raises a semantics problem brought about by big tech. In the 1990s, somewhere in Cupertino, CA, some designers and executives whose culpability will, I fear, be lost to history, created a taxonomy for Apple iTunes (and thus for the digital music industry to come) that collapsed all recordings down to three identifier fields: Song, Album, and Artist. This not only reflects the culture's bias toward song-based popular music, it reinforces it by mis-categorizing most aspects of sound-based music. There aren't many "songs" in composed or improvised music. Jazz artists generally call their pieces "tunes," as diminutive as that sounds. Classical and composed music refers to "pieces" and "works," often with subsections called "movements." Artist is a problematic term as well, because in classical, there are many artists involved: the composer, the symphony, the conductor, the soloist, and so on. Jazz bands likely have a leader, but there is no one "artist," because each musician matters. Be aware that the song/album/artist scheme at the very heart of the digital music world we now inhabit erases key aspects of musicality. It devalues the very kinds of musicians and works at the heart of this book and its idea of sound-based musicality.

So what does orienting toward more sound and less song *feel* like? How can we shift our focus? What could we be listening for if not the message of well-sung lyrics and our personal connection with a vocalist? It starts, I believe, by refreshing our awareness of sound as a physical phenomenon and our biological/psychological apparatus for perceiving it. That foundation is addressed soon in Chapter 5. But first, a few more tools and frames to make the journey toward deeper musicality as rewarding and rapid as possible.

Listen for . . .

. . . musical works from beyond the popular song form with no lyrics, whether jazz, ambient, soundtrack, or classical. Spend some time with popular music sung in languages you don't know, experiencing the lead voice as an instrument.

. . . the sounds around you at any given time with focus and attention to the smallest details. Challenge yourself to reach inside a superficially dull soundscape and be attentive to subtle changes—a siren, birdsong, a distant voice, a train.

3

GET OVER YOURSELF A MINUTE
How suspending judgement supercharges your taste

In a troubling episode of the PBS documentary series *Frontline*, sociologist and marketing expert Douglas Rushkoff profiles teens and tweens who've become literally addicted to online attention and approval. Some are breakout "influencers" with hundreds of thousands of followers and a deep-seated need to keep growing. Others are high school kids who post motivational videos to a tiny audience, hoping to go viral.

Rushkoff dubs this cohort "Generation Like," after the Facebook thumbs-up icon. The first *like* button reportedly was released on the boutique video platform Vimeo in 2004, inspired by the "digg" approval button at Digg.com in the early days of social media. MySpace didn't even have a *like* button until it copied Facebook's 2009 thumbs-up rollout. Soon, the *like* button, or its equivalent, was an assumed and central part of social media. For the audience, it was a source of gamified social approval. For the companies, it became valuable demographic data. This strange new world pushed people from thoughtful reactions toward the emotional and subjective. The social site formerly known as Twitter turned its *star* button (which to me implied "that's interesting") into a *heart*, which says instead, "I love that." And then it added real-time counters next to the hearts, so we could see how fast others' content was being hearted while we grew ever more anxious to post content that might do big numbers.

In our national music ecosystem, this tyranny of *like* is nothing new, predating social media and the internet itself. Record companies, radio chains, and popular media (especially television producers) developed simplistic and fixed ideas about us—the musical citizenry—in the late twentieth century. They profiled us not as curious humans with capacity for growth but as consumers of the artists and genres we already *liked*.

They weren't fools. They could see that ratings were stronger for familiar music than for obscure music and stronger for stars than for newcomers. Radio, a wide-open buffet of intermingled styles before the 1990s, built centrally programmed radio formats that were narrow-cast at specific age and lifestyle groups. Nothing about this is surprising given the realities and priorities of a market-based music business. What is surprising is that so many Americans, in the musically abundant land of the free, surrendered to this long game of marketing as the source of their musical taste-making. Obviously, some amount of legitimately grassroots enthusiasm churns the charts and makes new stars. I don't discount that in popular formats. But the marginalization—on radio and television—of all of the high-skill, sound-based genres was done to us, not by us.

Meanwhile, we elevated subjective values through our respect for personal freedom and autonomy. We are conditioned to honor everyone's taste as special and personal and largely out of bounds for questioning. And this is not wicked or wrong, but it is insufficient. Personal taste, as worthy as it is, gets overemphasized and mischaracterized in our culture. Opinion, being your sacred right, is thus a responsibility as well. What you *like* should be informed by what you *know*. Instead, the way we talk to one another mostly favors sweeping verdicts. "I love all music except country." "I hate hip-hop." "Classical music is boring." "Disco sucks." "I love rock and roll, put another dime in the jukebox baby."

The social internet, for all its problems, has brought some badly needed democracy to the exposure of more complicated and ambitious music, especially through YouTube. But that won't help you as a musical citizen if you don't take charge of your destiny. This is a two-step process. First is to appreciate just how powerful these cultural forces are and realize how many musical worlds and choices commercial media has hidden from us. What's harder, yet critical to building new layers of consciousness as a musical person, is to learn to resist the quick opinion reflex when exploring modern music. Drop your guard, cool your jets, and relax that twitchy trigger finger poised over your internal *like* button. You must, from time to time, set aside what you know to listen to new artists, genres and approaches. This is active listening, where vulnerability meets agency. Suspending judgment isn't the same as abandoning musical discernment. It's the key to developing it.

I'm asking you to trust that your horizons will open wider and faster if you put instant gratification on a shelf for a time and assume that there are parts of your musical self you do not yet know. Because this is true for even the most experienced musician. You've likely fallen in love with some music you didn't like on first impression, and if you've done it once, you can do it again. Life is long. Tastes change. So a lot of what lies ahead involves why and how that happens, whether gradually over years or in sudden epiphanies. Your current likes and dislikes might be stray data kludging up your mental RAM. Reboot your mind and see what happens.

The first time I noticed this happening to me had to do with the English pop band Squeeze. In high school, I fell for their tuneful quirks and humor. I loved "Pulling Mussels From a Shell" and "Tempted" and considered them in the top ranks of smart, energetic pop. So in 1985 when the key members reunited after a hiatus and released the album *Cosi Fan Tutti Frutti*, I bought it on cassette and on faith, sure that I'd like it. But honestly I found it odd. Some songs had key changes in midstream (rare in pop), making harmonic leaps that unnerved me. Some phrases didn't sound like they matched the next one. The beats were sometimes off-kilter, longer or shorter than I thought might make sense. But hey, it was in my car, so it played four or five times, and at some point, I got it. The curious chord changes became more exciting than their older music. Once they became familiar to me, the twists that had seemed so peculiar actually eased me in. And that began to open me up to more sophisticated and rewarding harmonic terrain in general.

Other music took me years or decades to reconcile. In my post college years, I had a friend who was deeply into Frank Zappa. He was a cool guy and he made it seem that liking Zappa was cool, because Zappa was such a rock and roll radical. So I let my buddy play me Zappa records—on several occasions! Did exposure to Zappa make me like his music? Thank you, no. I chafed at its tirades of notes and clashing timbres. The use of vocals seemed frequently and intentionally obnoxious. So Frank and the Mothers of Invention went on a shelf in deep storage in my mind. Then, over the years, on another track entirely, my interest in classical music expanded into contemporary terrain, where atonality, disorder and in-your-face gestures struck me as more interesting. And eventually, Zappa was reintroduced to me from a new point of view. Instead of hearing him try and fail to make super-artsy rock and roll, I heard him for what he was—an accomplished modern composer with command of classical, jazz, rock, funk and some sounds that were only in his head. I won't pretend that Zappa is in my regular rotation today, but I can dive lustily into *Hot Rats* (1969) or live shows on YouTube (his bands were super-skilled and well-rehearsed). And unlike a lot of Zappa devotees, I'm perfectly comfortable knowing something about him and not everything.

I ran into music that was too weird for me all the time when I was in my teens, from industrial rock, to free jazz, to twentieth-century Eastern European composers (a side road for my opera-loving dad). I went down blind alleys and up box canyons. On the other hand, there was no price to pay for a few minutes spent with something jagged and strange. I could turn the station or try another record, and I was free again. Through this stage though, whether by nature or nurture I don't know, my tendency in the face of music that was too disorderly or discordant or ugly was to almost never say "I hate that." Instead, I said, "I don't get that," allowing that possibly, one day, I would.

A refreshed outlook on the like/hate dynamic also means checking any bias you can detect against "old" music. You'll notice in some people—sometimes our younger brothers and sisters—a reflexive prejudice against music from decades past. Yet any music fan will chuckle to themselves over this particular set of blinders. Music most often has signatures of its time, and recognizing historic context is wonderful and recommended, but there's a reason that one form of praise we critics pay to music is to call it "timeless." That means this music has value and inspiration that feels intrinsic and potentially immortal. I personally don't hear anything dusty about Dusty Springfield or archaic about Art Blakey. The blues giants of the 1920s and '30s will always sound like they're singing to us personally, even if the recordings are a little noisy. Can you name something edgier than Stravinsky at the turn of the twentieth century? I'll wait.

I hope I'm not making it sound like exposure to new music or old music that's new to you is always a drag. Far from it! Love at first listen happens all the time in the musical journey. Sometimes a single example can swing you around and open up an entire genre that will feed your soul for the rest of your life. I feel like most often the big reveals happen in live settings, where the energy of the musicians is most vivid and infectious. I've seen this happen and experienced it myself at multigenre festivals, which are one of the most powerful vectors for discovery and taste-building.

At the same time, experience and science tell us that when it comes to music, familiarity breeds affection. It is inevitable and wonderful to carry favorite songs and artists from youth to old age. But the music business takes this too far, through vehicles like "oldies" radio, a huge commercial format. Billions of music fan hours have been squandered while the same 300 hits from the '60s to the '90s churn relentlessly in cars, offices, supermarkets, restaurants, and big box stores. Our amphitheaters and arenas are packed every year with rock and pop bands recycling their hits from three and four decades ago, while tribute bands of those bands do big business as well. For many reasons, some quite natural, music taste in so many calcifies about age 20, and the music business relies on and cultivates the notion of nostalgia as a lucrative lubricant for making the tired seem desirable. This is a trap and a key reason so many young, aspiring musicians in instrumental-heavy genres face a crisis of public demand for what they make. I'm with composer Ned Rorem, who said that music is "the sole art which evokes nostalgia for the *future*" (emphasis mine).

Challenging music evokes feelings inside us that are unlike any other art form. Difficult literature requires intellectual effort but isn't likely to bring on emotional distress. Strange visual art may leave us indifferent and possibly offended, but it's easy to ignore. Music, by design, burrows into our deeper brain apparatus, so it can provoke genuine unease, even fear. Complicating matters, people exposed to music that feels annoying, forbidding or harsh have no frame of reference to judge the quality of that music. What if it's just bad? It's like the time I tried sea urchin on a date at a sushi restaurant. To this day, I don't know if they served me spoiled food or if I tasted a good sea urchin and nearly threw up at the table anyway. (She hated it too by the way.) My point is that it's wise to explore new stylistic territory with examples of music that have been vetted and celebrated by experienced peers and critics.

Think of music as a ladder of complexity. Jumping up too many rungs at once can cause vertigo. Exposure to the right degree of difficult allows you to adapt, and it's not about how much music theory you know; it's about schooling your ears to grasp new sonic ideas and tonal dimensions. Listening builds connections among the many centers of the brain that process music, from its harmonic language to its associations in your memory. Neurons wire themselves in new ways with exposure to the patterns in unfamiliar music, encompassing broad forms, complex rhythms, new tonalities, and nuances of phrasing. Your brain's ready to accept a lot of musical expressions today and unready to easily appreciate others. The goal is an outlook of lifetime learning, curiosity, and accumulating insight. The path is a chain of epiphanies connecting concepts and generating new levels of music discernment and comprehension.

Taste is a muscle that gets stronger with brief bouts of stress. What sounds like disorder at one sitting can sound like genius with a little time. A liberal and playful attitude toward new sonic frontiers will guide you to a set of musical loves that are as personal as your fingerprint. While we're quite used to the beautiful idea that learning and loving new artists can bring us together with a wide, even international community of fellow fans (think Taylor Swift's near-universal appeal), it's also valuable and inevitable in a deep musical journey to come across artists who seem born to reach you and you alone. You are, after all, finding yourself.

Yet this doesn't mean you must expose yourself to everything, because you can't. I often refer to myself as a musical "omnivore" and I meet fellow omnivores all the time, but I'm skeptical when somebody tells me they like "everything." Music is just too vast to comprehend and love all styles from all places. So, as paradoxical as it sounds, being broad minded includes ruling out some styles, schools, and genres. I don't spend much time with indie rock and none at all with metal, and that's OK for me. There's more than enough great other music for a lifetime. Your results will vary. Just know that your taste and your curiosity are bound together. Indulge both to enhance both. I urge you only to make an effort to sort what you actually don't like from what you don't (yet) understand.

Listen for . . .

. . . musicians or composers you know are considered reputable and admired historically but whose music you find difficult, such as perhaps Arnold Schoenberg, Frank Zappa, or Ornette Coleman. Find a single work of less than six minutes, and listen to it four times in the space of a month.

. . . styles from early decades of the twentieth century that you've not explored, such as Dixieland from New Orleans, Delta blues, "hot club" or "gypsy" jazz pioneered by Django Reinhardt, or hillbilly string bands from the '30s. Try to put yourself in that time, when these sounds on record or radio were almost magical to people who'd not been able to hear them before.

4

BEYOND POPULAR
A new map of music

We all carry around a personal, default view of music that's unique to our upbringing and our inclinations. We inherit a core musical worldview, a sense of what's "normal," like we inherit a religious outlook or a culinary tradition. It's shaped by where and when we're born, how our community functions and our exposure to music and media in the first 20 years of our lives. The possible variety here is profound. For me, symphonic music is a comfortable home base, while polka is a bit exotic. For a woman from a blue collar family in Kenosha, WI, the reverse may well be true. How far we branch out from our birthright baseline music is up to us, and I offer this chapter as a new frame to help you do so with a new kind of enthusiasm.

We mostly express our musical comfort zones—what we like—as a matter of genre. We're led to see music as more or less fitting into stylistic categories called rock, classical, jazz, hip-hop, and etc. I'll have more to say about the virtues and limits of genre in a later chapter, but here I ask that you wipe this particular mental blackboard clean. I suggest instead a more holistic view that considers three ways or *modes* of music-making: popular music, composed music, and improvised music. These can be complementary, and they very often blend together, but they are distinct in their origins and their impulse. They present nicely as a Venn diagram, but one with fuzzy-edged circles, because all definitions and boundaries in music are fuzzy.

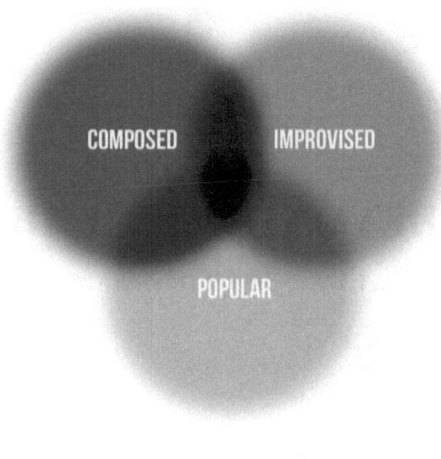

***

POPULAR

Popular Music is an established term in our field, a label that suits its subject in many ways. Sure, it has limits and ambiguities, but mostly it means what it says. It's people's music—music that a wide swath of humans grasp and like, in some cases enough to spend their money. The formal term is vernacular music, by the way. I think of popular music as akin to roots music, in that it springs from an ancient human need to communicate. Popular music in my framing encompasses tribal songs, work songs, traditional dance music and ballads, participatory church music, and the blues. It's also all the offshoots of those folk music origins. So it's teenagers learning by ear and bashing away at favorite songs in a garage. It's rock, country music, and hip-hop from the underground to their most commercial forms. Popular is the default mode of our national diet and conversation, a near synonym with song-based music as described in Chapter 2.

Music does not have to be commercially successful or even commercialized to count as popular music. Again, the modes are about the how and the why. Popular music is intuitive and inherited, learned more often by ear and demonstration than formal training. Is it weird to put Delta blues, James Taylor, LA hair metal, and Bruno Mars in the same basket? I don't think so. These genres and artists all trace back to the same headwaters, music based in humans bursting into song (and sound) for catharsis, communion, camaraderie, and attention. American popular music has been built into a powerful, influential music industry. And we have also held on to and cultivated our folk traditions and interfaced with other roots and popular music from around the world. It's quite a remarkable success story.

Because the overwhelming majority of popular music takes a song form, and since, as we've covered, song form is the center of musical attention in the modern USA, it's the one I'll spend the least time talking about in the pages ahead. And yet because our goal is to listen to *all* music with more insight and discernment, don't be surprised when I draw examples of advanced musicality from the realm of the popular, especially bluegrass, a genre that I've observed has high degrees of musical aptitude among its players and fans.

***

COMPOSED

Shift your focus please to the realm of Composed Music, where sonic art begins and lives as a form of *design*. From the earliest notated choral music of the fifteenth century through the highly conceptual rule-breaking and rule-remaking twentieth century, we can see a through-line of intent and control. Sound is organized by a single creator before anyone plays a note. Through the language of musical notation, works can be organized and structured with great intricacy and with potentially grand and highly nuanced effect. In contrast to popular music, where everyone playing brings organizing ideas and sound to the whole, composers define and refine every part, as well as the overall arc of a piece, and others execute and interpret it. The work becomes fixed in a text and can thus outlive the composer. It is like software that can be saved and run years later and far away.

At this point I need to address the anxious, inevitable question: Does my framework imply some kind of artistic superiority and/or higher intrinsic value of composed music? Mostly no, but partially yes. Here's how I would encourage you to think about it. Real world experience shows us that some music is better than other music. Some musicians are more creative, more intense, more magnetic, and ultimately more important in the story than others. I take that as a fact of nature, though I recognize that for many, an egalitarian impulse resists claims of superiority in art. I would beware of that kind of thinking. We can respect everyone's musical taste while not declaring music's value as entirely subjective, just because it's art and entertainment. Radical subjectivity flies in the face of evidence and the artistic calling itself. Why bother creating art if not to do one's best and to meet or exceed the standards one learns through listening and learning? Music school, after all, would make little sense if musical value was entirely personal. My agenda is to help us identify, appreciate, and cultivate the components of a holistic embrace of superior musicality, in whatever genre or field.

What we should not say, the myth we must put to rest (and one I grew up around), is that composed music or academy-trained music is inherently more valuable to human existence than popular music. While there is a sometimes useful analytical continuum from folk art to fine art, elite opinion has a poor record of drawing value lines. Once upon a time, only "classical" music was regarded as truly important and refined. Then over decades, jazz (disdained for decades as degenerate entertainment) demanded respect, until it too was knighted with fine art status by whomever is in charge of such things. At last and as well, blues, folk music, and bluegrass achieved so-called legitimacy, as scholars and arts gatekeepers recognized the masters and innovators in those fields. We finally figured out that while greatness is real, no genre has a particular claim on it.

I hasten to add that while I believe in certain kinds of stratification of musical value and excellence, they apply to music put forth in the marketplace, not to the millions of amateur musicians who play and sing for fun and community. These are just very different things with different standards and reasons for being. Young people writing songs for friends or posting on TikTok are making something of value that we can't compare to the work of Joni Mitchell. When someone decides they are a songwriter and releases an album, they will find themselves held to a new critical standard. Same again with mature, career artists whose mid- and late-life work can be compared to their past art and the art of those around them in the market.

So to recap, all three modes of music include musical genius and are capable of transcendence. However, each mode creates effects and ideas and sounds that the others cannot. The point is to know when you're hearing one or another and to recognize each for its own virtues and strengths.

For example, composed music is fundamentally different from popular or improvised music in its density and intensity of creative agency. Composing enables harmonic concepts, rhythmic ideas, and thematic development that are just not going to happen with musicians playing spontaneously. Music isn't better just because it's written out in scores, but a vast amount of the greatest music ever imagined *could only have been composed*. There is something special about it, and we risk losing that when we segregate it or dismiss it as archaic music for elites.

Some will protest that "all music is composed," but this is a semantics question. If you said in conversation that Carole King composed the song "(You Make Me Feel Like) A Natural Woman," I'd not object; it's a fine synonym for "wrote and arranged." But if you called Carole King a *composer* and started comparing her musical output to Mahler, that's an apples and oranges situation. She's a songwriter in the popular music field whose songs are enshrined as lyrics, melody, and chord changes. If a music director writes out fresh parts for "A Natural Woman" for a big ensemble, say at a Las Vegas show, we say they are "arranging" and/or "orchestrating" the song by Carole King. Composers use those tools too, but they do much more, conceiving every note, every motion, every textural and dynamic shift.

Composed music is my upgraded, updated term for classical music, in case you hadn't caught on. I believe it's a much better term, because it is more accurate, value-neutral, and period-neutral than "classical," which literally evokes antiquity. Composed music is less weighed down with historical and elitist baggage, and I think it ought to be a marketing and streaming music category. The aim is to encourage fans to listen to new composers and works, the way we push in popular music, and *then* explore back in time, rather than starting with powdered wigs and the viola da gamba. Composed music is not a Thing To Be Venerated but a strategy for music making that can only be learned through its language and practice. It's been proving itself for 500 years.

I'm aware, incidentally, that there are contemporary pieces that inject random chance into the performance (in some cases by literally throwing dice) or that involve the musicians in decision-making and timing based on moveable blocks of music. This so-called aleatoric music fits comfortably for me in the composed music cloud, because the composer made the rules, and the rules are transferable. Such pieces can be played 100 years from now from a score and be related to what they were at their inception, even if the context changes. But let's set aside meta-musical experimentation by academics and philosophers. These kinds of composing have their place, but they are remote to the subject at hand, which is the music you'll actually be listening to.

***

IMPROVISED

In the third mode, Improvised Music, sound is crafted in the moment with expressive intent. The artistic nexus is not the song (as in popular music), or the composer, but the player. This takes us to the realm of jazz and jam bands, where the point and focus is categorically different than mastery in the composed mode. Playing "correctly" and "well" mean different things.

"Jazz is about the power of now," wrote Wynton Marsalis in his 2008 book *Moving to Higher Ground: How Jazz Can Change Your Life.* "There is no script. It's a conversation. The emotion is given to you by musicians as they make split-second decisions to fulfill what they feel the moment requires." Marsalis is possibly the most famous jazz musician and ambassador of my lifetime, but he's also accomplished in composed music as well, having performed and recorded classical trumpet pieces. The same can be said of pianist André Previn, who was unusual in the '60s for his fluidity in both jazz and classical. He once said that in classical, "the music is always greater than its performance—whereas *the way* jazz is performed is always more important than what is being played."

Previn's observation anticipates the important question: If jazz is based on tunes or pieces that can be attributed to a "composer" (Wayne Shorter wrote "Footprints" for example), why isn't jazz composed music too? Well, some of it is. Big bands execute complex multi-part works through full scores, and some of my favorite works of all time are through-composed suites and works for jazz orchestra by the likes of Duke Ellington, Charles Mingus, and Maria Schneider, a contemporary master who should be known by more Americans. But most jazz—small group and solo—is about improvising on a tune. Unlike Beethoven's Ninth Symphony, "Footprints" or most other jazz tunes you could name has no standard reference score. Improvised music instead implies a compact among musicians based on some kind of framework. Perhaps it's an established work, like "Footprints," with that tune's melody and chord changes guiding the way. Or we might agree to play 12-bar blues in the key of A. Or we'll vamp on a few simple chords at a set tempo and see what happens as we play and listen to one another. Even no framework, so-called "free jazz," is a kind of framework.

When a high-level jazz ensemble plays a set, they tend not to refer to written music. By that point, they should have the melodic core and the harmonic language of their tunes comfortably in their head and hands. Traditionally, the performance is set in motion with a full statement of the melody, called the "head," and while many musicians will respect that melody note-for-note, some will begin recasting it right away. A tune's chord changes are roughly defined, but they are also negotiable. Much, but not everything, about "Footprints" is up for re-imagining. Indeed it's common to hear interpretations of standards that stretch so far, it is challenging to spot the source material, even though it's in there. There's more about this in Chapter 16.

A more recent form of improvised music comes from DJs and electronic musicians who sculpt and craft sound in real time, live performance. The scratching DJs from the first waves of hip-hop used their imagination to pull samples off existing albums, layer and juggle two or more sources against one another, and improvise rhythmic ideas with needles on records and fader boxes as their instrument. More recently, DJs use computers, synthesizers, and libraries of digital samples to spin webs of sound for live audiences. Such forms of improv can also be central to some popular record-making as well. In the studio, musicians play spontaneously for long stretches, capturing and keeping the best ideas, layering parts over one another, and editing the results into a satisfying whole.

The jam band movement sustains because of an ethos of playing in the moment, of conjuring musical moods and spirits for an audience that wants to be surprised and moved, often to dance. Phish, an extraordinary band no matter what their detractors say, uses songs as their skeletal structure, agreeing on the bones but letting everything else grow out of every performance. As they built their concept in the late 1980s, one tactic found guitarist Trey Anastasio (who studied music theory and contemporary composition in college) leading the band with a system of hand gestures. This subtle onstage conducting let the band shift from one feeling or sequence to another on the fly, giving the concert unbroken flow while retaining the freedom to play those concepts differently each time.

Phish, their forebears The Grateful Dead, and other jam bands, occupy a place in our Venn diagram where improvised and popular overlap. They're self-taught musicians who fit in the rock genre. They draw from and convey respect for American folk and world folk styles. *But their mission is to improvise.* In this way they are powerful musical hybrids. Dead and Phish fans like me value their instrumental novelty. We expect to be taken on a sound journey that goes far beyond the brief and pre-rehearsed instrumental "breaks" we hear in most rock or country songs. Jam structure depends on the song frameworks pulled from popular music, but it wouldn't have built such an audience and musical ecosystem without the improvisation. It's a mesmerizing balance of framework and freedom.

***

While some musicians excel across the modes, others have blind spots and personal capacities that inhibit mode jumping. Only the rare jazz artist is inclined to create large-scale, through-composed works for big ensembles. And many who work at high levels in composed music struggle to improvise, because it's not how they learned and not how their musical minds flow. Some popular musicians such as Sting and Paul McCartney have made forays into orchestral composing with mixed results, but it's worth mentioning some of the most acclaimed efforts from recent years, such as Jonny Greenwood of Radiohead and Bryce Dessner of The National.

In the middle of our Venn diagram, all three modes overlap, where lives, in my reckoning, some of the most elevated and distinctive music ever made. I mentioned Duke Ellington, because he was a genius who worked at the center of this fugue. His idiom or language was jazz, a fusion of popular music's blues roots and artistic improvisation, while his method was to compose for a big band or jazz orchestra, borrowing from classical icons like Bach and Bartok. Duke and later Gil Evans were pioneers of a hybrid of classical and jazz that critics in the 1960s started calling Third Stream music. Other musicians who commingle all three modes would include Frank Zappa and more recently Texas collective Snarky Puppy, whose Grammy Award-winning suite *Sylva* (2015) is a thrilling album that balances orchestral sweep and jazz improvisation with rhythmic language from hip-hop.

One thing music fans will discover as they explore the realms of improvised and composed music is that works tend to be longer than in popular styles. Instead of three to five minute songs, works can extend to ten minutes or more, and of course full symphonies can run for an hour. I recall that on the fantastic 1990s music appreciation show "Schickele Mix" from NPR (still available on the Internet Archive), host Peter Schickele would set up his examples by telling the audience how long they would be. This management of my expectations had a powerful effect on my attention span, and I began to understand how some musical effects depend on certain lengths of time. As you try new stuff, notice the length of works before you sit with them, and use the longer forms of composed and improvised music as a respite from the ADD culture we live in. Moreover, in jazz and classical, there are many five-minutes-or-less works, tunes, and movements to enjoy.

So, be mindful of the three modes and how they overlap and amplify each other. None of this is about trying to confine musicians and creators to categories. They'll do what they do. This is about how we listeners pay respect to the different skillsets and focal points of musical creation. We can explore not one, not two, but three whole fields of music-making, each with its own history and variety and crossover. The modes feed and inform one another. Appreciating the order and plan of Mozart's composed music makes the spontaneous order of Sonny Rollins's improvised saxophone that much more impressive. Feeling the freedom of Art Blakey playing jazz drums can set you up to wonder at the mastery of a notated percussion section in a symphony by Shostakovich. And we should celebrate popular artists who seek inspiration from the other modes, rather than borrowing only from other pop forms. It's like getting the gift of music three times over. Each mode has its pure examples, and vast bodies of great music are born in their overlap. Embrace the blur, the beautiful blur.

Listen for . . .

. . . works that are pure examples of the modes and others that are hybrids. Notice the unique powers of each mode to create works that stir different parts of your musical brain.

. . . aspects and elements of new music you discover that are drawn from popular forms, composed techniques, and improvisation.

Highly Musical Humans

Hilary Hahn

My first Highly Musical Human comes from not just the world of classical concert music but its very highest reaches, because in a genre field this overwhelming, one needs an easy and unmistakable place to start. Not being an expert in classical, I can't say anything new or revelatory about violinist Hilary Hahn, who may be the most famous soloist of her era. But she is as life-changing and thrilling as the many artistic traditions she embodies. Since emerging in the 1990s as a storybook prodigy, she's been a star who has performed the historic violin repertoire as well as anyone, and she has premiered new works by current and sometimes younger composers. She's won three Grammy Awards and played for presidents, so if you don't have much of a classical music life yet, she's an ideal way in.

Born in 1979 and raised around Baltimore, Hilary Hahn attended Johns Hopkins' music academy and played herself into Philadelphia's super-prestigious Curtis Institute of Music at age 10. One month after her twelfth birthday, she made her concert debut with the Baltimore Symphony, and she was a star by the end of the 1990s. Her recording debut with Sony Classical in 1997 (at 17 years old) was a chance to make a statement, so she chose the body of work she knew best from years of almost daily study—the famous solo Sonatas and Partitas by J.S. Bach, a titanic musical figure whom we'll address later. This is the first record I'd urge you to search up and sit with.

Here you get to listen for Bach's breakthrough harmonic architecture, with melodic line and counterpoint, as well as Hahn's youthfully enthusiastic but mature respect for the composing. Mind the contours of melody and the way the artist ties one note to the next with her supple bow touch. It almost goes without saying that her intonation (her pitch) and precise reading of every note are impeccable, but that's table stakes at this level. With the violin's rich tone nakedly audible, Hahn's varied dynamics and expressions are easy to hear: buttery, crisp, whispery, caramelized, authoritative, plaintive, amorous, and on and on. The "Chaconne" fifth movement of the #2 Partita in D minor blows my mind with its endless double stop playing, like two violins coming out of one instrument. These works have been in my life since I was 10, and they are foundational to western music.

Hahn has recorded all the great violin concertos, including Beethoven, Mendelssohn, and Samuel Barber (a personal favorite), as well as the important American composer Jennifer Higdon (challenging but enthralling). All are recommended, though these longer works take a high degree of commitment and concentration. So I'll point you to two more albums that, while accessible, will stretch your ears and probably surprise you. First is the *Sonata for Violin* and *Piano No. 2* by Charles Ives (1874–1954), a great example of early twentieth-century American music, in that it is harmonically floating without an obvious key center. Some will find this dissonant, but it's not ugly at all. It's haunting and pastoral. In fact I've chosen this one because I know Americana, and this is Americana. Ives titles the three movements not Adagio or Allegro but 1. "Autumn," 2. "In the Barn," and 3. "The Revival," evoking a country music tapestry. Ives said he was inspired by ragtime (then the hot new American pre-jazz sound), and the work quotes melodies from "Turkey In The Straw" and "The Battle Cry of Freedom." See if you can spot them in the 2011 release by Deutsche Grammophon featuring Hahn with pianist Valentina Lisitsa. The whole thing is less than 13 minutes long.

Finally, part of my book's agenda is to promote and elevate today's best musical creators and composers, and Hahn is all about that too, through frequent commissions. Let this spirit point you to a record called *In 27 Pieces: The Hilary Hahn Encores*, named for 27 short works for violin and piano by Hahn's friends and colleagues of all ages—a who's who of modern composing. This collection demonstrates that composed music, unbound by genre conventions, is as infinite as the human imagination. None of these works sounds like any other. You'll like some and dislike some, just like me. I never listen to more than a few at a sitting, because each is so rich and thought-provoking. They also show Hahn's mind-boggling technical skills—her speed, delicacy, control, and superhuman reach. I'm partial to: David Lang's "Light Moving," a pulsing dance of notes that delivers on its title; Mason Bates's "Ford's Farm," which evokes bluegrass fiddling; "Echo Dash" by the aforementioned Jennifer Higdon, in which the piano and violin chase each other in a fugue-like race; and "Two Pieces" by Valentyn Sylvestrov, which will put you in a more comfortable, romantic headspace than most of the others.

A person doesn't need to know music theory to be moved by a musician like Hilary Hahn. Yet knowing the basics should help you hear new things and widen your feeling for what's beautiful. That's what's next.

PART II

∫

HEARING

5

FROM THE SOUND UP
Your laudatory auditory system

n 1993, The Food Network became part of the cable TV menu
and over the next 25 years it synched up with the chef and
farm-to-table movements to help revolutionize food culture in
the United States. Food Network's most creative programming, like
Alton Brown's explanatory and scientific *Good Eats*, as well as some
of the chef contest shows, took viewers inside the multilayered culinary world and made them smarter about—and more aware of—the
power of their senses of smell and taste.

MTV, which switched on in 1983, had a dramatically different
effect on its purported field of interest. Instead of digging deep on the
subject of music, it made popular music more dependent on image
and celebrity than ever before. It excluded vast realms of musical
creativity from its highly influential playlist, including even hip-hop
until the network was shamed into programming Black music in
the late '80s. For decades after, artist discovery, development, and
presentation in popular music was shaped around its viability on and
for MTV and its imitators, VH1 and CMT.

What a paradox we have here. The Food Network wasn't even
able to present its actual subject matter—the food itself—over the
medium of television. It could depict lovingly shot dishes and the
hosts having flavor-gasms on camera. But we don't have Taste-o-
Vision yet. So the channel could only produce content *about* food,
and it changed the culture. The Food Network "took an American
public that largely didn't know or care about cooking and turned

them into foodies," wrote Jesse David Fox at Vulture on its 20th anniversary. Chefs became celebrities, and supermarkets of today, with their artisanal cheeses, duck breasts, fresh ginger, and international ingredients, look like specialty food shops of 30 years ago.

On the other hand, music *can* be presented on television, usually through live performance, but MTV did that relatively rarely and only in rock genres. Instead it played music videos 24/7, became a marketing partner of record companies and consumer brands, and made popular music more pop than it had ever been. It transformed what had been a robust, somewhat independent music business into a marketing behemoth aimed at teens and tweens. MTV could have presented information about music and how it works. But it offered almost nothing to make American music fans smarter or more aware of their potential as listeners.

No, MTV was something you watched, because much as we built our cities around the automobile, we've wired and organized our world to accommodate our visual brains. A great nation that was built in the age of radio had most of its aural attention hijacked by the irresistible medium of television. Imagery became the currency of advertising and entertainment. In our public spaces, our big box stores and our restaurants, the sonic environment is usually an afterthought. Hearing was enough; we weren't encouraged to truly listen. And this is what our sense of hearing is up against. Yet my experience tells me that discernment and appreciation in music begins with a feeling for the basics of sound and how we receive it. So let's take a close look (ahem) at listening.

***

Here's what most people know. Physical events send energetic waves through the medium of air. These sound waves reach our ears, where our eardrum and inner ear convert the pressure to nerve impulses that our brain interprets as information. All correct. But the musical citizen should appreciate the physics of sound and our extravagant, miraculous apparatus for perceiving and interpreting it.

Sound is dynamic and immersive, fluid and reactive. Even a quiet space is teeming with energy jostling every molecule of air, billions per cubic millimeter, in a complex, invisible dance. Any sound propagates in three dimensions from its source, and those waves interact and interfere with the fast fading echoes of the sounds that came just before. Sound strikes objects in space, like walls, and some of its energy bounces back as a reverberation, making for a complex acoustic situation. And here's where our auditory system takes over, starting with the visible part of our ears, those cartilaginous flaps that protrude from our heads with varying degrees of size and awkwardness. These are personal sound funnels called *pinnae*, whose form is integral to function. The folds and flaps imprint sound with subtle shadings, which our brains read as a kind of code to assist in sonic localization. With our eyes closed, we can tell the difference between a friend speaking to us from two feet straight ahead, or five feet away around a corner. We recognize sounds generated behind us because of the curling path they take around our pinnae on their way into our ear canals. And that's only the beginning of how our ears present a three dimensional picture of the world around us.

Our binaural hearing (two ears), combined with our unbelievably fast brain, gives us a kind of superpower. If a firecracker goes off 10 feet to your right, you snap your head in that direction without thinking. That's because even though the sound is traveling 700+ miles per hour, your brainstem is able to detect that it reached your right ear before your left and send a reflex signal to your muscles without even being processed cognitively. This built-in feature of being mammals is a product of evolution. Creatures with the quickest hearing, humans included, were more likely to detect threats in the wild and take evasive action. Those who didn't get eaten passed on their quick-reflex genes, over thousands of generations. Our herd was thinned depending on what we heard.

Further orienting us in the world is our amazing vestibular system, a pair of tiny gyroscopes networked into our inner ears. When we turn our heads, the inertial momentum is captured by tubes full of fluid oriented in three dimensions and converted into neural information. The ears, as a system, are constantly monitoring what's up and down, left and right, forward and back. Audio signals and spatial signals become woven together in our perceptive brains, somewhat like the dance between our senses of taste and smell. Music is composed and mixed across all genres so that the placement of different instruments plays a part in how it feels. Active listening makes a feedback loop with our sense of spatial orientation, an always-on form of mindfulness, whether we're enjoying music or a walk in the wilderness.

After sonic energy passes through the pinnae, it enters the inner ear, a narrowing series of chambers and interactions that amplify its signal strength. Sound reaches the eardrum, a stretched membrane that moves in response to energy. Ultra-sensitive, the eardrum can convey meaningful signals when displaced by the width of atoms. The energy is then transformed twice, instantaneously. First, the eardrum moves a set of three tiny, pivoting bones. Their leverage concentrates the energy by a factor of 22x before the third bone nudges the "oval window," the gateway to the cochlea, where sound energy moves through fluid. Coiled into the shape of a snail shell, our two cochleae are frequency detection devices. Special cells, usually likened to hairs, lie waiting in rows like sea anemones in a pitch black, ocean-filled cavern. Each set of hairs is tuned to a specific frequency, ignoring the rest but sending impulses down the auditory nerve when its frequency rings by, according to its strength. This Organ of Corti, which is about three centimeters long when uncoiled, enables all this transduction of energy by acting like a xylophone with thousands of tone bars. The highest audible frequencies "play" the bars at the opening of the cochlea and lower pitches have to travel farther in to reach their corresponding sensor cells. I've never known whether to think of this as miraculously complex or elegantly simple. But it works. And then it gets really weird and mysterious.

The processes by which the brain takes in this cascade of signals and assimilates them into something meaningful and possibly even beautiful and transcendent have been the subject of a flood of research in the past 25 years. One frequently cited finding emerging from the countless papers and books is that performing music involves the integrated activity of more parts of the brain than any other human pursuit. Listening to music, so they say, isn't far behind, because listening activates our motor cortex (as we imagine playing or dancing), our language cortex (as we process the syntactic aspects of music), and our higher cognitive functions as well, as we deduce factors like context and the artists' intent. In his wonderful and influential 2006 book *This Is Your Brain on Music*, record producer turned neuroscientist Daniel Levitin notes that "basic structural elements (of music) are incorporated into the very wiring of our brains when we listen to music early in our lives." From this, he asserts that music "can be thought of as a type of perceptual illusion in which our brain imposes structure and order on a sequence of sounds."

Notice too that the ears are not the only path for musical sound to reach our mind and soul. Dame Evelyn Glennie, the world famous concert percussionist who lost most of her hearing by age 12, perceives sound, including pitch and rhythm, through her feet, hands, and skin. She can make improvised tonal music with other musicians with no hearing aids, only a keenly attuned human body. She teaches these skills to young people with hearing disabilities, and she's a living symbol of how much our minds crave sonic sensory input. She'll come up again in Chapter 10.

At least as amazing, through selective attention, your brain knows that a singer's voice is part of the music but that the clinking of glassware or the bartender talking to a patron over your right shoulder is not. The mind integrates the direct signal from each instrument with its many reverberations, into an overall (hopefully) pleasant effect. And in a process that we'll discuss later that is too easy to take for granted, the brain infers a distinctly different sound from each cymbal, each guitar, each singer. From jostling molecules of air, we derive a coherent, meaningful, sometimes emotionally explosive inner experience.

***

One can't fully appreciate sound, especially music, without dwelling on and embracing the beauty of sound's opposite, sound's absence. "We need to regain quietude in order that fewer sounds can intrude on it with pristine brilliance," wrote audio theorist Murray Schaffer. It's a call to focus and discernment that shouldn't be overlooked. Notice please that neither Schaffer nor I are celebrating 'silence,' because that's a physical impossibility and a metaphysical bundle of problems. The right word is *quiet* I think, or *stillness*.

Working in radio has helped me hear quiet in new ways. When producing sound stories, we capture what's called *room tone*. After or before an interview, I record 15 seconds of the space we're in. We need this on hand because when we make an abrupt edit to a speaker, the background sound drops out too. The audience won't notice the background sound when it's there, but they certainly hear when it cuts off, because we're so attuned to sudden sonic *change*. Having room tone means I can fade the room out rather than cut it, attracting no attention. Through this, I've heard the rather dramatic differences among "quiet" spaces. Conference rooms in office parks have different hums and whispers than marble lobbies, old houses, hotel hallways, or barns. Restaurants and coffee shops are fonts of noise, but no two sound quite alike. Such backdrops surround us every day, all the time. Schaffer called this our *soundscape*, and he urges us to be mindful of it.

Perhaps you've heard of *signal-to-noise ratio*, which is a big deal in science and digital technology but also a core value for most musical people, even if we don't often use the term explicitly. Signal is what has meaning to you in the moment. Noise is the rest of whatever sound is happening that your neurons have to filter out. Our phones are a case study in signal-to-noise ratios changing over time, and not in a good direction. I grew up with copper landlines, when the voice at the other end was clear and distinct, even emotionally resonant, against a rather quiet background. Today's digital cell signals are often constricted and compressed, with a slurry of digital artifacts competing with the voice. Many people I know have grown to dislike phone communication over the years, in part because the brain gets literally tired of the extra work it has to do sifting the signal from the noise.

Therefore, quality music and active listening ask for a quiet space, just as a painting asks for a clean, blank canvas. There's nothing wrong with the hubbub of a concert venue for a rock or pop show or the conversations and revelry at a music festival. That music is amplified, and the atmosphere is part of the experience in the song-based world, even if some people could do a lot better respecting the concert experience of others. The sound-based music world though generally makes use of venues designated and designed for closer attention. Concert halls, jazz clubs, performing arts centers, and "listening rooms" cultivate an environment that gives the artists the best chance to achieve their vision and intent, because some of the most sensuous parts of music happen at the edges of notes and the transitions of silence to sound or sound to silence. In fact, researchers have found that our brains can become especially active during pauses in music, revving up so to speak in anticipation of the next signal. I'm aware that in Mozart and Beethoven's day, audiences could be rowdy and voluble throughout performances. That doesn't mean they had the best solution. Those people also used to submit to leeches to cure the clap. I believe we've made progress by creating forums and settings for quiet and active listening.

So with refreshed respect for our sonic surroundings and our auditory apparatus, let's get into the elements of musical creation and reception. Against a quiet background comes music—organized, controlled sound, created deliberately by a soloist or a group of people, sometimes just a few and sometimes more than one hundred. Behind this sound-making is a vast world of process and practice and commerce and culture. But set that aside for now and focus on three sonic elements, and because it's memorable and snappy to put things in alliterative lists of three, I call them Tone, Time and Timbre.

Tone is anything that has to do with pitch, including notes, melody, and harmony. If you can hum it or write it down on staff paper, it's tone. While tone is the stuff of the vertical staff lines in written music, where we represent pitches rising and falling, then *Time* is the horizontal dimension, the left to right motion and flow, energized by the phenomenon we call rhythm. Without this clockwork, music becomes a very weak tool for moving people, and to get a little meta about it, without the passage of time, no work can actually exist. Time comprises the temporal minutes it takes to experience a work, as well as the subdivided seconds that tie music to our heartbeats, brain waves, and dancing bodies. *Timbre* is the least understood and most subtle of our big three. For now let's call it sonic texture and color and save the rest for later. This T is far more essential to how we perceive and categorize music than we've been led to believe, and it is intimately related to how musicians shape and shade their instruments or voice for maximum emotional and musical effect.

But let's start with tone.

Listen for . . .

. . . soundscapes wherever you go, from natural environments to public places to your work environment. What's quality signal and what is noise?

. . . the quietest sounds you can detect. See if you can hear a cat padding across the floor or water dripping in another room. Do you perhaps have any tinnitus, an ever-present ringing or hissing in your ears? A visit to an audiologist for a detailed hearing work-up is good advice for anyone.

WATCH YOUR TONE
A pitch for intonation

The pipe organ was the first high tech musical instrument. For thousands of years, people blew air through or over tuned tubes to make notes, like Pan pipes. But when the super-organs came to the churches of medieval Europe, they were something else entirely—a source and symbol of raw power. Have you heard an organ fill a stone cathedral with its gargantuan, resonating tones? Imagine how that sounded in the sixteenth century, like the voice of God visiting your tedious life in a day-to-day soundscape comprised largely of animals, carts on cobblestones, human chatter, and the occasional war. I bet it felt pretty great.

Centuries later, I too had an organ induced epiphany in a church, which sounds pretty sketchy, but I assure you it was entirely musical in nature. As I've said, I take musical epiphanies seriously, meaning those *a-ha* moments when we recognize something new and useful about the art form and how it works. They are breakthrough insights that become habits of mind. Your goal is to take what you've learned conceptually about music and then put yourself in places where you're likely to hear music that connects with something you learned in the abstract. It might be chromatic soloing (we'll get to it) or syncopation or recognizing a motif. Epiphanies unlock a thing that once heard, you'll be wired to hear again and again, across all music.

Anyway, this story starts with my violin teacher's son Nicholas. Nick was almost exactly my age, and starting around middle school we became close friends. A better violinist than I was, he went on to a world-traveling professional career with a string quartet, but his gifts never intimidated me. I enjoyed being around (and performing with) a musician who was clearly special, and I learned a lot from him, his mom, and his family generally. Nick's father Joseph was an academic mathematician who had a second career as the music director for an Episcopal church in my neighborhood. And one Saturday when I was about 13, Nick and I got taken along to hang out while Joe took care of some business, which was to tune the organ that he'd be playing on Sunday.

Joe didn't let us get bored; he showed us how it worked. He pushed down a key triggering a pipe he knew to be in tune—his reference pitch—and he put a little wooden wedge in the key so the pipe would play continuously. Then he did the same with another key and thus another pipe, producing two pitches in the big church sanctuary. These notes were the same, but the second pipe wasn't perfectly in tune. He urged us to pay attention to the way the pitches interfered with each other, producing a warbling or beating effect. It was strong—a *whir-whir-whir* where before with one pipe there had been a clean tone.

So then Joe went to the base of the second pipe, where there was a little slider that subtly changed the length and thus the pitch, a fine-tuning device, because the organist has to be able to compensate when the pipe's base tuning is slightly warped by temperature or humidity. With a tiny hammer he tapped the slider, and we heard the effect on the relationship between the pitches. The whirring slowed down. The closer he got to matched tuning, the slower the beats got, until they vanished and the notes merged, seemingly into one.

In this ad hoc demonstration, I was hearing and learning a lot about pitch, tone, and frequency. When the pipes were just out of tune, I could internalize sound as a physical force in the room. I visualized, however crudely, waves rippling out from the organ pipes and interfering with each other. They became almost as tangible as the organ itself.

I knew something about tuning from years of violin lessons. Before I could do anything on the violin, my strings had to be cleanly in tune from low to high: G-D-A-E. Nowadays, electronic tuners show us visually if we're sharp, flat, or spot-on. But this was, let's say, before that. I had to tune by ear. My reference pitch was a tuning fork, a piece of metal cut and weighted to vibrate at the benchmark pitch of concert A. I would twist the tuning peg until my open A string was close to the tuning fork. Then I'd use these very handy fine-tuner knobs at the other end of the string to get it exact. I did not have a tuning fork for the other strings, so the game was to tune them in reference to the A. I'd play the A and D string together. This happens to be a perfect fifth, a vital harmonic interval (which we'll talk about soon), but I didn't have to know that to lock in the tuning of the D string. I could hear it and feel it. My two-note interval sounded nasty until I focused it with the D string tuning peg. Then it felt coherent and clean. That could be repeated with the high E and low G. Thankfully, a good violin holds itself in tune pretty well, so this wasn't a big tedious deal.

Intonation, the state of being in tune, matters to the integrity of musical performance. Musicians in the genres I follow and love really care about getting this right, sometimes at the expense of the audience. Stringed instruments, especially the ones with frets, can be uncooperative during shows, leading to pauses in the action. Jokes pass the time. "Mandolin is Italian for out of tune!" Tim O'Brien will say while tweaking his eight strings. The cliché fallback is: "We tune because we care." And a good one I heard recently: "Folks, tuning is like aircraft maintenance. You'll thank us when we're in flight." And indeed, when a bluegrass band, or an orchestra, or an organ is in tune, synched up so that the sound waves support each other instead of defeat each other, acoustic magic is more likely to happen.

Piano tuning (always done by professionals away from the audience because it takes quite a while) is fascinating, because each note is a composite of two or three strings vibrating together when struck by the piano's hammer. The tuner tends to want the bass notes to be perfectly matched for purity, but in the mid and upper registers, they will tweak certain strings by a fraction of a note, for a gentle and pleasing interference of the kind that Joseph showed us with the organ pipes. If you have a chance, strike a piano note around the middle and hold it. In the long decay, you'll hear gentle whirs in there, and just the right amount enriches the sound. When my acoustic guitar is truly in tune (sometimes it cooperates, sometimes not), it's strikingly more energetic. It sits lighter in my lap and it resonates with more wood and air. For the player and audience, slightly imperfect tuning isn't necessarily going to ruin a good show, but it all feels sweeter if it's right.

All this said, clean and perfect western scales are not an end in themselves and not the only way. Great music is overflowing with notes that are bent, slid, slurred and shaded. The blues depends on microtonal angst. Bill Monroe's high tenor notes in his bluegrass songs sounded more emotional and intense by being just a shade flat, very much on purpose. Because the voice is more flexible and expressive than any instrument in its use of tuning nuances, Auto-Tune software, an invention of the digital age, is controversial among musicians and superfans. My feeling is that Auto-Tune is simply a tool, one that's been used with subtlety and sometimes with intentional, dramatic intent (famously in Cher's innovative "Believe"). It has also been overused to absurdity in pop music and mishandled in country music, where the blues bedrock of the genre is incompatible with the idea of "fixing" notes. So as you develop your ear for pitch, you'll be able to hear when music is in tune for real, unfortunately out of tune, out of tune on purpose, or pitch-corrected with software. And again, I will disclaim that this conversation and the harmonic material ahead is centered on western and American musical forms. Other cultures have music based on different scales and pitch vocabularies instead of our 12-tone system. That's important and all out there for you to discover, but it's beyond my scope.

Let's untangle and embrace some terminology to get out of this chapter with the most tools for the road ahead, a few common words I've been using without good context: frequency, note, and pitch. They are close in their meaning, with fine points. The most scientific and precise is frequency, which refers to the number of sound waves (or cycles) per second generated by a vibrating body, measured in the unit hertz (Hz). Humans can hear frequencies as low as 20 Hz and as high as 20,000, and we tend to lose the high end, about the top 5,000 Hz, as we age. Music folks (especially audio nerds) are aware of the frequency ranges in our assessment of music. The bass extends up to about 250 Hz. The midrange, where we hear voices and melodic instruments, goes from there to about 4,000 Hz. Above that is the treble, which encompasses the highest notes on the piano or violin and then further up to where we hear the sizzle of cymbals and the sibilant sounds (like the letter S) in the human voice. Certain frequencies of sound were designated as "notes" through a complex series of attempts to set standards in Europe and the US, ultimately settled by some accounts in the 1920s. Middle C is 261.6 Hz. The A note you hear from that oboe when an orchestra tunes up before a piece is 440. If a given note is skewed above its reference, we say it's sharp, and if skewed too low, we say it's flat.

One remarkable feature of pitch and frequency, which will come up in more detail later on, is that when we double any given frequency, say from the 440 A to 880, it also makes an A, one octave above the reference pitch. Cut the frequency in half, down to 220, and you get an octave lower. The 110 hertz A is pretty low, but you have to go down two octaves below that, to 22.5 hertz, to reach the lowest note on a standard piano. They are all the note A, octaves apart. If you don't already have a feeling for what an octave is, run to YouTube and do a search for a demonstration, and you'll quickly get it. Octaves are the anchor points of the western scale.

Of course you'd never say, "I loved that passage you composed, Max. You chose just the right frequencies." You'd use the word *notes*, because notes are what players play and what singers sing and what composers select. *Pitch* is a word sort of in between, sharing some meaning with the concepts of both note and frequency. To say "pitch" implies an objective tone that could be named or could be said to be sharp or flat against a reference note. Singers sometimes use a harmonica-like tool called a "pitch pipe" with reeds tuned to all the pitches in a 12-note scale. This can give, for example, an a cappella singing group a common reference pitch as they start a song. Here's a good place to point out that if a singing group sets their reference above or below the officially named pitches, they can still be in tune with each other. They'd be making use of *relative* pitch versus *absolute* pitch, and this will sound good to most people, except for the rare folks who have what's called "perfect pitch."

Yes, perfect pitch is real in a modest portion of our population (in societies with aggressive public music education the incidence is apparently a bit higher, so there's evidence that it can be both inborn and taught). It basically means a person can identify a pitch by name without any reference and/or sing any note—a D or a G or an F#—on request. It's an explicable psychological phenomenon that's far less weird than some of the things our brains can do. Some superior musicians have perfect pitch, but I've read that it confers little extra advantage of musicianship or musicality, though such people tend to also have an advanced inner ear that allows them to imagine and identify complex chords, which would be cool! For us mortal fans though, it's safe to pay perfect pitch little mind. But what I would warn against is downplaying or dismissing your own ability to hear pitch and intonation. It's weirdly common for people to claim (often with a kind of exaggerated resignation) that "I'm tone-deaf!" as a shorthand for saying they don't think of themselves as very musical. This is like setting out to climb a mountain and deciding to carry a 50 pound sack of potatoes for no reason. A small number of people do have brain irregularities that hurt their pitch perception, a form of what's called *amusia* by the doctors. But you almost certainly don't have that. You can discern pitch if you lean into it, which takes listening and attention. The best path to internalizing intonation is to sing notes out loud, steadily and with care, to match reference pitches from any instrument. Find a private place and sing, note by note, training your ears and your body. You'll start to hear music differently I suspect. You may not have perfect pitch, but singing as accurately as you can will help your overall musical trajectory to be more perfect.

Listen for . . .

. . . music that's out of tune for some reason, maybe a songwriter with a less than perfect guitar, and try to discern the specific offending note and whether it's sharp or flat.

. . . music that uses bent pitches below or above the true pitch for dramatic and emotional effect.

. . . your own voice singing pitches from a reference. Sing out loud with a piano and pay attention to the feeling of your body vibrating in tune.

7

CARRYING A TUNE
The marriage of melody and harmony

On the page, notes look like flocks of blackbirds arrayed on parallel power lines—or Arabic poetry, or some kind of 3D chess instructions written in Morse code. Country music pioneer Jimmie Rodgers called them "flyspecks." These hieroglyphics have bewildered nonmusicians and frustrated music students for eons. And yet, musical scores represent a pinnacle of human invention, a symbolic language that allows complicated musical works to be composed and codified, like literature or law, for a journey across time. The next two chapters are about notes—how they work and sound together when creators organize them into melody and harmony. And we're not going to read any music on the way. Just as one doesn't need to read Aramaic to grasp the Bible or read code to use computers, there are ways to internalize and appreciate the way music functions without knowing A flat from D natural. Yes, we'll encounter more terms than perhaps any other part of the book, but I want to at least introduce you to the rules of the game, in order to make music more accessible and rewarding. This is about the stuff the musical citizen should know without getting too far in the weeds. The terms are cool to learn anyway, because they are concepts that have implications beyond music.

Like so many people, I first experienced harmony in church. There I was, as a little kid, taking in the first live, ensemble music in a resonant space I probably ever heard. (This was a Presbyterian church by the way, so it was anything but funky. But in a way, its prim austerity made for a good elementary music education.) I was led to understand, in the first structural insight I was given about music, that the organ and choir made chords, while the congregation sang the melody. Simple enough. At some point, sensing I was old enough to grasp the idea, my mother urged me to listen to her as she deliberately sang a "harmony" line to the melody of some hymn. Her voice was easy to single out against the background as she complemented the melody. And I got it. I couldn't have made up my own harmony line at the time, but that would come later. First I had to name harmony and grasp that there was such a thing.

The melody seemed to need no explaining. It *was* the song, or the hymn, or whatever. Melodies were fundamental to everything I heard, from "Old MacDonald" to Sunday morning hymns to Elton John on the radio. How does a song *go*, musically speaking? The melody is what we think of. And as I grew up and found I could remember melodies with accuracy, Mom told me that I could "carry a tune." Perhaps it's significant that the first instrument I played, the violin, is essentially melodic. While it can play two notes at once, playing chords is not what it was designed for. Where my later study of the guitar would give me access to the harmonic side of music, the violin set me out on my journey, for better or worse, with a melody-forward idea of music.

Later, in my years of befriending country, folk, and jazz musicians in Nashville, I heard them talk about their deep and inspiring reverence for melody. They really think about it, as did their heroes. The late great banjo player Earl Scruggs heard from his mother when he was young and learning that he needed to think less about his fancy rolls of notes and more about a clear melody. He pushed himself to do just that and revolutionized the technique banjo players have used ever since. Mozart himself (who sure could compose harmony) said, "melody is the very essence of music." And 150 years later, just before an anti-melody revolution in modern music, the great progressive Stravinsky echoed Mozart, saying that "melody should keep its place at the summit of the hierarchy of all elements which constitute music."

Melody and harmony, while distinct, are integrally related and bound together in a complementary, yin-yang sort of embrace. A common analogy is made to a painting's foreground (melody) and background (harmony), but we need to disturb this simple conception a bit, first by asking more rigorously what is a melody exactly? It's like asking what's a sentence? Both melodies and sentences are linear sequences of deliberate choices drawn from a limited set of variables, with unlimited possibilities. Every melodic moment represents a choice for the creator, a pitch giving way to one of four options: a higher pitch, a lower pitch, the same pitch again, or no pitch at all. Rests are every bit as essential to melody as the notes, as are the durations of all the notes and rests. In this sense, even simple melodies are microcosms of music. Rhythmic and harmonic content are integrally bound up. So no wonder people have been singing single-line melodies to themselves to pass the time for millennia. They are as nourishing as oxygen or water. Or words.

Melodies are as long or short as they need to be in each musical situation. Melodic passages that recur in a work, often with variations or extrapolations, are called *themes* or *motifs*. Related to these are riffs, common in rock and pop, like the guitar statement that kicks off the J.J. Cale song "Cocaine." Riffs are too truncated to be considered a melody, but they generally establish the kernel of the melody to come. If a melody is too long or unresolved, it can lose us and feel unsatisfying. Melodies can be easy to follow or perplexing or difficult, and this is influenced by several factors. Country, folk, and pop melodies have a strong form, with repeating phrases, easy to count sections and a kind of symmetry. But in other genres, some melody is very fast, with notes piling on notes in torrents, and while extreme versions of this can leave melody behind for sheer texture, I've noticed that people can be put off by the speedy melodies found in some jazz improvising. While we all seem born to follow simple melodies, learning to follow and enjoy complex, prolonged and densely packed melodies can take time and exposure.

Melodies play diverse roles, dominating the foreground of some works and merely suggesting themselves in others. Melody can be played by a soloist or a section of an ensemble. They can feel like soliloquies or exhortations or provocations or sermons, because melody is as diverse and impressionable as any mode of human speech and rhetoric. So I encourage you at this point to sharpen your melodic focus. Pull up songs you love and listen to regularly and try to isolate the melody from the lyrical content and backup. Give it the attention it deserves and feel the interaction with the other elements of the music. Notice when there is or isn't melody happening on a record. While a lot of great progressive music of the past 50 years eschewed melody for more abstract concepts, emphasizing chords or textures instead, we're going back with this meditation to an especially melodic era. There's a critical consensus and even some research finding that in mainstream pop, melody has grown more simplistic and dull in the past few decades.

As with musicians, some melodies are better than others. But what's the criteria? How can we presume to declare one chain of notes, rising and falling and rising again on a trip through time, superior to another? Classic pop and classic country music are rich with melody, while current pop and country are less so, so let's look to American standards to think about that question. "Somewhere Over the Rainbow" is melancholy yet majestic. "When the Saints Go Marching In" is streamlined and ripe for improvisation. "Ain't Misbehavin'" fused early jazz with Broadway. "Time After Time" is a pop melody so seductive it's been recorded by dozens of artists since Cyndi Lauper wrote and recorded it. The great country songs are anchored in melody, so the great ones like "Cold, Cold Heart" or "Crazy Arms" are tunes that millions of non-musicians have sung to themselves or at karaoke for the sheer pleasure of feeling the melody unfold. My gold medal hall of fame melodies would also include the magic old jazz number "Begin the Beguine," the country/soul song "You Don't Know Me" and the show tune from *My Fair Lady*, "On the Street Where You Live."

Let's talk about that last one, a love song written by composer Frederick Lowe and lyricist Alan Jay Lerner and premiered in 1956. It has broad, sweeping lines and intricacies that make it a good lesson. If you are a dedicated show tune fan, perhaps you can conjure "On the Street Where You Live" in your mind's ear clearly and accurately, but that would make you rare. I'd recommend pulling it up on a streaming service (Nat King Cole, always a good choice for melodic pop like this, has a great version). Listen again with fresh ears. Pay attention as it develops, considering every note and rest. Don't trust your imperfect memory here. Get the song in your head for real and do your best to hum or sing it out loud.

Notice that the melody doesn't start on the first beat of the measure, but the third beat. There's a little two-beat pause just before each key phrase begins, a reminder that melody is made of rests as well as notes. Once underway, the melody starts on the home key note then rises, with three scale steps, like a major scale, and then it hops up a bit, by three more steps. Then it falls, in a mirror image of the first phrase. Then it begins to repeat itself, but the leap reaches farther and higher, to a note that insistently repeats, starting with the second syllable of the word "pavement" and continuing on the words "always stayed" and then there's a toggle back and forth before a fall that echoes the first fall. Then the kicker, patiently set up by Mr. Lowe's composing, as the line soars with the words "All at once (leap!) am I, Several stories high," before taking the stairs down to the end of the verse (and the hook of the song) through the line, "Knowing I'm on the street where you live." While this mighty melody spoons intimately with the song's lyrics, it stands on its own, leading many a jazz artist to cover it with instruments only.

That said, melodies that relate to and resemble human speech tend to be robust and relatable, explaining why some melodies can be described as "lyrical," as paradoxical as that sounds. Quality can also come from balance, general symmetry, dramatic timing, thoughtful development, and a feeling of climax and anticlimax. It's in the graceful bridging of one note to the next, starting with small steps and then introducing larger steps in both directions. And here we arrive at the most important thing I can share with you about melody and harmony in the grand scheme. We are taught mostly to think of music as a sequence of notes and chords, but you'll feel and hear more by focusing on the *intervals*.

***

Intervals are everything. *EVERYTHING*. Notes are powerless without a relationship to notes before and after them in a melodic line. And chords, where harmony comes alive, are best thought of not as stacks of notes but as the sound effects made by the intervals separating the notes. The notes we hear relate existentially to each other, to the home key of the piece, and to the departures from that home key. You may have heard the sage but possibly perplexing musical advice that music is truly found "in the space between the notes." This can be taken two instructive ways. It could mean the pauses where no note is played, or it could mean the harmonic intervals between the notes as they flow by. That's the space between the notes we're going to think about now.

Our minds respond to intervals as a factor of both innate biology and experience. Some intervals are more "natural" sounding and obvious than others, starting with the easily understood octave. As we discussed in the previous chapter, octaves are made by doubling the frequency of any given pitch. These 2:1 relationships are easy for us to hear. Now I hasten to say that an innate human sense of octaves is a matter of some dispute at the fringes of the musicological world, but I'm persuaded by the case that our brains are very good ratio-detecting machines and that it's no coincidence that our near universal experience of pleasant sounding intervals has something to do with orderly mathematical ratios. You are free to explore the counter-theories.

To make sure we're all on the same page, let's review some basics. Connecting each octave, the western scale has eight notes or pitches, double counting the key note at the bottom and top. Most of us know the common major scale, tunefully represented in the *Sound of Music*, as Do-Re-Mi-Fa-Sol-La-Ti-Do. Musicians represent this with "scale degree" numbers for notes, one to seven, not counting the octave at the top. Most of the scale notes are a whole tone or whole step apart, but not all of them. Between the three and the four (Mi and Fa) is a half step. Same with Ti and Do up there, as the seven resolves to the octave. There are many other scales with all manner of intervals on the way from the root to the octave, each with its own feeling.

Octaves are harmonically weak, creating no color or sense of motion. We start to generate chords with the highly potent scale degrees three and five. And where scale degrees are expressed as numbers, we speak about their *intervals* as "thirds" (one to three) and "fifths" (one to five). The opening of the song "Blueberry Hill" by Fats Domino is a great way to sing and hear this. The melody rises from its home note to the third, then the fifth, then the octave, tracking the four words "I found my thrill . . . ". This is a great one to sing and internalize, because it spells out the bedrock chord of western harmony, the *major triad*.

I want to keep terminology to a minimum in this book, but this major triad idea is as simple as it is important, a name for something we already feel or know intuitively. It rather obviously means *three*, as in three pitches, stacked into the most elemental of chords, spelled one-three-five. (The octave, being a repeat of the home pitch is not considered part of the triad.) We could play all three notes of the triad at the same time, making a chord, or we could play them in sequence (as in the song we're talking about), which we call an *arpeggio*. Either way, the major triad becomes a kind of home base, and much harmonic complexity can be heard as variations on or additions to this foundational three-note chord.

To feel the power of intervals, imagine making a small change to the "Blueberry Hill" triad. Take the pitch of the word "found" (the third in our triad) and drop it down by a half step. It's the smallest move we can make in the western scale, just one adjacent key on the piano. Yet with this tiny gesture, the triad's nature is transformed from *major* to *minor*, the well-known (if oversimplified) contrast between a bright and upbeat feeling to a sound that's darker and sadder. This is elementary terrain for musical people, but it's good to be reminded of what a dramatic change in emotion and harmonic meaning can be achieved by shifting just one interval by just one half step.

Some of y'all may be losing the thread by now, but let me offer this reassurance. Music is to be heard and enjoyed, not named or analyzed. Yet it's useful to at least appreciate how musicians think. So let me offer more of a metaphor or framework for the inner game of intervals and the feelings they can evoke. Let's call it *tonality*. Different works of music across all genres, and often passages within works, have different tonalities, resulting from the way intervals are deployed in their chords and scales. Now that we've flagged the commonplace tonalities of major and minor, let's build on that. I learned for example that some music (I've heard this in some Celtic folk and some rock and metal) is constructed to scrupulously avoid thirds. And think what that means. Without any thirds or flat thirds of the root note, there are no cues telling your ears that the work is major or minor. Such music floats ambiguously in between, a beguiling tonality of its own.

Another tonality you might conjure up in your mind's ear is built on a certain modal scale with the wild name Phrygian Dominant. Don't panic or remember that. What's important is that this is a scale Hollywood composers turn to for scenes with camels striding across the Sahara desert. It's a western scale that coincides just enough with the harmonic language of North Africa and the Middle East to conjure those sensations and associations in the mind. This effect works because of certain intervals that are emphasized and others that are carefully avoided so as to keep a consistent tonality in play.

Other tonalities define the blues. Musicians learning any form of popular music practice "blues scales" to get those intervals deeply ingrained. You know them when you hear them coming out of the voice or guitar of B.B. King, and the sharp musical citizen will perk up when a blues scale emerges in other genres, such as the classical composing of George Gershwin. In related terrain, different approaches to tonality mark sonic boundaries between different schools of jazz: smooth, soul/funk, hot, or contemporary (where tonalities can be quite dense and complicated but so alluring). Composers turn to still other tonalities to evoke scenes in what's sometimes called "programmatic" composing, like a haunted house, a heroic Western movie vista, or a serene meadow in the Alps. While those are simple stories tied to visual media, heavier music presents us with a vast range of much more diverse and complex tonalities that seduce us for their own sake.

When I said earlier that melody has harmony baked in, I meant that the choice of notes/intervals that make up a melody strongly imply the chordal structure behind them. Consider a simple melody from the heart of country music, the Carter Family's "Wildwood Flower." As its opening line rises up, it hits all of the notes of the home chord, with some passing tones along the way. A musician could deduce the home chord of the first two measures by hearing the melody "spell" the essential notes that make the chord a C major. As it proceeds to the third measure, the notes spell or imply a different chord, a G major seventh chord, and then in measure four, we're back home to C major. Now be aware that this is the most simplistic version of the chords implied by the melody. A savvy musician would play other, nicely compatible chords behind the "Wildwood Flower" melody to create a new feeling and mood with this technique of *chord substitution*. This is also called *reharmonizing* a tune, and the concept will return later.

But let's wrap this chapter with possibly the most important thing you can do to bask in the harmonic convergence of melody and harmony, and that's to listen deeply and often to the music of Johann Sebastian Bach. He is the Alpha Dog and the Chairman of the Board for western harmonic potential. "Bach is Bach, as God is God," said the composer/critic Hector Berlioz, and he's far from alone in his high regard. Bach was a visionary on the order of Isaac Newton or Leonardo DaVinci, i.e. one who revolutionized his field and whose insights and techniques are studied to this day. One biographer, John Eliot Gardiner, said this about the composer's marriage of melody and harmony in his book *Bach: Music in the Castle of Heaven*: "Certainly no one before Bach (and only a handful of composers since) had used this point of intersection so fruitfully: melody underpinned by rhythm, enriched by counterpoint and coalescing to create harmony, itself a composite of consonance and dissonance that register in the listener's ear. Looked at another way, it is astonishing how the harmonic motion seems to carry the full freight of melodic ideas on its shoulders."

I'll talk about the vital concepts of consonance and dissonance soon, but please linger now on that word counterpoint. Counterpoint means setting one melody against another in a kind of woven pattern of notes across time. The technique can be found in popular music, as when the Everly Brothers move their vocal lines in opposite directions or past each other, flipping who's singing higher or lower. In most classical composed music, counterpoint is ever-present, because it gives melody more impact. And in Bach, counterpoint is the mesmerizing heart and soul of the music. Whether in his choral, orchestral, organ, or small ensemble works, counterpoint can be clearly heard through crisply articulated scales and heavy use of arpeggios that generate forward motion. Bach even uses counterpoint brilliantly in works for solo instruments, which would seem impossible, since it takes two melodies to contrapuntally tango. Yet in the famous and essential solo cello suites and violin sonatas and partitas, the lone string player, using mostly single lines, *implies* two or more moving parts. The mind's ear hears melodies that aren't really there. And the heart is embraced by a divinity made of nothing but immaculately arranged intervals.

Listen for . . .

. . . pieces that are major or minor in their dominant tonality. Some popular songs, "We Can Work It Out" by the Beatles is a good example, shift from major verses to a minor chorus or bridge.

. . . the distinct tonality of the blues in songs like John Lee Hooker's "Boogie Chillun."

. . . the difference in the tonal language of a smooth jazz track by sax player Dave Koz with that of a contemporary saxophonist like Joshua Redman.

Highly Musical Humans

Nir Felder

Given my listening habits and musical passions, I had to include a jazz guitar player in my list of HMHs. Instrumental guitar music could not be closer to my heart. The obvious recommendation would have been Julian Lage, a Bay Area native who is among my favorite contemporary musicians. He is to his field what Hilary Hahn is to hers—famous and critically acclaimed. But I'm going to go with Nir Felder, a New Yorker who, at 42, is five years older than Lage and a bit wider ranging in his guitar pursuits. I figure if I told you about Lage, you'd have only a small chance of discovering Felder by association, but if I tell you about Felder, and you like his music, your reckoning with Lage will be inevitable.

Felder, growing up in the suburbs of New York, picked up a $250 Fender Stratocaster guitar and started teaching himself, influenced by Eric Clapton, Stevie Ray Vaughan, and other blues/rock. During four years at the Berklee College of Music in Boston (a popular finishing school for jazz guitarists), he received an important scholarship. He moved to New York City and quickly became known as an outstanding and versatile sideman for live gigs and recording sessions. His list of credits is huge, but a sampling of names—Diana Krall, Kacey Musgraves, Kamasi Washington, Chaka Khan, and Common—suggests his range and repute. For his original material, NPR tagged Felder as the "next big jazz guitarist" in 2010. Sony Masterworks took him on, leading to his 2014 debut as a featured artist and bandleader.

That album, *Golden Age*, is bold and absorbing, with spoken word from historic tapes of Malcolm X, Barbara Jordan, and Richard Nixon woven in with a deft quartet. But I'd recommend you start with Felder's second album, simply called *II* from the summer of 2020. It's not your grandad's swinging jazz. Like the instrumental music I listen to most widely and hungrily these days, it's a bit cinematic, rock-influenced, highly varied, and often defined most by texture and feel. The artist uses studio overdubs to construct a soundscape over a core of jamming with his band. Amazing drumming from Nate Wood drives and sparkles behind Felder's rich and playful guitar. It's free-feeling but never too far out—a fine example of contemporary music that I'd think almost anybody could relate to.

I'd also point you to the first place I heard Felder, an album I fell for during the 2020 pandemic called *Soundtology*, led by keyboard player Kevin Field. Felder trades guitar duties throughout this album with another well regarded player and composer, Mike Moreno. To zone in on Felder's playing, I recommend "High Crane Drifter" with its 1970s rock fusion overtones and the epic "Quran Quran," where Felder establishes the mood and melody up front over a tricky time signature and delivers a gracefully unfolding solo about three minutes in.

Instrumental guitar music is rich terrain for new listeners. Felder has many excellent contemporaries, such as Kurt Rosenwinkel, Wolfgang Muthspiel, Molly Miller, Rob Luft, and Gilad Hekselman. As for their forebears and influences, I have a lifelong love affair with Bill Frisell, Pat Metheny, John Scofield, Joe Pass, Jim Hall, Kenny Burrell, and Wes Montgomery. To know them is to bond with an important American tradition that has fans all over the world.

As for Felder, he tours the world and works on various projects, still playing that $250 guitar he first purchased. "Jazz is one part high art, one part folk art," he told *JazzTimes*, "and I don't know how much sense it makes to make folk art on a $15,000 instrument."

PART III

∫

HARMONY

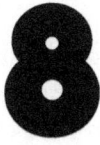

CHORDS AND THEIR CHANGES
Harmonic structure, progression, and resolution

ll this harmony/melody business only works on our hearts and minds because of the mechanics that hold music together as it moves through time. I didn't get this until I took bass lessons as a teenager. For years I'd experienced written music defining my part on the violin, but my bass teacher did something different. He wrote out songs or tunes as sequences of chords in a grid or *chord chart*, which mapped out measures and sections. It was music, but it was unlike anything I'd seen. A generic blues in the key of C looked like this:

	C	F7	C	C7
F7	F7	C	C
G7	F	C	G7 :	

Here, the vertical lines indicate measures, with four beats in each. For simplicity, every measure contains one chord, and the progression through these chords is what musicians call the tune's *changes*. Every 12 measures (or "bars") the cycle returns to the start and repeats (cued by the double dot), hence the term for the classic "12-bar blues." This is an almost painfully simplified chart, as songs usually have multiple sections, designated A, B, C, etc., but this example has just one repeating A section. A band could play this progression over and over until deciding collectively to play an outro/ ending. Simple though it seems, this charted chord sequence backs up a huge number of blues tunes, including the widely known "Sweet Home Chicago." An adept band can elaborate on these changes with complementary chord substitutions or extensions. But we're keeping things simple for now, through triads like C and F. I'll address those vital seventh chords shortly.

I remember feeling like I was let in on a secret when I saw this charting system. I'd spent years learning pieces by rote from written music, and I'd sometimes perform with a piano playing the chordal accompaniment, but my teacher never informed me that those pieces by Vivaldi, Mozart, etc.—not to mention symphonic works— had underlying chord progressions. What I remember being shown was a melodic way to hear classical music, and the powerful effects of harmonic motion were something I felt more than I understood. That said, charting the chords of a classical piece is terrain for experts, and this new framework came along just when I needed it—to understand the logic of jazz and pop songs. Charts guided my job as a bass player, because I had no pre-written part. My role was to anchor the harmonic backbone of tunes. Sometimes I would learn bass lines note for note from records so that I could be part of a band doing reasonably authentic sounding covers of songs by the Police or Talking Heads. But more often, especially as we started writing original music, the notes I'd play were up to me. I'd need a map, hence these charts.

The rudimentary way was to play root notes, the anchors of a C, F, or G chord, and the obvious chord intervals, the fifth and third. This is why the bass, especially for country, blues, bluegrass or folk, is a good instrument for adult learners to pick up. Following roots and fifths can be adequate support for jam sessions, while more advanced players use passing tones, "walking" lines, and other techniques to make the music more interesting. Either way, we often refer to the bass player and the bass line as "holding down" the harmony of a piece of music, and whether it's a symphony, a jazz band, or a rock and roll outfit, the bass generally makes the lowest notes you hear. Even when music comes from a solo piano or guitar, focusing on the lowest notes is a great strategy for a listener trying to hear more in a piece or song.

Keys

Most of the music you hear is described as "tonal" because it has a tonal center called a key, meaning it's built around and in relation to the home base chord. The blues charted above starts and ends with a C chord and is thus in the key of C major. A key, like a chord, can be major or minor (and I don't know about you, but I have major love for minor keys.) Rock and country songs are most often rooted in simple keys like C, G, A, or E. Why those, and not E-flat or C-sharp minor? Because some chords, and thus keys, are easier to play on certain instruments. On a guitar, those keys are easier to finger, where F, for example, requires extra dexterity. You should be aware that the key of C is seen as the simplest and most central key in western music, because it has no sharp or flat notes in its major scale and is thus represented by the white keys on the piano. Why history chose our home key as C and not A is a story too wonky to get into, but it's what we were given. Bluegrass, an interesting exception in popular music, makes heavy use of the harder-to-play key of B-flat, because genre father Bill Monroe found that the key suited his voice at the top of his natural register, evoking his signature "high lonesome" sound. Meanwhile, brass band music uses E-flat and B-flat a lot because those keys are natural to how horns and saxophones are built. Guitar players tend to cringe at playing in E-flat, but B-flat is so important in jazz that I taught myself to play comfortably in the key.

Composed music uses all the keys quite fluidly. You can find string quartets and symphonies set in just about any key you could name, and pieces usually shift keys for lengthy passages for a more scenic harmonic journey. Pop songs sometimes shift keys in midstream too, an emotional trick called a modulation, as in the climax of Celine Dion's "My Heart Will Go On." (The tactic is oft regarded as cheesy and manipulative, but hey, it works.) The freedom composers have to make artful use of keys and key shifts is something that comes with training, and it's one of the things that sets composed genres apart for more attentive listening.

Historically, different keys have been thought to have inherent moods and tonalities. It is said that C major has a quality of innocence and delight, while G major is especially pastoral and calm. A-flat major has been used to evoke death. I hope you know the bit in the movie *Spinal Tap* where Nigel Tufnel explains that his moving piano ballad "Lick My Love Pump" is in D-minor because it's "the saddest of all keys." The joke was not without a rationale. Composers have long turned to D minor for melancholy works, yet whether it's more melancholy than A minor or E-flat minor is esoteric and unknowable.

How does this affect me, the listener, you may well ask? Well, I'd say what's important is to feel the harmonic home base note in any given tonal piece or song, which is called the *tonic*. This is second nature to musical folks, but if you're getting oriented to harmony, try to sing the tonic of songs you like, and listen for whether the song is keyed major or minor. (The key's letter name is not important.) Don't cop out and tell me you're tone deaf; we've been through that. You almost surely can, and moreover you should attune your ear, body, and mind to that anchoring place, so that the departures from and returns to that key center have more impact.

Chord Progressions

There's another set of number relationships that musicians use, and I admit this can get confusing. I've been using numbers to indicate scale degrees, like being three steps (a third) or five steps (a fifth) above a reference note. But musicians also give numbers to *chords*, so they can chart them out relative to the home key chord. It's called the Nashville Number System, for its origins in Music City studios in the mid twentieth century when sidemen had to play along with a song they'd just learned and that might need to shift key to help the singer find the perfect range. So if a song is in C major (like "Wildwood Flower"), we can name the F major chord a Four chord and the G major chord a Five chord, because those chords have root notes that are four steps and five steps respectively above the home key chord of C. The Nashville system uses standard whole numbers, but I learned the jazz way, which uses Roman numerals. That makes F a IV and G a V in the key of C. In every key, there are seven relative chords, and for fascinating reasons we won't get into, those chords are naturally either major or minor. In C, the D chord is minor, so I chart that as ii. Again, there's no need to know the deep theory, but I'm about to talk about chord changes, and I don't want you to be confused between a IV chord (F major in the key of C) and a fourth (the note F above C).

Chords, progressing through a work's changes, lend tonal western music its structure and flow. Each chord has its own characteristics and colors and feelings based on its own intervals and its sonic relationships to the chords that came before it. Every chord you hear going by in a progression has a root-3rd-5th triad at its heart, whether major or minor, but it's usually got more notes than that. A triad is like the chassis of a vehicle. Just as body panels and performance parts are attached to that frame to determine the role of the vehicle, be it sedan, sports car, or pickup truck, extra tones and intervals are attached to the triad chassis to create chords that serve different purposes. Truth is, triads are actually pretty boring to the musically minded person. They are common in country and rock and roll because it's simple music, and we listeners engage with popular music less for harmonic dazzle and more for the emotional expression of the singer/leader. But even simple songs with simple triads, like that blues at the start of the chapter, can't work without the assistance of some vital next-level intervals, starting with the incredible seventh.

This interval, seven steps above the root note, might be the most mystical and important in our music. A natural seventh is a half step below the octave of the root, and half steps create tension. Like a leading question, the seventh is a "leading" tone. For reasons grounded in a mix of biology and culture, western music is built around the ear's desire to hear those tension notes resolve to the home key. They are said to be unstable, whereas the key chord is stable. Composers and improvisors think deeply about how to manipulate the tensions made by those non-home, unstable intervals and chords. Music generates cycles of tension and resolution at micro and macro levels.

It might be most easy to grasp it in country music. If you hum "Hey Good Lookin'" by Hank Williams to yourself, the song starts on the home key chord, rises to the Two (II7) chord on "How's about cookin'" and hits the Five (V7) chord on "Something up with" and then, with that nice feeling of coming home (C) on "me." This progression suffuses popular music. It's going on in some way, with decorations and variations, in virtually every song you've ever heard. One (I)—Two (II)—Five (V7)- One (I).

The nerdy term for the V7-I feeling is a *dominant-tonic* relationship, and it is more common in music than you can believe, because for, um, reasons, this harmonic shift is extremely compelling to our brains. It's the final two chords of "The Star Spangled Banner" and "Happy Birthday." Returning to "Wildwood Flower," every line concludes with the V7-I resolution, a G7 chord to the home C. You've heard symphonic movements end with big V7-I conclusions. Composers have all kinds of ways to manipulate the "closure" effect of this dominant-tonic resolution, called a *cadence*. Cadences happen mid-song, at the end of choruses for example, and certainly at the end of most pieces. There are several kinds of cadence, the most interesting being a "deceptive" cadence when the composer sets your ears up for that closure feeling and then says "psych!" by shifting to a new chordal journey, delaying the gratification of coming "home." Incredible variety and motion is made possible with the strategic use of seventh chords and dominant-tonic cadences.

Inversions and Voicings

Tension and resolution is the heart and soul of tonal music, the basis for making our brains follow harmonic progressions and get satisfaction out of that movement. This core principle can take an infinite number of forms and shadings and feelings because of the many other intervals composers and creators have to work with. For example, a major triad plus a sixth interval has a color that can evoke the tonalities of throwback swing jazz and bossa nova. As a guitar player, I had spent years learning dozens of songs in country, blues, folk, and bluegrass without being aware of this 1-3-5-6 chord. I never suspected anything other than a basic major or minor chord could be the home base key of a song anyway. When I took lessons to get myself to a new level where I could play jazz tunes and the closely related genre of western swing (think Bob Wills and his Texas Playboys or Willie Nelson), learning how to finger sixth chords became crucial. My playing didn't sound authentically in the style without this particular tonality. It went from sounding square and bland to sounding groovy and sophisticated.

Before we talk more about extended chords and the magic of more challenging intervals, it's time to recognize the concept of *inversions*. These are happening all the time in music, and listening for them opens up new frontiers. Inversions refer to different ways of stacking the notes in a chord. A pianist plays an easy A6 chord: 1-3-5-6. Then she shifts and plays the same pitches, but instead of making the one the lowest note, she puts it on top of the stack, resulting in 3-5-6-1. Then she can try another version of the chord, with 5-6-1-3. These inversions are so cool because they sound different *and* similar to the original at the same time. Inversions serve the same function in the music's harmonic flow, allowing what we call different chord *voicings*. There are a lot of possible voicings, and each has its own personality. You wouldn't think this simple restacking of intervals/notes could make that big a difference, but it does.

Now, to break up this theory with some specific advice, I urge you to spend quality time with R&B from the 1940s and '50s, because not only is it a golden age of American innovation, it's an era that put the principles I'm talking about—rich chord changes, inversions, the melody/harmony marriage—front and center. Your ears will grow and your heart will swell listening to the composing and arranging in the music of Ray Charles ("Don't Let the Sun Catch You Cryin'"), Etta James ("A Sunday Kind of Love"), Bobby "Blue" Bland ("Who Will the Next Fool Be"), and Ruth Brown ("I'm Beginning To See The Light"). Listen here for the flow of chords, unusual voicings, and bass lines that define the harmonic progression with savvy note choices.

While these nuggets come from the world of vocal music, the role of chord inversions is sometimes even easier to focus on in instrumental jazz from the same era, such as Lester Young and Teddy Wilson playing "Our Love Is Here to Stay" or the historic duo of guitar wizards Lonnie Johnson and Eddie Lang playing the dazzling "Guitar Blues." In such music, the soloist will command the most attention. But focus on the backing instrument that's playing in the middle—the piano or guitar—sketching the harmonic motion with subtle rhythmic gestures that give the soloist space and groove to express themselves. We call this technique *comping*, derived from accompaniment. And it would be impossible to do well without inversions, because it would be boring to repeat the same stacked chord voicing over and over. If I'm filling two measures of an A6 chord, I can opt to play it *here* or slide up the neck a few frets and play it *there*, or *there*, or *there*. Learning all the ways to play chords is part of learning the jazz vocabulary. But comping can pop up in many genres, potently in bluegrass banjo. The master of this was Earl Scruggs. People forget to listen to him carefully when he's not taking his own solo. But his support of fiddlers, mandolinists, and singers— his comping—remains highly prized and influential.

When I've tried comping in jazz ensembles or played rhythm guitar in folk situations, I learned something important when I understood that *a part of a chord is often more powerful and musical than a full chord.* New guitarists learn chord patterns that use full strums across all six strings for the kind of G or E chords you hear in folk or country music. But for jazz, my role as a guitar player is to *suggest* harmonic motion without crowding out other instruments. If the bass player is playing the root note of a chord, I offer the music little if I play the root as well. I might just pop off two notes, but if it's the fifth and sixth of the chord, it will have punch by bringing the most potent intervals to the mix. You may know how in drawing, you can suggest a whole wall of bricks by drawing a few bricks here and there? This has the same effect. Judicious use of chord tones without playing full chords is usually the most musical place one can be.

Listen also for something called *chordal melody* in which instruments or singers make chord changes that imply a melody in the listener's mind, but an elusive one. If I asked you to sing back the melody, you might realize that it's not so easy to identify because of the whole chordal sound together. This is common with guitar and piano, the most chordal instruments, but also it's a thing with choral music or small harmony groups. A great example is the Crosby, Stills & Nash song "Suite: Judy Blue Eyes" from 1969 where the voices are coequal on those opening lines "It's getting to the point, where I'm no fun anymore." There is no stand-alone melody, but the chords evoke a melody in the mind. Orchestral composing does this all the time—multiple parts state chordal melodies without a standout lead voice, using all manner of inversions and voicings across strings, brass, woodwinds. It takes an accomplished artist to compose or execute passages like this, but for the listener, they don't require practice to be sweet on the ears.

In popular music, harmonic flow and chord changes support the song, expressed in melody and word. In sound-based music, the harmonies are more of a main event. Melody may be forward, suggested, implied, or absent, even as the intervallic movement, rhythm, and timbre do most of the heavy lifting. Immense thought goes into crafting harmonic passages in instrumental music with more elements than a song-backing track can or should have. Standing in the foreground, there is more agency, more responsibility on the composer(s) and fewer restrictions and more potential to make chordal surprise happen. That's where things get wonderfully weird.

Listen for . . .

. . . the home key note of songs you know and like. Sing the root note out loud and notice if the song's key is major or minor.

. . . the chord changes in those songs, not what they're called but just when they happen.

. . . chords that are more complicated and colorful than basic triads.

. . . small musical gestures that imply full chords.

. . . chordal melodies, when the harmony implies a tune with no dominant melody.

DISSONANCE IS A DRUG

Harmony and its acquired tastes

If you were here in my studio and willing to exercise your ears for a bit, I'd sit you down in front of the stereo, bring you a drink, and play for you "Teenie's Blues" from one of my favorite jazz albums, *Blues and the Abstract Truth* by Oliver Nelson. I'd play the famous "Dance of the Young Girls" from Igor Stravinsky's *Rite of Spring*, and a bit of Bartok's Violin Concerto #1, and perhaps "Invisible," the first tune from the first solo album by saxophone visionary Ornette Coleman from 1957.

You could tell that none of this is music for children. It has no sing-song melodies or calm, easy-listening chords. Depending on your experience and taste, you might find this music extra-stimulating and rich with intrigue, or you might find some of it harsh and unpleasant. You might try and try again to enjoy it and still not like it, but not because the music is bad. All of these are recognized masterworks and many of us certainly love hearing them. All this means is that we're leveling up our concept of what makes music work on us and what makes it pleasurable or peculiar.

I heard music that was challenging, abrasive, and disorienting throughout my life, with varying degrees of acceptance (pursuing the aforementioned ethos of "I don't get it" versus "I don't like it"). My understanding of more complex and sophisticated harmony came from two directions. The first, which anyone can do, was simply more listening and more exposure. The other came from learning the guitar. With that as a window, I'll try to briefly carry you up the harmonic ladder from simple to strange.

I learned my basic major and minor chords—those 1-3-5 triads about the time I went to college. I (sort of) figured out how seventh chords worked in music's flow by learning songs from James Taylor and Neil Young songbooks with those little chord diagrams that show you where to put your fingers. With my bass lessons as my guide, I made use of the number system to chart out rock, folk and bluegrass songs I learned by ear and then songs that I began to write myself. All this time, like almost any student guitar player, I noodled around, trying to find tasty, unusual harmonies on the guitar neck. New guitarists find, for example, that if you take a basic open E major chord and shift that fingering up the neck, you get some exotic sounding intervals. I had no prayer or intention of naming them; I just liked how they sounded on my ears, reminding me of delicious tensions from artists I loved like R.E.M. and Thelonious Monk.

Years later, when my curiosity about jazz on the guitar grew too loud to ignore, I took those lessons in Nashville when I learned how to introduce sixths into my vocabulary, along with a few other vital color tones. It was liberating. Fireworks went off in my mind as I heard myself making those succulent chords I'd heard others play. My ears grew more in a few months than they had in the previous years. I could play timeless tunes like "Right or Wrong," "All of Me," "Faded Love," even the essential, highly transferable chord changes of "I've Got Rhythm" by George Gershwin—in any key.

Now we're caught up to the meat-and-potatoes harmonies that powered mid-twentieth century American popular music. But all along, in composed music and jazz, harmony was on the march, and I heard edgier sounds in progressive improvised music that made me hungry for more, and maybe you are too. Onstage comes a new family of intervals, the ninth, the eleventh, and the thirteenth, which if you'll notice are nothing more than extra thirds—a third above seven, then above nine, then above eleven. These intervals (and their flatted and sharped neighbors) offer new worlds of color, contrast, and tension. Learning to play or compose with extended harmony is hard, which is why we have conservatories. But for the listener, it's about opening up to the pleasures of richer, stranger tonalities. Some intervals are easy on the ears and others more challenging, and with that, we enter the realm of *dissonance*. It's a funny word because while it's widely used and understood, we almost never hear anybody use its opposite, *consonance*. Consonance is just assumed I guess as the default mode of enjoyable listening, so why give that a name? It's not as if people say, "Hey, that's dissonant! Play some nice consonant music!" Rather, people vote with their ears and put distance between themselves and music they find gnarly. And yet if they run from dissonance through their lives, they are missing something pretty huge.

There is no clean line delineating consonance from dissonance, just as we can't find an exact point where sweet becomes sour or happy becomes angry. It's a continuum, and Aaron Copland points out helpfully that dissonance is context based, "according to the period in which you live, according to your listening experience . . . and the place that it holds in the piece as a whole."

Let's take those in turn. It's not lost on you, I'm sure, that from the mid-nineteenth century and through the twentieth, music became ever more complex and experimental, as composers and players sought innovative ways to express themselves. Thus, harmonies that once sounded shocking and hard to understand to the general public became familiar and interesting. The "Rite of Spring" I mentioned earlier is famous for having caused a minor riot at its premiere in Paris in 1913, in part because of its uneasy friction and discord. Today however it's widely performed and a core influence on music commonly heard in film soundtracks, TV commercials, and musical theater. One generation's dissonance is a new normal for the next.

Copland also speaks about where and how dissonance is deployed in a work, and we're all accustomed to this, whether we know it or not. When things get anxious or scary in a movie, the music will shift from sweet and easy harmonies to degrees of dissonance to sell the story. We are emotionally engaged, and we expect that the music's going to return to its basically consonant default at some point, so we are more open to weird intervals at times like this. At a more micro level, sophisticated music of all genres will regularly use dissonant chords as role players, as passages, as dashes of color or depth in a larger, conventional-sounding whole. The famous and much-analyzed opening chord of "A Hard Day's Night" by the Beatles is a semi-dissonant chord that's been grabbing our attention since 1964. There are chords in songs by Stevie Wonder ("You Are the Sunshine of My Life"), Joni Mitchell ("Blue"), and The Roots ("Step Into the Realm") which, if played in isolation, would sound pretty edgy or jagged. Yet in the context of the music, those "off" notes are guiding the ear into the next chord and the next, setting off little bombs of tension that get resolved in a way that makes us stay tuned in and excited. One of the reasons Kurt Cobain's songwriting for Nirvana was considered so bold and novel was his use of unorthodox intervals ("Lithium"), and that's why today you can find jazz artists covering Nirvana songs, while the songs of, say, Garth Brooks, while very nice, don't come with enough harmonic intrigue to inspire the modern improvisor.

Copland's most important point about dissonance has to do with listener experience. To me, this has always been best expressed through analogies to food and drink, where the idea of an acquired taste is well understood and valued. Children often love coffee ice cream but cringe at black coffee. With time, many grow into appreciating the bitter layers of coffee itself. Few who love whiskey savored their first sip of the drink. A culinary journey, one of life's great pleasures, is going to force you into a lot of firsts, with unfamiliar spices, novel textures, and offbeat ingredients. As somebody who's had tripe and congealed duck blood in Sichuan hot pot, I can testify that this is a whole bunch of fun and adventure. Even the new tastes we don't enjoy stretch our palette and our sense of what's possible. And there's a well understood process of neural development in which the brain adapts to novel stimulus with exposure. What we initially think is bad can become tasty and eventually a favorite thing.

Music is too grand, too rewarding, too invigorating to live a life confined by easy listening. Frank Zappa is rumored to have said that "music without dissonance is like a movie without a bad guy," and while I can't confirm that, I'm just glad anybody said it. Getting stimulated by contrast and tensions in harmony and melody is one of the key pleasure centers for the active listener. I'd argue that in sound-first music, dissonance—or at least surprise on the harmonic level—is why we love it so much. When music writers like myself reach for words that suggest the tonal feeling I'm talking about, we come up with *angular, bent, rubbing, tense, weird*, and *edgy*. They're not adequate, but we hope to convey an element of drama or danger.

The reason this chapter likens dissonance to a *drug* is that harmonic complexity works on us in similar ways. If we get too big a dose at the start, we recoil. Yet if we experience well-measured departures from our norms, we get enjoyment. With time we grow accustomed to a baseline dose of dissonance, and we need a little more to get the buzz. Jump too far too fast, and it becomes unpleasant again. This is not, I stress, an endorsement of narcotics. Rather it's a reminder that responding to music can invoke drug-like brain states in our limbic systems, looking for all the world on brain scans like someone in the thrall of sex or heroin. And yet music is safe, affordable and inexhaustible. Just say 'yes' to dissonant music.

Think of it as a ladder of sonic strangeness. At the bottom is music for children, consonant to the point of agonizing sweetness, all thirds and fifths. We climb up a few rungs to the salty harmonic terrain of popular music, with its seventh chords and its major and minor triads. Most people are completely comfortable hearing a traditional jazz band playing standards with extended chords and color tones. The question becomes how far are you willing to climb after that?

The next tier of dissonance, the next dose from our benevolent drug dealer if you will, is even more detached from the tonality of a home key and its related chords. For every key, there are notes that "work" and other notes that are by definition out of the key. Only a few of the notes of the 12 scale tones are truly "out" in any given key, but when somebody hits them in a performance, we notice them. Perhaps they're played by mistake and are just wrong, but there is a way to make those "out" notes work, and it's called *chromatic* playing, a word that carries with it nice connotations of light and photography. Chromatic playing makes use of all 12 scale tones, deftly and artfully (one hopes) blending the non-chord tones into a larger sonic fabric. Its counterpart—the consonant norm—is the *diatonic* approach. Meaning "through the tones," diatonic playing employs the "safe" or "in" notes against the chord progression, as you'd hear in the playing of most lounge jazz or blues bands. This dichotomy is so wired into musicians' conversation that we often describe an instrumentalist as "getting out" when they leave diatonic harmony behind and get a little crazy.

Jazz improvisation emerged in the early twentieth century as a basically diatonic musical form. Players mostly stuck to a song's chord intervals and melody notes when improvising. This is easy to hear in Dixieland jazz, with multiple lead instruments playing interwoven solos on tunes like "When The Saints Go Marching In," or in early iconic works like Louis Armstrong's famous "West End Blues" from 1928. Then in mid-century, as musicians sought more avenues of expression, they began to play more chromatically, employing more "out" notes as part of the art. This can range from a few passing tones spicing up a basically diatonic approach to the kind of caterwauling that leaves the tonal center far behind (and much of the potential audience along with it).

I mentioned "Teenie's Blues" at the outset of this chapter, and it's a good onramp to dissonant jazz. It opens with two choruses of solo bass, so if you listen attentively, these 41 seconds orient your ear to the harmonic center and the chords of a 12-bar blues. But then the song's head comes in, and it's wild—three horns playing together rhythmically but clashing harmonically. The melody of the song—a chordal melody—is uneasy, crunchy, frictional—and to my ears, beguiling and thrilling every time. Meanwhile, the blues form gives us a place of stability. Your ears may need a few passes to get into it, but you'll earn your first dissonance merit badge.

Chromatic musicality influenced composed music too, to say the least. Indeed, much of the harmonic stretching one hears in later twentieth-century jazz had already been introduced into classical music years before. Beethoven's chordal language grew increasingly dissonant over his life. Impressionist period composers like Debussy and Ravel made a beguiling blend of novel-feeling tonalities that are lush and lovely with well-chosen contrasting tones and chords just under the surface. In their time, they sounded pretty out there, yet audiences could feel something special. Then came the rise of the modernists—Bartok, Stravinsky, Ives and onward—composers who brought in color and texture and harmonic thrills that were not on anybody's radar in the prior centuries. The hugely influential Arnold Schoenberg (1874-1951) conceived of a new *atonal* language that obliterated the very concept of key-based, diatonic music. He created rules for himself and others, such as devotees Alban Berg and Anton Webern, who adopted his "serialism" or "twelve-tone" concept. And even this music, while disorienting to most western ears, doesn't define the outer limits of dissonance. Some music in the twentieth century became defiantly disordered and brain-shattering as an intellectual exercise. This world is not without its interest, but I regret every time that some impressionable person heard examples of "modern" jazz or composed music that sounded scary and off-putting from this ultra-avant-garde realm. Because it's not the whole of it, and the astute listener will find plenty of sweet spots in the contemporary canon.

This radical, experimental approach isn't only harmonic in its dissonance; it's structural and rhythmic too, with passages and sections that feel downright chaotic. And for sure, a lot of avant-garde music goes too far for me and leaves me no way in. It can feel like an assault. At the same time, this world is work-by-work, composer-by-composer, and I have occasionally been surprised and won over by some forbidding stuff. Some difficult music starts to sound more engaging after a few minutes, when its hidden patterns and ideas become clearer. Sometimes it's about finding an artist that you like in one context who becomes more able to lead you over a hill into something more tricky. I have a years-long passion for the late saxophone genius Wayne Shorter. His conventional jazz and fusion earned my trust, so that I'm more willing to sit with some of his most challenging works. Contemporary guitarist Nels Cline in concert can feel on some occasions like a back scratch and other times like a mugging. But as I said in Chapter 3, what sounds weird and perplexing in one era of your life and journey can become quite appealing later on.

We all crave the pleasure of beloved, familiar music, but musicality also implies a mindset of respect for progress and those who shake up music's harmonic and rhythmic conventions. My experience is that as one listens and collects over years, a curious craving sets in for adventure. I want to hear musicians boldly expressing something they feel, and that can include anger, anguish, and confusion. Sure, they can get too far from shore and leave us lost, but there are countless examples of great artists finding the balance between the comfortably familiar and adventurous stretching. My hope is that you get what you need from music exactly when you are ready for it.

Listen for . . .

. . . dissonant moments snuck into otherwise harmonious pop or rock songs.

. . . passages where a soloist, such as a guitar or saxophone, slips from diatonic playing (the "in" notes) to chromatic playing (the "out" notes), and notice the effect that has.

10

TIMBRE

The umami of music

Jamey Haddad drops an extra-large duffle bag on a studio floor. It goes *"shhhrank"*—a cluster of mysterious sounds suggesting textures inside the canvas sack: wood, metal, bells, plastic. It's an incidental noise but one pregnant with the possibility of music. Haddad, a professor at Oberlin University's music school and the percussionist in Paul Simon's band, is an authority on the rhythms and rhythm instruments of the world. He has a vast collection from his travels and this day he is arriving in Nashville with a sampling, chosen for a two-day session of composing, improvising and recording. His musical collaborator is my friend Casey Driessen, a former student of Jamey's and one of the most accomplished fiddle players in the world. He's a Berklee College of Music graduate and instructor who explores the overlap of bluegrass and jazz. It's 2013, and I am filming this encounter, a documentarian fly on the wall.

Jamey's instruments begin to emerge from the duffel bag and several rolling road cases: thin skinned rim drums, hand drums, wooden clappers, cymbals, tambourines, and shakers—more shakers than you'd ever dream could exist. So many, because no two sound the same. One shaker had a rough roar, another a brittle whisk, another a thicker slap/splash like a hand striking water. You can imagine in your mind's ear the differences between shakers made of tin or iron pipe or a length of bamboo. And each of these vessels could be filled with lead BBs, plastic fragments, or kernels of dried corn, imparting an ever-expanding palette. Jamey and Casey didn't know what they were going to play in advance. Whatever parts and sounds and feelings were going to be worked out together would be imagined in real time. The personality of one shaker could work perfectly for an idea they were working on, where another would stifle the music's energy or mask the sound of other instruments. They wanted to have choices, for these are people who believe that these choices, as subtle as the swish of some beads in a box, have meaning—the difference between random babbling and speaking clear prose.

With only two violins (one with four strings the other with five), Casey seems to have fewer sonic options than Jamey, but when they begin jamming together and working out ideas, Casey's advantages in sound shaping and making become clear. For one thing, he can make sustained tones. With his bow and the proper technique, he can make notes that last indefinitely without a break or pause, whereas most of Jamey's percussion instruments emit a flash of sound that rapidly decays. Here we had a dichotomy in these two musicians' vocabularies. One seemed to specialize in leading edge cracks, whacks and smacks. The other in notes and tones and pitches. But it wasn't so simple, because these are especially exploratory musicians. Jamey had some drums and mallet instruments that were tuned to pitches and cymbals that rang and sustained. He and Casey worked to make sure they were playing the same tonality based on the ringing of the drum heads.

This borrowing played out in reverse as well. Casey, you see, is a specialist in a bow technique called *chopping*, which turns the fiddle into a rhythm instrument. With flicks of the wrist and application of the right pressure with his bow hairs on the violin strings, he produces a *chock, chock, chock* sound. By dragging the bow against the strings forward and backward rather than the conventional side-to-side motion, he makes a *hiss* sound. Then he can juggle the chocks and hisses into complex patterns that suggest a tiny drum kit. It is this passion for rhythm on the fiddle that has led Casey to propose this session with Jamey in the first place, to see how a tonal instrument and rhythmic instruments could cross over and play in each other's terrain. For me observing, this became an extraordinary experience in hearing musicians manipulate and search for subtle and extreme uses of tone color or *timbre*. (TAM-ber is the easiest way to say it.)

Timbre is, in my observation, the least appreciated or talked about aspect of music. It is the mellow fruity voice of a trombone, the velvet bloom of a piano note, the bright clarity of the acoustic guitar, the woody aura of a cello, and on and on. Even similarly designed instruments—cello, viola, violin—have different timbres to the attentive ear. An electric guitar player can coax wildly different sounds from one instrument. It's the fourth dimension of sound. Where does timbre come from and why does it work? On one hand, the answer is esoteric and mathematical and nerdy. But I found that learning a bit about the physics of this aspect of sound really opened up my ears and helped me swim inside tone and appreciate more abstract and sophisticated music.

The classic illustration of how timbre works starts with Pythagoras working it out 3,000 years ago—with a vibrating string. A string has several variables—its length, its tension and its density. All of these will affect its pitch when plucked, struck or bowed. Every stretched string will have an inherent resonance and will vibrate at the same frequency whether it's plucked in Boston or Burma. It's a fact of physics, like the laws governing the acceleration of falling bodies or swinging pendulums.

So let's say I've plucked the open A string on my guitar. We can hear it (thanks to the amplifying wooden box with the sound hole in it) making that familiar, slightly low A note. We can see the string vibrating in an oblong blur from one end to the other, and we can place a device next to it to measure the frequency of those vibrations, in this case 110 Hz.

Here's where it gets weird and interesting, because vibration is a lot more complex than we can easily discern. What the naked eye can't see is that the string is simultaneously vibrating in two halves, or nodes, and each node vibrates at twice the frequency of the full string, producing its own pitch at 220 Hz. The full string's 110 Hz tone is called the fundamental, while the fainter 220 pitch is called the string's *overtone* or *harmonic*, this first one being an octave. We're just getting started with these vibrations-within-vibrations thing.

That same string is vibrating in quarters (at 440 Hz), and even in thirds and fifths all at the same time. Each of these sub-vibrations rings out, producing a cascade of overtones. The fundamental pitch is what we *think* we're hearing, but the actual *guitar* note we're registering is a unique mix of all those overtones, faint as they are. And here's a bonus fact about this phenomenon that blew my mind and that gives a clue where our harmonic system comes from. The third harmonic in the series, where the string vibrates in three nodes, produces a fifth of the fundamental. The fifth harmonic, where the string vibrates in five nodes, produces a third. We can measure this and with special techniques we can even hear it, but how about that? The third and the fifth, the ingredients in our all-important triad chord, are hiding in every note we play.

Controlling and manipulating timbre happens in basically three ways. It starts with the design and construction of instruments, something I'll get into in the next chapter. A well-made guitar has a richer tone than a poorly made one because it's more capable of producing clear, cohesive overtones. Next, we players influence timbre with our technique and touch. For example, if I pick my guitar in the very middle of the string, it sounds slack and dull, but if I pick it in the optimal place just by the sound hole, it sounds livelier and brighter. Then if I play right next to the bridge, the guitar sounds metallic and edgy.

Then we get into the wide world of timbre manipulation tools. Centuries after Pythagoras noticed the harmonic series in strings, humans invented circuits that could carry acoustic vibrations over wires with electricity, and we discovered that loads of sonic information could be embedded in those pulses of voltage. That meant we could record and reproduce accurate timbres, and we could modify and shape them with circuit design. That's what happens when an electric guitar player adjusts their tone knobs, drawing out more treble or bass. You've no doubt seen guitarists use racks of floor pedals, each of which is tailored to sculpt the sound's overtones to produce something new and personal. We also invented synthesizers, which actually generate tones with an oscillating device and then pass them through rows of circuits that make the sounds edgy, smooth, fluffy, metallic, voice-like, etc. Later, with digital technologies, we could convert that sonic and timbral information into code, and control of timbre became even more radical and limitless.

As much as composers and musicians think about harmony and rhythm when creating music, timbre gives them an even more expansive set of tools to reach us. Think about the dazzling passage that opens the symphonic version of George Gershwin's "Rhapsody in Blue." Find it on YouTube and listen if you can't recall it. It's not a horn made of metal. It's not a violin made of wood and propelled by strings and a bow. Gershwin (or possibly his arranger Ferde Grofé) chose a clarinet—a woodwind instrument uniquely textured to make that clear, cutting part, with its trills and its long slide, rising from down low to a soaring blue note. And so it is with all composers, every measure. Every time we hear a flute rise above the orchestra for a solo, or a rack of tom-toms being deployed for their tonal report, or a string bass thumping along as the foundation of a jazz band, you're in the presence of timbre deployed artistically and strategically to make the music speak.

Timbre touches us in intimate and personal ways, or it can if we let it. We're talking about minute frequency combinations and sonic colors rubbing against the microns-thin membrane of your ear drum and entering your brain. It's serious business. That means that some sounds will charm you and others will leave you indifferent, while others can chill your blood. Therefore, you should expect to have deep personal and private reactions to timbres of various instruments or vocalists. Noticing timbres and how they make you feel is a great way to live deeper in music.

For my part, I love mallet instruments, like the vibraphone, with its piquant attack and its glowing tones. Same for the woodier sounds of the marimba and the African balafon. In a related family of sound, I'm drawn to the acoustic bass, with its broad-shouldered box of wood and string. And this gets us into stringed instruments, where I spend so much of my time, from bluegrass fiddle and banjo to classical or jazz violin. Such magnificent voices! Of course I love guitars, in their mind-boggling variety. A Spanish classical guitar sounds different than an American dreadnought acoustic guitar or a small-bodied parlor guitar. They sound different when played by fingers or a pick. The range of timbres in electric guitar has fueled popular music's many genres for a century, and the chiming clarity of the pedal steel guitar stirs something powerful, whether in its home base of country music or in ambient jazz. I find reed instruments friendly and appealing, with their subtle complex buzz, whether in a clarinet, a saxophone, or an accordion. I love drone instruments like the Indian hand-pumped harmonium or a well-designed synthesizer soundscape.

This is my list, my personal aural signature, and you can cultivate your own. Down deep, we come into this world attuned to certain types of sounds, and I think it's a joy to discover what those are. Also, what *don't* we like? This is just as important to know, so you can let go of your anti-timbres. Personally, I'm not a fan of the flute. I find classical flute too clean and metallic, and a piccolo feels like a pencil in my ear. Apologies to my flautist friends. I'd fight for your right to flout your flutes. But something about air blown over a hole has a signature that leaves me cold. Your mileage will vary. Nor do I like most male falsetto singing, when they use their head voice like the doo-wop singers of the '50s or the obviously talented and important Bee Gees. It's proven extremely popular over the decades, but it's not my sound. But then there is so much to love and explore with the human voice, the most timbrally diverse instrument of all. I recognize singers whom I know are fantastic but who don't reach me tonally. There are singers who sound rough and raw who move millions. I have personal favorites, who feel like intimate companions, whose voices may or may not appeal to people I know have good taste. So while there's no way to generalize about the qualities of the voice, I'd like to tie the way you hear singers to a new way of hearing instrumentalists. Some fans can identify jazz soloists on sax or trumpet or piano from a few moments of one of their solos. I am pretty good at naming bluegrass guitar players with a blindfold on from the way they sound. And what makes Sonny Rollins or Wayne Shorter or Joshua Redman sound unique? What tells me it's Doc Watson and not Billy Strings? There are many factors, including note choices and phrasing, but a key signal comes from timbre, from the special voice and sound of each individual. And it's not all that different from distinguishing between singers, like Ella Fitzgerald versus Beyoncé. Great artists sound like themselves, whether singing with their throats or their instruments.

Timbre is closely related to *tone*, which I used rather glibly in my tone/time/timbre construct early in the book. Yet one important meaning of tone for us players has to do with not just the innate timbre of our instruments but our ability to draw out the richest and most expressive version of that sound. I struggled as a boy to get tone from my violin, which is challenging on a box of wood and strings that can screech and scratch. Now when I play my acoustic guitar, I feel like those lessons and a lifetime of tonal attention really have come into focus. I use right hand technique to strike the strings with authority and intent, which lets them vibrate fully. I keep my chest and right arm from clamping the body too firmly, so as not to dampen its vibrations. I think about holding down the fretted notes as cleanly and as long as possible, without squelching any ringing string. Timbre is the underlying vibrational phenomenon. Tone is the quality of the sound made by a player.

Now why did I open a chapter about overtones and timbre with instruments like shakers and drums that don't make extended notes? Because every instrument has its own sonic signature, no matter how long or short its notes and no matter what role it plays in music. And because I want you to be extra sensitive to the effects that different drum and percussion sounds have in music. A snare drum isn't just a snare drum! Listen to any song with a snare keeping the beat and ask yourself: is that a natural drum or an electronic one? Is it crisp or splatty or thuddy or something else? Can you hear the body and tone of the drum resonate, or only the report of the drum head? My heroine Evelyn Glennie, the deaf percussionist we met in Chapter 5, says the snare drum is her favorite instrument, for reasons both cultural and timbral: "In Scotland, the snare drum is very prominent in Highland bands. The Scottish style of playing is in my blood. It's a very powerful instrument, but it can also be soothing, like velvet," she has said. Hearing her solo freely on a snare drum, easily found online and in her bio documentary *Touch the Sound*, is revelatory. She mines a single drum—one we think we know—for infinite sound and variety.

I also want you to think about the timbre of drums because there is so much power in leading-edge sound, also known as the *attack* part of a tone. After the attack, sounds are then divided into phases called *sustain* and *decay*. You're never going to need to break down the minutia of a single note like that, but just realize this. The attack of any note carries a huge amount of information about its timbre. Even with the long notes of a violin, a flute, a tuba, the leading edge is vital to your perception. When researchers trim the attack off of common instruments in experiments, people's ability to recognize one from another drops off considerably. We crave the onset of any note—the rosined acceleration of a bow over a string or the felty hammer strike of a piano—to really grasp its purpose and placement. As these notes sustain and release, they become complete gestures and thoughts. You are not, I assure you, tasked here with microscopically breaking down every note you hear to be a better music fan, but I do urge you to take the time to consider these details, to be aware that they exist and that great musicians are deploying timbral nuance they've practiced their whole lives.

Listen for . . .

. . . instrumental sounds you like more than others. Ask yourself what sonic characteristics you find attractive.

. . . the timbral choices in a good recording of "Rhapsody in Blue." Why might Gershwin have chosen piano, clarinet or brass instruments for various passages?

. . . leading-edge sounds in stringed instruments, horns, drums. How much of your feeling comes from the attack, versus the sustain and fade out of notes?

11

GOOD VIBRATIONS
The resounding power of resonance

I have a memory fragment that seems random and peculiar, but I've realized it stuck around in my noggin for a reason. I was 10 or 11 years old, and my violin teacher took a pause from having me saw noisily through the notes on the page. I think she wanted to get me thinking about tone. She held her violin in the air in front of me with her fingers muffling the strings. Then with her other hand, she tapped and knocked the violin body at various places and asked me to listen to how it changed from place to place—solid and thuddier near the edges, more tonal and light near the center, especially on the back. I had no idea what it all meant at the time, but yes I could hear the different sounds. Years later, I learned that violin makers "tone tap" the component tops and backs as they carve and refine them before they're assembled together. The experienced ear can hear minute differences in the pitch of the taps, and these guide the luthier in shaving off microns of wood here and there until the frequencies reinforce each other rather than fight each other when the finished instrument is vibrating. The desired outcome evokes a musical and acoustic quality that's closely related to timbre and tone, and that's resonance.

The verb *to resonate* derives from Latin *resonare*, meaning *to sound again*, or in a sense, *to echo*. Over time, it grew from its literal sense of repeating something back to the lovely metaphoric connotations we know today: emotional response, empathy, or historic import. If an event or a work of art has impact on society we can say it had a resounding effect. Things resonate when they affect one another through space, time, and proximity, one hopes in a positive way. Resonance means comprehension, amplification, and natural rapport. Similarly, sound begets sound through the phenomenon of sympathetic vibration.

My mother spent much of her life as a working harpist, so in our living room where I grew up was a golden harp, six feet tall. When I was a toddler, I discovered that if I shouted or sang into the back of her instrument, through the sound holes into its big teardrop shaped body, the chamber would sing back. It wasn't an echo so much as an amplification of my voice and activation of the harp's sounding board. Some of my calls produced a muffled, atonal response, but if I sang certain pitches, the harp chamber would come alive, ringing even louder than my own voice. What was happening here, I'd later learn, was that I was setting the harp's strings in motion through the physics of induction and sympathetic vibration. Strings have a natural resonating frequency as we talked about in Chapter 10. They lie there quietly, but they want to vibrate at their natural pitch, and all it takes is a little energy to get them to wake up. We can apply that directly, by plucking or bowing, but it can also just be acoustic energy in the air. Even now, if I shout toward my acoustic guitar hanging on the wall, I can set its strings in motion and hear it answer me.

What this tells me is that music lives as *transfers of energy*. An instrument's vibrations are passed into air pressure waves, which strike the ear drum, transferring the waves to a liquid medium, and once again via the cilia to neural impulses. If recording or amplification is involved, we have transfers from acoustic to electric to digital and back again. None of this happens without natural resonance. Instruments are resonating machines that in various and remarkable ways amplify small energy vibrations into large ones. The harp, one of the oldest instrument designs of any kind, suspends strings in a frame, one side of which is a wooden box roughly the shape of a boat hull. When the strings are plucked, they set the sound board vibrating. The other side of the harp body is rigid and has sound holes. The vibrating wood top creates a pressure load in the harp body. When that pressurized air squeezes out the holes, it shoots like water through a gap, helping it project into space. What's wild and worth pausing over is how much information those tiny pressure waves can contain. Is it a gut string harp or a steel string harp? Our ears can tell. Were the strings plucked with a fingernail or a finger pad? Our ears can tell that too. The quality of the instrument determines how much of that information carries into the room around the instrument. In every instrument is an insight about resonance.

Violins, cellos, and basses pass their string vibrations to their bodies through a wooden bridge that holds the strings in place and a sound post beneath one of the bridge's feet inside the instrument. The post transmits the energy of the bridge to the back of the violin, which generates the most signal. Acoustic guitars have no sound post, but their bridge works in a similar way, setting the top in motion, creating pressure in the body that's forced out the sound hole.

Pianos are remarkable sound-making devices whose machinery is weirdly like a drum crossed with a guitar. It's a drum because each key activates a hammer that strikes courses of tuned strings, and in some contexts, the piano is actually classified as a percussion instrument. It's like a guitar because it has a wooden sounding board—a thin, piano-sized piece of spruce suspended beneath the rigid steel frame that holds the strings in place. "It is the largest single piece of wood in the piano, a five-by-eight-foot slab of planks that is rounded off at one end," writes James Barron in the book *Piano*. "It will function as the piano's amplification system, a pre-electronic triumph of physics. Without help from a single audio cable or input jack, it will transform relatively weak vibrations of the strings into sounds powerful enough to fill a concert hall."

Another way to leverage resonance and make quiet signals louder is to compress air in a chamber or tube and then let it out through a bell or a horn. An entire family of instruments (and stereo loudspeakers) works this way. And it's quite something to consider that what starts as musicians pursing their lips and making a buzzing sound can be amplified by brass tubing and a flared bell to be loud enough to damage someone's hearing at close range. In this genus, trumpets occupy the higher registers, French horns the mellow middle, and tubas the bass. Valves controlled by the fingers allow the musician to generate a range of pitches. And then there are the reed instruments, where the initial vibrations come from blowing over a carved sliver of bamboo or wood. Here we find clarinets, oboes, and saxophones—all sounding different depending on their size, shape and material.

Drums vibrate from a stretched skin over a frame, and depending on how they're designed, they can die out with a quick smack or they can ring true and be tuned to pitches. Many percussion instruments don't have or need resonating assists, because cymbals, castanets, cowbells, wood blocks, etc. generate loud signals to begin with. Yet the percussion family is also full of instruments that play with natural amplification and sound shaping. Marimbas pair the direct sound of felt mallets on wood with reverberations generated by devices below the tone bars. In some traditional designs, it's a wooden box that echoes the sound up and outward. In modern marimbas, every tone bar has a tube below it, and each of those pipes is tuned, by length, to match the pitch of its tone bar. The resonating effect of that is improbably rich. This principle gets built on with the vibraphone, which emerged in the 1930s. Its system of amplifying pipes includes a spinning axle that opens and closes the pipes like valves, at varying speeds controlled by a foot pedal. The result is a cascading warble that's like nothing else in music, something to seek out in the music of Milt Jackson ("Reunion Blues" with Oscar Peterson) and Gary Burton ("Common Ground" with Julian Lage).

I'm fascinated with the devices and inventions people have come up with that use science and natural acoustics to amplify and enhance instruments. The banjo came from Africa with a gourd body and then evolved into basically a skin head drum with strings stretched across it. In the nineteenth century, a rigid back with forward facing sound holes was added to make it louder with more attack, just the ticket when bluegrass came along in the 1940s. The acoustic guitar got a higher-volume version in the 1920s with the introduction of the resonator guitar. Here, a shallow aluminum cone is positioned inside the body (which are either wood or steel), just under the bridge where the strings are played. The signal is amplified and pushed out with a bright metallic timbre that's well known in the acoustic blues. But my favorite might be the Hammond B3 organ, made famous by Jimmy Smith, Booker T. Jones, and many southern soul and rock bands. The mechanism behind its tone is too complex to get into, but it's well known for amplifying its sound through a companion "Leslie" speaker. Inside its cabinet, outward facing speakers are on a rotating drum, whose speed is controlled by a foot pedal. Their spin imparts a natural tremolo that is just magical and core to certain styles of American music.

We don't need instruments to experience resonance and sympathetic vibrations. When we sing in a tile bathroom, we hear our voices amplified and made richer and rounder. If you experiment, you'll find that any given room will amplify some pitches more than others. As we adjust our pitch, we find the natural resonant frequencies of the room or the shower stall. The effect is called *reverberation*, of just *reverb*, and it's top of mind in the design of concert halls and recording studios. Players and engineers want spaces that are neither dead-feeling like a small home bedroom nor too "live" with a lot of decay, like a large stone church. Concert halls depend on this reflected sound to make an orchestra feel vibrant and loud enough without amplification and getting the balance right is a matter for highly trained acoustic designers. In recording, artificial or induced reverb is added to parts through a crazy array of fascinating methods. The old school way is to run a part, like a vocal or a lead guitar, through a speaker placed in a resonant space—a concrete box or sometimes a stairwell or elevator shaft—and then rerecorded through a microphone to a new track with its new echoing saturation. A variety of more controllable reverb effects are added with carefully designed pieces of gear—pedals, studio rack devices, reels of analog tape, tube or solid state. It's a world unto itself. And for decades now, digital workstations have used modeling to simulate an infinite variety of reverb effects "in the box," as they say. And it's probable you've never heard a recording that didn't make use of one of these methods, because reverb just makes music sounds richer, rounder and fuller.

We also experience resonance day-to-day in our appreciation of different human voices. It's why Morgan Freeman makes big money as an actor and a voice-over artist. Radio DJs speak with resonance as a job qualification, meaning their chest cavity is poised and full and the throat is relaxed and they probably have a big sinus cavity. Opera singers train to hold and shape their pneumatic physiology just so, controlling airflow from their diaphragm and lungs, up the larynx, past the soft palate, through the nasal cavity, out the mouth through sculpted lips, where the music finally is released. This is how carefully they think about this stuff.

You'll do well to think about it too. What does a sound reveal about its origins? Was it sung, bowed, plucked, struck, or blown? Did it pass through wood or metal or plastic? Perhaps it was electronically generated? How distinct is the sound's leading edge and timbre, and how influenced is it by the resonance of the room or space it was made? Getting in touch with the nature of the sounds will bring the music closer and engage more of your sensory and emotional response.

I find this way of hearing and feeling—this attention to resonance—especially provocative when listening to stereo systems, which I'll discuss in a later chapter. A good hi-fi system excites the room with a quality I like to call bloom. There's more resonance than seems possible, a life force that suggests the musicians and their instruments are actually in the room with you. This essence informs the comparisons between digital and analog music. Analog music is entirely made of waves, electric impulses, or moving fields, whether over wires, in grooves, or in the air between speaker and listener. When analog becomes digital, the waves are converted by a computer to ones and zeroes and captured as a high resolution sequence of samples in a file. Because we take so many pictures per second, and computers are so fast, high-quality digital is remarkable. But for some, there's a purity issue, a chain of custody issue. I love and listen to digital music, but I can hear more resonance and color and organic energy listening to records. I can see why some want their music to be all analog, from source to ear. Otherwise it doesn't ring true to them.

Listen for . . .

. . . the feedback from your voice singing in a shower or tiled room. At what pitches does your voice become louder and more reverberant?

　. . . musical instruments modified for extra resonance, volume, or reverb.

Highly Musical Humans

Allison Miller

Before we embark on three chapters about rhythm and the art and lore of drumming, let me introduce you to a drummer, composer, and bandleader who straddles worlds I love and live in—jazz and Americana. Allison Miller is a New Yorker in her 40s, active since 1999 and now recognized as a major figure of her time in improv-based and composed music.

Miller grew up in the DC area and played the drums from age 10. Even before she graduated from West Virginia University and moved to New York, she was spotted as an up-and-comer by jazz watchers. For interest and a livelihood, Miller also took road gigs with singer-songwriters, starting a decades-long job with Natalie Merchant in her post–10,000 Maniacs life. That led to shows and recording with Brandi Carlile, Ani DiFranco, and Toshi Reagon. Meanwhile, Miller was playing all over New York in creative, stretchy combos, and she developed as a composer. Now, to hear the music executed by her band Boom Tic Boom is to go on a journey that'll get you tuned into today's most respected contemporary jazz.

Her debut as a leader arrived in 2010, and I first heard her on the acclaimed and adorably titled 2016 album *Otis Was a Polar Bear*. But I'd suggest diving in with 2019's *Glitter Wolf*, an hour of beauty, energy, and remarkable collective creation, guided by the sometimes intricate compositions of the drummer/leader. I'll be honest, it can be clanging at times, as with Myra Melford's wildly burning piano solo on the Miller staple "Congratulations and Condolences." But there's also heaps of sweetness, funk, and light. I think you'll love the slinky, shifting rhythms of "Malaga," where Ben Goldberg delivers a great clarinet solo. The blend of wind instruments with the violin of Jenny Scheinman (another favorite musician of mine) is a field day of timbres. One of Miller's best drum solos comes most of the way through the brisk "Daughter and Sun."

Miller joined a supergroup of leading jazz women in 2020 called Artemis, named for the "Goddess of the Hunt," which is the custom-written first tune on their self-titled debut, Miller's one original on that album. All the musicians involved across now three Artemis albums are major players in today's scene, but one to note is the now-famous singer Cécile McLorin Salvant, who delivers a can't-miss take of Stevie Wonder's "If It's Magic" on album one. "Big Top" by pianist Renee Rosnes is catchy and humorous with its circus allusions, and it's a key tune to listen to how Allison Miller gives each little section its own drum treatment. Hear what she does and what she does not do, i.e., play a dull cyclical beat or hide in the background. The album's closer "Sidewinder" offers a chance to hear a 1960s standard, written by trumpeter Lee Morgan, come to life in the 2020s, with Miller laying down a laid-back groove and some of today's best musicians enjoying themselves.

Lastly, I'd recommend more Miller and Scheinman, because the drummer and violinist have a special, long-term collaboration going, and I think Scheinman shines as a jazz artist and as a singer songwriter. Their top collab is called *Parlour Game*, with Carmen Staff on piano and Tony Scherr on bass. I love this 11-track ride, an exceptional example of creative contemporary ensemble music, whatever you call the genre. "116th & Congress" is a floaty delight. While that one is composed by Scheinman, Miller co-writes on "Michigan," another beautiful mid-tempo piece.

Miller suggested to me in an interview that we may make too much of the distance between the genres in which she's worked. "I don't think I approach it that much differently. I try to play what the music calls for," she says. "In fact, I think that probably the singer-songwriter work I've done over my career has influenced me more than anything else as far as how I approach jazz."

PART IV

GROOVE

12

FIRST TIME
A White kid discovers Black rhythm

I want to tell you about two artists, one local and one national, who changed the way I heard the world and propelled me on a lifelong fixation on the mystery and magic of musical time.

First is Beverly Botsford, the go-to percussion player in the artsy southern city of Durham, NC, where I grew up. She worked with a variety of soul, funk, and reggae bands, popping up at street fairs or campus concerts through my formative years, the kind of working musician I'd meet many of later in life. For me, she was a figure of cool mystique with long brown hair and a drum key on a leather thong around her neck. Her chief instrument, as I remember, was the congas, the waist-high hand drums essential to any Afro-Caribbean ensemble or funk band. I noticed that not only were her congas tuned to different pitches, she could conjure different tones from a single drum depending on how she struck it with her fingers and palms. She could also rub her finger along a drum head and make it sing like a bowed string. That knocked me out. Her percussive notes rang out clean between the beats of the kit drummer. Beverly, I'd later learn, was playing counter-rhythms that generated the mesmerizing quality we call *syncopation*. Syncopated rhythm is the surest way to get people dancing. Beverly, who still works in the area four decades later, has inspired a lot of dancing in her time.

I had a more sudden rhythm epiphany in the presence of Buddy Rich, the world-famous jazz drummer (and infamous narcissist/prick though we had no way of knowing this at the time). When

I was about 12, my mother, normally a devotee of classical music, took me to see the Buddy Rich Big Band at Duke University. And it was overwhelming. For one thing, there he was—the drummer—at the front of the band, not at the back and not supporting the music but propelling it. With his giant toothy smile and blur of limbs, Rich made long, uncontested bombing runs of groove, leaning hard on the ride cymbal with his right hand as the heart of the time-keeping. His snare drum issued forth an impossibly exciting range of sounds. I'd heard drum rolls in the manner of marching bands before, but Buddy's were completely different, like ferocious rivers of white water. He'd spike their roar with crisp accents like rifle shots that played with my sense of where the meter's home base was. It was a fusillade of syncopation, colored by splashes from a variety of cymbals. For a private school, violin-playing, academics-oriented kid from the mid-South, this was radical, subversive, and a glimpse of something I needed to be around.

What was that thing that I was hearing—and more to the point feeling—in the hard swinging big band jazz of Buddy Rich and the funky soul of Beverly the conga woman? I sensed a spiritual aspect even then, because I was drawn so magnetically toward it and still am. It was worldly and deep and ancient. But its true nature didn't reveal itself for many years, because the story of American rhythm isn't taught in school, and it's only transmitted to those who offer themselves as students. This vivacious feeling stood in stark contrast to the rhythmically simple stuff I was playing in my youth orchestra or hearing on the radio. Classical music's meters—especially the Vivaldi and Haydn that I was exposed to early—mostly plodded through typical one-two-three-four measures without variety or surprise. Meanwhile, rock and pop music had a strong, sustained beat, but its meters were also symmetrical and right angled, dominated by the thump of the bass drum and the sock of the snare drum. Any such music I came across in normal life—Fleetwood Mac, The Eagles, the Stones—for all their sonic variety, usually felt lashed to the same simplistic time-keeping.

The truth is that I was waking up to the sprawling and remarkable story of Black music in America. Buddy Rich and Beverly were both

White, but they'd inhabited a world of rhythmic movement and energy that made my own native musical surroundings sound lifeless by comparison. Remember that rock radio around 1980, at least as far as I could hear, was overwhelmingly White. So was MTV during my high school years. My parents and peers didn't talk about James Brown or George Clinton, let alone about jazz drummers Max Roach or Elvin Jones, or New Orleans funk band The Meters. I had to find my own way through the mass-market miasma to a more exciting rhythmic world, by way of records by Stevie Wonder, Santana, and Earth, Wind & Fire, through a year or two of drum lessons, through engaging with the jazz community in my town and going to shows, ever in search of a deeper, more elusive groove.

Yet still, I didn't understand the debt and would not for years. American popular music exploded as a social, artistic, and economic force in the twentieth century because it had a beat, a pulse on long-term loan from the rhythmic language that African Americans had been nurturing for centuries. I don't diminish for a second the monumental achievements of Europe and the West in innovating and codifying the harmonic and melodic side of music. Indeed jazz became possible (to simplify a nuanced story) when African American rhythm and song styles met the tonalities of Bach and Debussy and Ives on American soil. Black time overwhelmed the staid oompah cadences of old Europe, making so much possible. That's not to overlook the rich rhythmic traditions from all over the world—the taiko drummers of Japan, the thrum of Celtic folk, and the fractal complexities of Indian classical music. I mean only to celebrate the American rhythmic story that is so indispensable to a contemporary concept of musicality. In my country, Black music became the swing of the blues, the collective pulse of pop and rock, the syncopation of funk, and the flow of hip-hop. This success is an artifact and legacy of slavery and its aftermath. It's ignorant to ignore that and unfulfilling to not study it through that frame. American musicians and music fans can't grasp the mystique and magnificence of rhythm in general without this reckoning.

"The most apparent survivals of African music in Afro-American music are its rhythms," wrote scholar LeRoi Jones in his great 1963 book *Blues People: Negro Music in White America*. "Not only the seeming emphasis in the African music on rhythmic, rather than melodic or harmonic, qualities, but also the use of polyphonic, or contrapuntal, rhythmic effects. Because of this seeming neglect of harmony and melody, Westerners thought the music 'primitive.' It did not occur to them that Africans might have looked askance at a music as vapid rhythmically as the West's."

Rhythm is often paramount in what makes a genre or style distinct. The celebrated record producer and writer Joe Boyd discovered over his long, globe-exploring career that rhythm is ultimately how nations, regions, and tribes express their signature sounds. And these signatures deserve respect and protection. In an interview we did about his book *And the Roots of Rhythm Remain*, he singled out Paul Simon, whose lyric is the source for his title. Simon, he said, sought out world music inspirations (from South Africa for his great album *Graceland* in particular) and did a respectful job adapting his music to *their* heartbeat. Meanwhile, other pop musicians have scouted for affects, textures, and melodies from advanced musical cultures overseas only to set those elements to a more generic "mid-Atlantic" rhythm, taking what they wanted like magpies but leaving out the essence of the music they'd appropriated. "Because it's all about the rhythm," Boyd told me. "And the rhythm is what endures. When melodies and playing styles and instruments travel around the world and get fused and mixed and borrowed and stolen, the *rhythm* of culture remains."

In the next three chapters, I'll describe the fundamentals of rhythm, introduce you to a number of important drummers and styles, and offer insight into how to watch and feel drummers play. Keep in mind however that this is a part of music where theory matters less than experience and a cultivated feel. Only through wide and engaged listening to our polyglot culture can the galaxy of American and world rhythm across all genres come alive. And if you take that journey, you'll probably be blown away as I have been by just how many ways there are to make music move.

***

The brain is an organizational, pattern-recognizing organ, so it's alert and oriented when music is divided into evenly spaced events. We thrive, as does music, on semi-predictable repetition. It's also a temporal organ that operates in part on cycles of high frequency oscillations. Through unconscious processes, humans are almost uniquely capable in the animal kingdom of feeling an inner clock, a steady beat (though some birds seem pretty darned good at it). Based on all I've read, I strongly suspect that rhythmic feeling is wired deeply in the human mind and genome. While many people claim to be or seem to be bad at rhythm, I'd suggest that, as with self-misdiagnosis of tone deafness, rhythm is down in there for nearly everyone. I think most rhythmically estranged people can find it and feel it with a shift of point of view and some fun, constructive clapping, tapping, dancing, and whacking on things.

A musical piece or tune flows through time at a velocity agreed to by the performers, which we call a *tempo*. And tempo is one of the most critical aspects of interpreting a piece of music in any genre. Musicians, besides using terms like "a little faster" or "pretty slow" just like any of us would, sometimes speak of tempo in terms of beats per minute (BPM), something most of us are familiar with from measuring our heart rate at the gym. For musical understanding, a good reference point is to know that most disco and house dance music hovers between 100 and 130 BPM, the pace of a brisk walk. (Think of John Travolta, in *Saturday Night Fever*, striding down the avenue to "Stayin' Alive" at 103 BPM.) These tempos inspire physical motion more than most, but you'll hear great music at every tempo between lows around 60 BPM and frenetic highs of 250 or more—if you're into punk polka for example. Music with a pulse needs the *right* tempo, and musicians and producers discover that a mere two BPM difference faster or slower can transform a track from good to great. Hits have been made and missed over shades of difference in tempo.

Musicians stay together by following a map (written out or mental) of connected units called *measures*. Each measure has the same number of beats, commonly four, making a matrix or grid that is filled in with notes whose duration is expressed as fractions of the measure. We call it 4/4 time. A whole note lasts all four beats. A quarter note (what you're counting when cycling through *one-two-three-four*) lasts one beat—a quarter of the measure—and so forth, into eighth, sixteenth and even thirty-second notes, though those get a little impractical. Notes are juxtaposed with rests with the same divisions and names, and these silences are every bit as critical to generating rhythmic feel as notes are.

Music set in a so-called waltz time is expressed as 3/4, implying three beats per measure with a quarter note defining one beat. Most folks know a waltz when they hear one. "The Blue Danube" by Richard Strauss II is the stuff of legend and TV commercials. Waltzes are almost unheard of in pop music, but they're common in country and roots music where they are part of dance hall culture, from "Waltz Across Texas" to "Bartender's Blues." The astute listener will be able to hear the difference between 3/4 songs and 6/8 songs, including "The End of the World" or "Norwegian Wood" or "Hallelujah." These 6/8 songs have a see-saw quality with sets of three beats on either side of a fulcrum. They offer a rhythmic sway commonly found in doo-wop music. *One-two-three-Four-five-six*. And so on.

Connecting with music begins with being able to identify the *downbeat*—the ONE—in a piece and then to count through its measures, whether in 4/4 or in 3/4 time. For most musically engaged people, finding the one is second nature, but for those who don't find this obvious, I can think of few more useful or accessible exercises for becoming a more active, involved listener.

You may feel better knowing that there are seasoned professional musicians who don't know quite what *finding the one* means, but they know what it *is*, at least according to a story from the realm of funk music, as told in the Cinemax animated documentary series *Mike Judge Presents: Tales from the Tour Bus*. One day a half-century ago, a newly formed teenage band in Georgia got hired out of the blue to play for fast-rising funk pioneer James Brown. The bass player, William Earl "Bootsy" Collins, played too many notes without enough clarity of purpose for his demanding new bandleader. Brown told young Bootsy—ordered him—that whatever else he did, he must always, always play hard and firm on the ONE of every measure.

Bootsy didn't initially understand what he meant, until he figured out that measures could be counted: ONE-two-three-four. All his life he'd *felt* that strong first beat in the music, but he'd never encountered the theory of the subdivided, counted-out measure. Now with that mental tool, he was oriented and able to set a landmark for the listeners and dancers—and for Mr. Dynamite—in every bar. Of course James Brown's funk depended on a lot of other things happening in between the ONEs, especially the syncopated drumming of Clyde Stubblefield, sometimes joined by a second drummer. And Bootsy, having done his emphatic job, had something to build off of for the rest of every measure. (Amusingly, because Bootsy was frequently on LSD in those early days, the ONE became a cosmic concept for him, a mantra of unifying force and love, which it kind of is. Later, when Bootsy joined Parliament-Funkadelic with George Clinton, he discovered that Clinton didn't know about counting one-two-three-four measures either! Which means that they both learned the *feeling* without the terminology, which is a lot more important than the other way around.)

Some beats in the bar get emphasized (sometimes, but not always, the ONE), while others are played softly or dropped out, and this dance between *strong beats* and *weak beats* does more to determine the vibe and feeling of music than just about anything else. They are woven into song based music by the accented syllables of the lyrics. Strong and weak beats can be set for a whole tune or they can vary from moment to moment in the hands of an improvisor. A jazz drum solo is mostly a flux of strong and weak beats as the drummer controls dynamics and shifts emphasis to conjure a feeling. In reggae or certain reggae-influenced rock songs like "Bring on the Night" by the Police, the accents are on the *offbeats*, another important concept. The chopping guitar chords seem to say one-AND, two-AND, three-AND, four-AND as the verses cycle along.

The power of subtle shifts in this kind of emphasis reminds me of a running joke in bluegrass circles, worthy of a bumper sticker, that goes: "friends don't let friends clap on one and three." It's funny because it plays off of a common divergence between the way the band and the audience feel the strong beats. If a band plays the old standard "Rocky Top," it's incredibly common to hear members of the audience start clapping along on the ONE and THREE. Problem is, the mandolin and guitar are chopping on the song's strong beats, the TWO and FOUR. This rhythmic dissonance causes the motion of the music to seize up and become conflicted as the band and crowd work at counter purposes. The rhythmically hip members of the audience look sideways at the ONE and THREE clappers. And then the ill-advised clapping along peters out and everyone tries to forget what just happened. Another way to grasp the lesson is to imagine a Black gospel group going full tilt on a Sunday morning. The choir and congregation will clap along, and if you count, you'll discover the claps are happening and will only work on the TWO and FOUR. Getting this wrong could have consequences for your soul.

So we've now encountered the dominant song meter of 4/4 and the less frequent but still widespread 3/4 time. But some of us music lovers get unreasonably excited by songs or passages in outlier time signatures—songs where the measures have five beats, or seven, or thirteen. Such works can throw some listeners off balance with their asymmetry, but others relish the wobbly weirdness. The most famous example of this breaking through is pianist Dave Brubeck's "Take Five," a sleeper hit in 1959. The entire tune is in 5/4 time, yet drummer Joe Morello made it swing with a crafty quintuple feel that feels like *ONE-two-three-FOUR-five*. If you haven't heard it in a while, listen again, especially to Morello's legendary drum solo, and feel how those mystical measures captivated America. That jaunty feeling, along with the melodic saxophone of Paul Desmond, the song's composer, propelled "Take Five" to its historic status as the first million-selling jazz single. Other beloved popular songs with odd, yet natural sounding times include The Beatles' "All You Need Is Love," in 7/4 and the opening of the Allman Brothers' "Whipping Post," which is in the surprising time of 11/8.

These nonstandard meters had been used in classical music for ages, but largely in brief stretches or as transitional measures between passages in 4/4. More expansive examples can be found in Tchaikovsky's Sixth Symphony, whose second movement is in 5/4 time, a feeling that observers called a "limping waltz." Igor Stravinsky composed extended use of 7/4 time into his Firebird ballet of 1910. These thought-provoking works influenced the genre of prog(ressive) rock in the 1970s, when bands like Yes, Emerson, Lake & Palmer, and King Crimson went to town with elaborately constructed, hard-to-count suites. Pink Floyd did rather well with its song "Money" from the titanium selling *Dark Side of the Moon*, which is in 7/4 time. You should put this record on, find the ONE, and count along. It's not as fun counting money, but it's fun.

For some reason, odd meters in prog rock and jazz fusion came to be regarded as the province of nerds and over-intellectual White guys, and I resemble that remark. But I'd point out that this engaging rhythmic hack also shows up in folk music. "Clinch Mountain Backstep," a traditional fiddle tune made famous by the Stanley Brothers, has an extra beat dropped in to each cycle in the B section, making for a delightful hook. Later, progressive bluegrass artists Béla Fleck and Sam Bush composed tunes with 5/4 ("Blu-Bop"), 7/4 ("Laps in Seven"), and other odd meters as well. Music like this is catchy in a whole new way. Electronic dance music tends to keep things in 4/4 or 2/4 time, but it also drops beats and adds beats of silence to build tension and release with emphatic returns to the ONE. So keep your ears out for uneven beats; they're hiding in places you might not expect.

Another good idea as you ponder music in new ways is to ask yourself where is the rhythm actually coming from in a band or ensemble. Of course it's coming from everybody somehow, because every note contributes to the overall motion of the music and its pulse. Yet if you listen carefully, maybe you'll hear a musician who's out of time and holding the band back! The drummer is likely to have a dominant role, but give an ear to the *bass player*, because often they're doing even more of the work of keeping a band rock solid and propulsive. In jazz, the bass player often carries most of that time-keeping role, while the drummer uplifts and decorates the beat with accents. We call the vital partnership of drums and bass the *rhythm section* in a band, a role that can also include a piano player or guitar player, depending on the setting and arrangement.

We can also think about the placement, intensity, and purpose of the rhythm in various kinds of music. On one extreme is punk rock with its wall of fast, insistent, and rather monotonous groove. Metal has a similar ferocity but much of its excitement comes from sudden stops and starts and hard-stabbing accents that lend variety to the thunder. Disco, new wave, house, trance, and EDM bring their audience along with a more robotic pulse that's often called four-on-the-floor. What these genres have in common is a generally unsyncopated rhythmic flow, which is why I'm personally less drawn to them.

I've mentioned syncopation several times, so let's define it. It means accenting beats in places that rub against the clear four-four grid. The dictionary calls it "a temporary displacement of the regular metrical accent in music caused typically by stressing the weak beat" (which is a rather square way of thinking about a rather hip thing, because you can't make funk without it). As I've noted, music of African derivation, as well as most Latin music, thrives on syncopation.

A related concept is polyrhythm, which is when one rhythmic pattern is superimposed over another, creating a shifting, slipping feeling that lets the listener follow or dance to any number of cyclical beats working together in one piece of music. I heard a life-altering example of this in my college years when I took an ethnomusicology class as an elective. The professor knew of a drum ensemble there in Chicago with members from Ghana in West Africa, and we saw them perform. The ensemble drummers took on assigned cyclical beats. Each was simple in itself, but when they all played together, the different patterns locked together in a kind of tapestry of time— polyrhythm incarnate. The master drummer was the only musician who was free to improvise. He'd create washes of sound on his large drum in sympathy with his group, and his calls signaled the ensemble drummers to shift to new patterns. The effect was stunning. I heard them again during a festival on a beautiful spring day on the shores of Lake Michigan, and I danced like a fool with bare feet and a lot of joy.

While popular genres lean on steady pulses throughout each song, composed/classical music makes much more flexible use of time. In orchestras, it's up to the conductor to push and pull the tempo for expressive purposes. Classical scores suggest a tempo for each section, but there is so much room for interpretation that different performances or recordings of full symphonies may vary by minutes in total duration. Notice also how composers shift the focus of the time-keeping around the ensemble as different instruments carry the heaviest rhythmic responsibility from passage to passage. The music will sound light if it's the first violins keeping a quarter-note pulse, and it will have more weight if it's the double basses and tympani punching out whole notes down low. In smaller ensembles like a string quartet, the musicians push and pull time together through listening and intuition, ideally as if they are one organism. Classical time almost never "grooves," but the creative manipulation of tempo works on us in surprising ways.

It's easy to think of rhythmic feeling as relying on consistency and accuracy, in other words hitting notes precisely on time, like a metronome. Rushing and dragging are both just bad, right? Actually though, advanced musicians play around with the beat with dramatic effect. When I got to Nashville and started learning the finer points of bluegrass music, I heard musicians talk about playing *ahead of* or *behind* the beat. It might also be expressed as leaning in or laying back. Often we'll hear a mandolinist consistently play the TWO and FOUR chop a few microseconds early, giving the music a feeling of acceleration, but without actually rushing. Conversely, the bass player can play a few microseconds behind the beat on the ONE and THREE, giving the band a relaxed feeling, but without dragging. Done at the same time, the push-pull effect can be truly seductive. Such expressive techniques chafe against the perfection of computer generated beats, and sometimes over-eager recording engineers will use digital tools to move "imperfect" beats to conform to the grid, but the resulting "perfection" can lack life and energy. The musicians I know and most admire tell me that they admire other musicians who know the pulse and how to massage it. Whom do they most want to play with? Musicians who "have good time."

And then there's dancing, which is how so many people most viscerally experience and express rhythm. Yet I won't get into it, because dance is its own vast and sophisticated subject that spans traditional ritual, formal ballet, modern dance, club life, jam band hippies, and having fun on TikTok. Dance is as universal and varied as humanity itself, and our bodies speak to us in different ways. I've lost myself in dancing to live music at various times in my life, but dancing is not integral to the experience of music for me. So perhaps my advice is to let dance guide and enhance your musical journey to the degree that you feel it and on a case-by-case basis. Some of the greatest music in the world is not suited for dancing. Some of the best dance music is far off the mainstream radar—like New Orleans funk or Cajun and zydeco, which for me is the most bodily infectious of all. And remember that it's more than OK to let music's rhythm work on your insides and on your mind. Whether your body is moving or not, the important thing is to feel it.

Time and music are bound together mechanically and physically, mathematically and spiritually. There is no playing or listening without the commitment of time, and our ability to understand and communicate music depends on subdividing time in a sharable schema. I think of music as one way that humans can take some measure of control back over ruthless time. We borrow its steadiness for relief from our otherwise arrhythmic lives. Rhythm can be explicit or implicit, strict or loose, forward or backward leaning, propulsive or calming. What I find most remarkable is how entirely distinct rhythm is from harmony, while the two are so mutually dependent. Harmony and rhythm are made of different raw materials, serve different purposes, and are processed by different parts of the brain. Rhythm divides time in even slices, in twos and fours and 16s. Its frequencies are measured in tens of beats per minute. Harmony depends on odd ratios, of threes and fives and sevens, with frequencies measured in hundreds or thousands of cycles per second. There is harmonic music that exists free of rhythm (like ambient music that ebbs and flows without a pulse). And there's music made almost entirely of rhythm without much harmonic content, like that West African drum ensemble. Yet what we crave, what we humans have made so much with, is a golden braid of harmony and rhythm. Like a double helix. Or a marriage. How people thought to fasten those two phenomena together into an art form is for me a source of endless wonder.

Listen for . . .

. . . the true source of the time-keeping in a song. It's often the bass, not the drums. And if there's no drummer or bass player, who is the keeper of the pulse?

. . . strong and weak beats, polyrhythm, and syncopation. Try to clap out a complementary part more complex than simply clapping on the strong beats.

. . . works of music in unconventional or irregular time signatures.

13

SECOND TIME
A brief history of musical time

To grasp the possibilities that await you as a listener in the realms of time, it helps to know something about the journey of American music from a rhythmic point of view. So welcome to the most historical and chronological chapter in this book. It's a story and a listener's guide meant to describe how different genres evolved out of rhythmic ideas and combinations. Our rich musical culture has had many beats. Feeling them pays respect to the many strains of our heritage.

African music became African-American music on Southern plantations and in countless church houses before and after the Civil War. But one good place to start the story of the American beat is Congo Square. Starting in the eighteenth century, slaveholders in and around the bustling, international city of New Orleans gave enslaved people Sundays off, and as early as 1740 they began congregating to trade, play drums, and dance in a clearing along Rampart Street in what would become the Tremé neighborhood. Traditional rhythmic music from different parts of Africa and the Caribbean mingled together in a jam session that lasted decades. While the tradition was snuffed out in the years before the Civil War, Congo Square was like a fermentation still for the layered rhythms, the call and response, and the collective spirit that would evolve into brass band parade music, second line, jazz, R&B, and funk.

An early landmark on that road was ragtime, a genre that fused European harmonic language and marching band music with syncopated (or "ragged") rhythm. Scott Joplin became the movement's best known composer, with his seminal "Maple Leaf Rag" emerging in 1899. Fellow pianist Jelly Roll Morton became a star out of New Orleans, while James Reese Europe and W.C. Handy enriched the sound with full bands that toured the US and Europe as pioneering Black popular musicians. Meanwhile, what we now think of as the drum kit—integrating bass drum, snare drum, tom-toms, and cymbals—had begun to come together in the late 1800s for use in pit bands or stage orchestras. Such simple inventions as the kick drum pedal and mounting hardware for cymbals and other percussion instruments opened up new prospects for drummers and their role in bands. Details about this leap forward, as well as many of the rhythmic innovations over the next century that are described in this chapter can be found in Matt Brennan's fascinating book *Kick It: A Social History of the Drum Kit.*

"Drummers faced a wide variety of challenges—of space, labour, and status—in their lives as professional musicians. This was the context in which different drummers, particularly those based in the United States, independently reached the same conclusion: life would be easier if they played several instruments at once," writes Brennan. The evolving drum kit "gave them a competitive advantage for securing gigs (why pay three musicians to play bass drum, snare drum, and cymbals and percussion when you could just pay one?), and saved space in overcrowded orchestra pits. It might even gain them some much-needed credibility amongst their peers. The innovation would ultimately unleash creative possibilities for drummers that no one could have imagined at the time."

Ragtime evolved into jazz with the advent of midsize bands organized by visionaries like cornet players Bix Beiderbecke and King Oliver, who mentored the incomparable jazz founding father Louis Armstrong. Where ragtime had a strutting, striding rhythm, the 1920s saw the rise of the feel called *swing.* It's a rhythmic sensation so potent and popular it gave its name to a "swing era" in early jazz, becoming a verb that meant producing a good, easy sensation in the music—and a noun for the abstract quality that good popular music should achieve, what one source calls "an irresistible gravitational buoyancy." In clinical terms, swing is defined by accented emphasis on the second and fourth beats, a *ting-ting-a-ting* pattern from the percussion, a "walking" bass line, and a slight hesitation every two beats that breaks up the monotony of four even counts. Almost any kind of groove-based music can "swing" in this broad, eye-of-the-beholder sense, from marching band to old-time fiddling to Tom Petty and the Heartbreakers. But before and during WWII, swing was the dominant popular genre and a showcase for increasingly technical and daring drummers.

Baby Dodds from King Oliver's band inspired Gene Krupa, a charismatic virtuoso band leader of the 1930s. Krupa, who was White, and Chick Webb, who was Black, emerged as the first star drummers in American popular music. They took blazing solos and set new standards for what was possible with four limbs and a set of drums and cymbals. Coming up just behind them was Buddy Rich, emerging as a child prodigy who was exploited by his parents making a sensation and good money in vaudeville as "Traps, the Drum Wonder." As a young man, Rich played with the Artie Shaw big band and drove his boss crazy with his showy, loud, and extravagant playing, drumming that seemed indifferent to the band or its musical cohesiveness. He'd wind up working for a variety of ensembles but found his biggest impact and fame leading his own big band, which he did for most of his latter career, playing everywhere from PBS specials to *the Muppet Show* to Duke University, where I saw him perform.

After WWII, music and its business changed and accelerated, producing two new genres that seem superficially to have little to do with one another but which share some rhythmic genes—bebop and bluegrass. Bebop represented a reclaiming of jazz and blues-based improvised music by Black artists from the overwhelmingly White swing big bands. Pioneered in Harlem by trumpeter Dizzy Gillespie, sax player Charlie Parker, and pianist Thelonious Monk, bebop was musically challenging, harmonically progressive, and intolerant of mediocrity. It was also concert music for attentive listening rather than for show or for dancing, and for those who saw this revolution unfold from tables in cozy cocktail clubs like Minton's Playhouse in Harlem, it was rhythmically hot and physically enthralling.

The standout drummer in the movement was Kenny Clarke, who emerged in the late 1930s as a sonic innovator. He's said to have been the first jazz drummer to keep steady time with the ride cymbal instead of the bass drum, which freed the snare and bass drum up for off-kilter accents and surprises (sometimes called "dropping bombs"). Clarke took care to complement the band's inner voices (as opposed to only the soloist), enriching the music by spreading around the listener's attention. He could play with feathery finesse or with explosive power. But that right hand technique would become his greatest innovation, writes Brennan: "Clarke's new way of drumming—playing a shimmering 'spang-a-lang' swing rhythm on the top cymbal complemented by accents on bass and snare— would eventually be universally adopted by jazz drummers, and is now taken as the default mode of playing jazz time." (At least it was before hip-hop and funk made huge twenty-first century inroads into the genre, which we'll get to.) Clarke led a new vanguard of remarkable American drummers, including Max Roach, Art Blakey and Roy Haynes, that gave the instrument more personality and a more dramatic and costarring role in the music while refining the drum solo from the crowd-pleasing showpieces of the big band era into flowing, dynamic expressions. As Max Roach said, the new jazz "liberated the drummers from having to play a certain way. The *musicality* became dominant" (emphasis mine).

Meanwhile in the winter of 1946, Bill Monroe and his Blue Grass Boys brought a new lineup to the Grand Ole Opry in Nashville featuring young five-string banjo player Earl Scruggs. With a syncopated three-finger roll that suggested the firecracker accents of a swing snare drum solo, Scruggs synched his banjo up with Monroe's sharp mandolin chop on the two and four and the bass player's striding emphasis on the one and three for a new American groove. Country music fans, comfortable with the gentle swing and shuffle of honky-tonk music, which was made largely without drummers in the '40s, found the timing and riverine flow of bluegrass absolutely thrilling. The music also resembled bebop jazz in its balance of group music-making with individual soloing, a dance made visible as bluegrass bands cycled in and around a central microphone, taking turns in the foreground with graceful choreography. The key musical ingredients in bluegrass—the blues, big band swing, and Anglo-Irish fiddle music—each had their own rhythmic heritage. Fused together, they made a wonderfully flexible template that could, depending on the song or section, swing hard, spank like rockabilly music, or cruise forward like a fast locomotive. With further evolution in the decades to come, bluegrass would begin to inspire dancing on the jam band circuit.

The most impactful rhythmic revolution in postwar America was rock and roll, but it wouldn't have happened without rhythm and blues, the versatile catch-all for the rich and wide world of Black popular music of the 1940s and '50s. It's impossible to briefly summarize this complex evolution, but one fair point is that much of R&B's pulse, including the mainstay feeling called boogie-woogie, was propelled by piano players generating sensations traceable to Congo Square and New Orleans. Professor Longhair and Fats Domino might as well have been drummers, given how they animated music with their powerful piano hands, while their drummers (when they played with one) supported the time rather than necessarily generating it. When Elvis Presley latched on to R&B grooves under the ambitious production of Sam Phillips in Memphis, his first expressions of rock and roll didn't even use a drummer. But it did have the sharp emphasis on the two and four, called a *backbeat*, which had a long lineage in R&B and Black gospel. The backbeat, defined almost always by the snare drum, became the heartbeat of American culture and a common feature of all popular music. But it's taken many sonic forms. In rockabilly, a sound that influenced country and rock, the bass fiddle is deployed as a percussion instrument with a pronounced slap on the two and four. Wherever the source, the backbeat was danceable, sexual, and revolutionary in its time, while now to our modern ears, it's omnipresent and unremarkable.

Elvis found himself playing with a drummer by accident on an early gig with the house band of the Louisiana Hayride radio show. He liked the drummer and his vibe so much that DJ Fontana became part of the Elvis rock and roll sound. Johnny Cash's backing band of bass and guitar the Tennessee Two became the Tennessee Three with the addition of drummer W.S. "Fluke" Holland, who'd played on the Carl Perkins hit "Blue Suede Shoes" and who helped make room for drums in country music. Earl Palmer of New Orleans drummed his way into the Rock and Roll Hall of Fame for his seminal sounds with Fats Domino, Little Richard, and others. But nobody inspired more new drummers or established the instrument's potential in rock and pop music with more impact and reach than Ringo Starr. The Beatles were compelled to fire their first drummer and good friend Pete Best to meet the exacting standards of producer George Martin. Ringo, who'd impressed John, Paul, and George as a skiffle drummer in the British "beat" scene, kept jaunty, exciting time in the early years. Then, as the Beatles remade themselves several times over in the next stunning decade, Ringo's dynamic interplay showed how integral the drums could be to songwriting and record making. Just listen again to his creative enhancements to "She Said She Said" or "Come Together" as two examples of his unifying vision.

***

Black American music continued leaping forward in the 1960s with the triple threat of R&B, soul, and funk, genres defined by their rhythmic concepts as much as anything else. Every American should know Al Jackson, Jr., the subtle wizard on the kit in the house studio band of Stax Records in Memphis from 1962 into the early '70s. With exquisite timing and inventive touches, he propelled countless hits by Otis Redding, Sam & Dave, Rufus Thomas, and more, even as that same studio band released progressive instrumental music as Booker T. and the M.G.'s. Meanwhile, James Brown hired and fired drummers almost whimsically, but he found his most historic heart-beat with twin drummers Clyde Stubblefield and John "Jabo" Starks. Their interwoven sound was rooted like a tree on the bottom, crisp and snapping on top with complex snare patterns, fancy use of the hi-hat cymbals, and decisive bass drum, setting the template for funk. New Orleans developed its own funk feel in the mid '60s with the rise of The Meters, powered by the slippery grooves of Joseph "Zigaboo" Modeliste. Fusing second line parade band feeling with a rock-oriented stage show, the Meters crafted a feeling that's been part of New Orleans culture ever since, with Stanton Moore of the band Galactic as a terrific source for that sensation today.

Those '60s innovators—Ringo, Al, Clyde, and Jabo—made history on drum kits of the same lean and understated design as the jazz drummers of the 1950s (bass drum, snare, at most two tom-toms, and a couple of cymbals), but as rock and roll came to embrace excess for its own sake, the drums and drummers followed suit. In the arena rock era of the '70s onward, double bass drums became common (though the idea was pioneered by a few jazz big band drummers), along with a dozen or more tom-toms and even more cymbals. Drummers like Terry Bozzio (Frank Zappa), Neil Peart (Rush), and Mickey Hart/Bill Kreutzmann (The Grateful Dead) performed on risers surrounded by gear. It gave the musicians more notes, more timbres, more options, and the trend mirrored the growing complexity and showiness of progressive rock and metal. Drum solos became a staple of rock concerts in the '70s, and let's just say quality control in that department was spotty. For every Lars Ulrich (Metallica) and Stewart Copeland (The Police), there were scores of artless thunder gods flexing their muscles and banishing the muse of dynamics to hell.

Jazz got thicker too, first through "hard bop," an Afrocentric response to "cool jazz," a mellow movement of the '50s that often relieved its urbane White audience of feeling anything too strongly. Art Blakey, the quintessential hard bop drummer and bandleader, embraced and integrated what he'd learned from a couple of years spent in Africa in the late '40s, giving him an unmistakable force and polyrhythmic seductiveness. The music had fewer tricky chord changes than bebop and made room for funkier rhythms and riff-based improvisation, leading to a kind of sister genre called "soul jazz."

One icon who embraced both was Miles Davis, who as part of his lifelong shapeshifting went all in on funk jazz fusion with his landmark albums *In a Silent Way* (1969) and *Bitches Brew* (1970). The drummer on the former was Tony Williams, a young genius who'd been tapped by Davis in 1963 to be part of his great quintet with Herbie Hancock (piano), Wayne Shorter (sax), and Ron Carter (bass). I've sometimes thought of Williams as my favorite drummer of all time, and I can't recommend this body of work enough for overall dynamics, freedom and musicality. *Bitches Brew* featured two extraordinary drummers in Jack DeJohnette and Lenny White, the latter of whom became a leader and star in the jazz/rock fusion movement that the Brew album signified. There's too much to say about this period, but I'd encourage you to explore it because this is when jazz was liberated from the ting-ting-a-ting swing feel that dominated for decades and became a malleable, groove-based music that is perhaps more relatable to rock, pop and country fans. It's hard to believe this dazzlingly interesting rhythmic language emerged in the same decade as disco, a simplistic and four-to-the-bar beat that took over the world's dance floors and never entirely went away.

***

Hundreds of recorded tracks from hard bop, soul jazz, and fusion became source material for the next great rhythmic revolution in popular music, the New York–born genre of hip-hop. I know far too little about this sprawling realm of music, but I can tell you what fascinates me about it from a musical perspective. For one thing, its seminal grooves came from an inspired fusion of (sampled) old records and the novel technique of scratching, in which LPs, twin turntables, and their needles became a musical instrument. DJs identified "breakbeats" from solo drum passages on vinyl albums—mostly from R&B, soul, and jazz—and "juggled" them with impeccable timing, bouncing between one turntable and the other. By scratching the records back and forth, they evoked a new realm of sound. Over this, rappers built on the natural syncopation of speech, spinning their urban poetry in a patter that was admired as "flow" when it was good. The evolution and progress of rap is easy to hear, between the rather singsong cadences of 1980s hip-hop versus the bar-crossing, slip-slide of rappers of the '90s and beyond. Certain rappers or MCs have been hailed as particularly innovative in their use of inner rhymes and rhythmic complexities, notably MF Doom, Mos Def, Eminem, and Kendrick Lamar.

Hip-hop, a genre that rarely was backed by traditional bands with live drummers (The Roots with Questlove being a notable exception), also became a forum for the widespread use of drum machines and the computer techniques of sampling and sequencing. Synthetic drums introduced a mechanical precision to beats that is quite different from human-kept time but has its own particular energy. A synth-based pulsing or "motoric" quality was the foundation of Krautrock, a sound that emerged from Germany in the late '60s and '70s via bands like Neu!, Can, and Kraftwerk. That evolved into a family of electronically derived, steady-pulse genres, including new wave, trance, techno, house and EDM. Computers also assisted artists in these realms with looping, an essential tool in the hip-hop craft of "beat making," in which combinations of live recorded drums and synthesized drums can be layered and set against one another in interesting ways.

One universally acknowledged maestro of beat making was the late great James Dewitt Yancey, the Detroit producer, songwriter, and musician known as Jay Dee or J Dilla. He was a multifaceted artist worth deep study, but his top-line claim to fame has to do with his idiosyncratic use of drum machines, chiefly his famous MPC3000 sampling and sound effects unit from Akai. He had the insight to turn off a feature in the digital device that "quantized" its finger-triggered sound pads, which is to say "perfected" them by moving them to their closest line on the rhythmic grid. Without the quantizing, Dilla could play the machine more like a natural drum, leaning over or behind beats and placing them with human feeling rather than machine precision. He pushed the boundaries of being off the grid so that many of his most famous beats—indeed his signature sound—had a staggered or "drunk" or "slugging" quality, a kind of counter-groove that became integral to modern hip-hop.

Once again, a pop format circled back and changed jazz, where starting around 2000, the head bobbing beats and slugging feel of hip-hop became part of improvised art music. "We've now got a whole generation of jazz musicians who have been brought up with hip-hop," sax player Kamasi Washington told *The Guardian* in 2016. "We've grown up alongside rappers and DJs, we've heard this music all our life. We are as fluent in J Dilla and Dr. Dre as we are in Mingus and Coltrane." The trio Medeski Martin & Wood brought this fusion to rock and jam band culture in the 1990s. In recent years, I've binged on brilliant jazz with hip-hop roots, including the creative drumming and remixing of Chicago's Makaya McCraven and leaders in the London scene like drummer/producer Yussef Dayes. I find the fusion of these two African American art forms one of the most exciting developments in modern music, and I wish I saw more evidence that the public, especially younger folks, understood that in this and other ways, the almost perfect music known imperfectly as jazz keeps evolving and embracing new ideas.

My survey leaves out many important and wonderful rhythmic traditions from around the world and around the nation. The grooves inherent in Cajun, zydeco, Appalachian old-time, polka, and Texas border music are all magnificent parts of the American story. Latin music from many countries of origin has thrived in the US in its pure forms and through influence on pop, jazz, and folk music throughout the twentieth century, including a major bossa nova craze in the '60s.

Likewise, there are countless great drummers I couldn't weave into my narrative for sheer space, but I'd recommend you seek out the history-making work of session and touring icons Steve Gadd, Dave Weckl, Jim Keltner, Hal Blaine, Buddy Harmon, and Vinnie Colaiuta. My favorite drummers today include Nate Wood, Jay Bellerose, Tyshawn Sorey, Antonio Sanchez, and Brian Blade. And listen for the beat in history's cracks too. Check out videos of Karen Carpenter, known so well for her lovely voice, playing her first and favorite instrument, the drums. Her percussion career fell victim to the sexist forces that also leave my list of twentieth-century heroes exclusively male. That's changing in jazz though, where I'd point you to drummer/composers Terri Lyne Carrington, Allison Miller (already profiled), and Eva Klesse.

And while you're at it, fight against the forces in the industry and culture that leave drummers anonymous shadow figures who have been made to feel at times like interchangeable machine parts. Listen for drummers' unique voices and styles. And seek out music that foregrounds their contributions. Drumming and beat-based music have been pilloried and condemned since they began to make commercial inroads in the early twentieth century. Drummer jokes can be amusing, but treating drummers like jokes is not. Great drummers are great musicians, and they're integral to one of the most universal responses we have to music. In the next chapter, I'll talk about how to listen for the nuances and gifts of individual drummers.

14

THIRD TIME
The call of the drum

I was about 14 or 15 when I heard a drum solo that messed with my head. It was on the radio of all places, a program I'd listen to on a station out of UNC Chapel Hill to fuel my growing interest in jazz. I don't remember the tune or the band unfortunately, but I remember how this solo made me feel. I realized after quite a few measures that the drummer had only touched his cymbals, not his drums. Then came more cymbals. More time went by. More cymbals, lightly touched, not smashing or crashing. I started to think maybe he's going to play a *drum* solo using *only his cymbals*. And that's just what happened. The soloist came to the end of a phrase, and the rest of the band came back in. I haven't encountered an all-cymbal drum solo since that I can think of. But at the time it struck me as almost like heresy or sacrilege. Drum solos, I thought, were supposed to be big and bold and punchy and cracking and syncopated and funky. But the fact that I remember this very different vision for a drum solo all these years later suggests it got a rise out of me. It made me listen harder and longer, eager to know what was going to happen next. And isn't that the point?

What makes a drummer good? How do we recognize excellence or its opposite? Well, my little anecdote suggests that one measure is the ability and willingness to surprise, to defy easy expectations with legs, arms, and sticks, amid the seeming monotony of keeping time. But there's more, and in this chapter I try to describe how you might listen more insightfully to drummers and percussionists and how to foreground them, even when they may be sitting in the back of the band. Sensitivity to musical time brings rewards that are esthetic, physical, and spiritual. I'd suggest that there's a drummer inside of all of us, including you.

Let's stipulate what great drumming is not necessarily about, which is power and speed. The 2014 feature film *Whiplash*, while a rare and welcome story about jazz in mainstream culture, depicted its student protagonist as under immense pressure to play faster and more technically by his domineering instructor, played with fierce intensity by J.K. Simmons. Jazz musicians know this is a distorted and angry picture of their art form. Nor is great drumming dependent upon being a flawless human metronome, able to precisely identify and keep any beat. Like perfect pitch, that is a skill that some drummers have and that one might *like* to have in one's tool kit, but robotic drumming is only one approach that only sometimes works with certain types of music. More than these, great drumming is about establishing a cohesive, evolving mood and feel, and that is best accomplished by sounding like a team player rather than a dictator.

In pop, rock, country, and blues music, drummers are more often support players, solidifying the beat, working in attentive synergy with the bass player and in so doing basically disappearing. The rhythm section conjures what musicians call the *pocket*, or the steady heartbeat of a tune, the groove in which everyone should be gliding forward together. With everyone's focus on the song and the singer, one might imagine that beyond not rushing or dragging, there's little a drummer can do in these genres to impress. But if that were true, we music fans wouldn't have such particular respect for certain influential rock/pop drummers such as Charlie Watts of the Rolling Stones, Stewart Copeland of the Police, or Levon Helm of The Band. For Watts, it was a sense of swing he brought to even the hardest rocking songs—a subtle stretching of time that came from his upbringing in jazz. Copeland was technically exciting and progressive. He brought world rhythms and tricky backward patterns to the reggae rock of the Police. The amazing Levon Helm was for me an ideal song-based drummer, because his deep country style conveys the essence of American roots music with threads from the New Orleans street and rural back roads. Levon's beats conjure the blues with sway, swing, strut and snap, pushing the bass drum against the drag of the snare drum. His snare beats seem to take forever to arrive, but when they do, it's with a quick hand, and their sonic-boom snap keeps the music shooting forward like a maglev train. Also, being a good drummer, he conceives different parts (with hi-hat, ride cymbal, etc.) for different sections of each song. Listen to "The Shape I'm In" on *The Last Waltz* soundtrack for a clinic in building a performance. Listen for how he uses the bell of his ride cymbal as he pushes the band to a big, horn-saturated climax.

Drummers in popular genres may have their best shot at individual expression during *fills*, the decorative transitions between sections in songs. The drummer plays a steady part through the verses and usually greets the arrival of the chorus with a series of drum figures capped off with a cymbal crash on the downbeat. So what are we listening for? For one thing, notice how early the fill starts. Some are almost inaudibly quick, just a couple of beats, but they can be more interesting if they start two or three measures early with a nice runway to do stuff. Beginners play sixteenth notes on a couple of toms with a cymbal crash on the one. So if you hear a version of that, you're not in the presence of greatness. A good fill is like a miniature painting, neatly framed. It should have syncopation in it, with strong and weak beats, which can be expressed by what we call *ghost notes*, softer, almost suggested beats that develop suspense. I've noticed good drummers sometimes swinging their stick toward a drum only to stop it before the strike, as if rethinking the need for that note just then, yet the listener feels a *suggestion* of that note and its place in the flow. Depending on its timing in a song (a singer's first chorus versus capping off a two minute keyboard solo for example), the fill should be as subtle or showy as the moment calls for. And then just watch to see if the drummer does something actually surprising and weird. Maybe they'll only use their cymbals.

Everyday drummers in bar bands or wedding bands tend to play formulaically and to treat every song basically the same. But when we listen to song-driven music, we like to hear a band where every member respects what each song is trying to get over. Kenny Malone, the late, great session drummer from Nashville (and one of the sweetest guys you could meet) became known as the drummer on Music Row who always asked for a lyric sheet. He played with empathy rooted in the song's story and emotion, and he seemed to treat every cymbal strike as a gesture from his heart. That gets at perhaps the most important thing that a pop drummer can achieve— to match and guide and enhance the overall energy and story of each song. A good band creates a flux of dynamics and power, with the drummer holding everything together, controlling the tempo when some want to rush but accelerating the band in a deliberate way if that's where it's all got to go.

What about drum solos? Popular genres have been hot and cold on them over the years. In the arena rock era of the '70s and '80s they were commonplace, for good and for ill, as I noted in Chapter 13. In pop country music, drum solos tend to be perfunctory and short—just a bit of flex and flash. The Grateful Dead's drum solos stand out for me as exemplary because they were an integral part of the show (noted on every set list as "Drums") and because the band's improvisational ethos gave drummers Mickey Hart and Bill Kreutzmann more time and expressive freedom than almost any other rock band.

But let's say you're at a show—of any genre—and to your surprise there's a longer drum solo. Don't go to the restroom. See if the drummer takes you somewhere. Once again you'll be listening for use of dynamics, probably the most expressive tool in the percussionist's bag. Rhythmically, the drummer will cut up the beat into all kinds of slices and boxes, hopefully with a plan. Are you hearing a theme and variations? Is he or she using creative repetition that lets each idea sink in? Weaker musicians bash away without a sense of direction and design. One wants to hear a kind of narrative arc. Sometimes I imagine a drum solo as a spoken sermon, with phrasing, punctuation, and sentences of varying lengths. Can you hear deliberate use of the pitch and voice of each drum? Also listen for staggered, displaced, or strange beat patterns that seem out of time. Wait for the idea to complete itself, because the effect can be like watching an acrobat do a flip and land on a tightrope. Drummers can create tension and release as surely as melodic musicians.

In jazz, drum solos are more often expected as part of the fabric of a complete tune. As I've said, the jazz ethos is based on equal voices for all, and in general, if there's a drummer, there will be drum solos. That means you'll hear more variety and personal voice, more selectivity in the touch of the sticks on more parts of the drum kit. Jazz drummers simply train with more focus and knowledge of music history, because they're carrying the torch of the blues and the African roots of jazz to its highest levels of expression. They can do more with less, generally playing on small kits but producing more colors and ideas than rock drummers do with big racks of equipment.

Something to notice on this spectrum is the jazz drummer's expansive, expressive use of the snare drum, which is often at the heart of a drum solo, as I saw in my revelatory experience with Buddy Rich. As we heard from Evelyn Glennie in the chapter on timbre, the snare drum has many voices, depending on where the drum is struck. Struck on its rim, it offers dry metallic timbres, and trained drummers know how to strike the rim and drum head at the same time with one stick, creating a staccato blend of the note of the drum and the bite of the rim. Soloists can play with that "rimshot" sound and blend it with tom-toms and cymbals in ways that feel like the whole kit is levitating. Drummers can also switch off their snares, the array of wire springs below the drum that make its characteristic crunching sound, and then play with the naked ringing sound of the drum, which has a tone all its own. Jazz drummers often use wire brushes instead of sticks to soften their attack and give a lush texture to ballads. Don't tune the drummer out when the music is slow, because pushing the groove forward is harder in the lower BPMs than on up-tempo songs.

Creative use of texture and timbre is key, whatever the genre. When I see an Americana band with a drummer who starts striking the sides or rims of their drums, or who has shakers on their wrists or ankles, I feel like I'm in good hands, because it means they're not stuck in a box. Creative drummers switch up their sticks, sometimes using felt mallets or brushes or fine wooden dowels bound together in what are called bundle sticks, to offer a lighter touch. I've seen drummers keep the beat on the snare drum with clusters of seashells or lengths of chain. They'll pick up a shaker with their left hand and keep the beat going with their right. They'll make creative use of the hi-hat, that ultra versatile part of the drum kit that claps two opposing cymbals against each other with a spring-loaded pedal. Drummers use them for an ever-present tick-tick-tick sound when closed, for an open-closed *swish* sound that became a signature of disco drumming, and for a distinctive jangle and splash made with the stick on semi-closed hi-hat cymbals. Every cymbal sounds different too. Some are designated as ride cymbals for steady rhythm or crash cymbals for emphasis and exclamation. Tom-toms can be tuned, and while in pop music the tones of drums are generally muffled to the point of deadness, in jazz one tends to hear their pitches ring out, complementing the harmonic feeling of the performance.

We should also notice and admire the unique stamina drummers bring to the bandstand. They're usually doing the hottest and most physical work for the duration of a show, and for many great bands including Springsteen's and Phish, playing three or more hours is the norm. Drummers (at least the ones who don't work major tours with crews and techs) generally have the most gear to carry, set up, and tear down from gig to gig. It's hard work. Yet as I discovered getting my drum set in seventh grade, drumming is incredibly fun, so often the most qualifying feature of a cool drummer—the thing above all else that gives me trust and draws my attention—is a smile.

As for you, there's no better way to gain a deeper understanding of groove than by making beats. I'd encourage anyone to play with the many online or phone app tools that let you manually put synth drum parts on a grid, a simplified version of what pop and hip-hop producers do when producing rhythm tracks. You can build a simple pattern with bass drum and snare and then start layering percussion parts on top of it—hi-hat, shakers, claps, congas, etc. Take heed to how dramatically the feeling of a beat can change with small shifts of various components or by adjusting the tempo up and down by a few BPM. Try to achieve syncopated grooves or polyrhythms by sliding beats around on the grid. Turn certain instrument tracks off and on to see how it changes the vibe and see if you can keep the vibe with fewer parts rather than more. It can be a seductive exercise, one you can do on the screen of your smartphone.

Of course rhythm is a physical, full-body experience, so you should bang on things in the real world too. If you've ever felt like playing the drums, I recommend you do whatever you can to make that a reality. It's cathartic, fascinating, and a relatively fast ticket to being able to make music with others (compared with the learning curves of guitar, keyboard or songwriting). And yet you don't need a full drum kit to live in rhythm. Get a hand drum—a djembe or a pair of congas or even bongos—for a hundred dollars. Cultivate the different pitches and timbres you can get out of them by striking them in different ways and places. Even cheaper, wonderful rhythm instruments might be lying around your home or garage. An empty jug from an office-sized watercooler is a remarkable hand drum, with quite a few notes and voices in it. Five-gallon buckets make powerful sounding drums, and you may have seen street musicians beating joyfully on sets made from them. We eat a lot of Asian food at home so we have a drawer full of chopsticks made of bamboo, wood, and plastic. They have a light touch, and I bounce them off a variety of items in the kitchen seeking out great percussive effects.

For soundscape writer W.A. Mathieu, the idea is to draw out the sounds of the physical world, to grow closer to nature and to mankind by asking how objects speak. "Everything has a sound," he observes in *The Listening Book*. "Don't be shy. A tap with your finger might reveal a holy book. Take secret pleasure in the fragile sound of glassware. A life drummer cannot pass a window, a fence, a pole, without knocking or stroking out the sound of it. These tones need to escape, to break out. The voices of metal especially have to be released. Let nothing be safe."

Highly Musical Humans

Christian McBride

While he's one of the most famous bass players, composers, and public advocates in jazz, Christian McBride isn't a household name, but only because jazz isn't a household thing. Now in his early 50s, he's won eight Grammy Awards, played with most living legends, led bands small and large, and championed the genre in many forums, including NPR's *Jazz Night in America* program. So his résumé is loaded, but it's his enthusiastic collaborative spirit and wide-ranging musicianship that make him a one-man gateway into what's happening in improvised music.

As I suggest elsewhere, bass players are sometimes our best guides to what's going on both harmonically and rhythmically in a piece. Focusing on McBride's bass parts is like appreciating a gothic cathedral from its foundation and buttresses out. Christian's own foundations came from greats like Ray Brown, sideman to Oscar Peterson and one of the masters of note choices and flow. While I think of McBride—a product of the fusion and hip-hop eras—as less polite and refined than Brown, he is rooted in the fundamentals. And he plays with an edgy, animated tone that marks him as a modern musician. With diverse skills and a radiant positivity, other musicians love to play with him.

McBride was born in 1972 and grew up in Philadelphia, a top music city that launched jazz greats McCoy Tyner, John Coltrane, and drummer "Philly" Joe Jones. Christian's school friends included the brilliant jazz organist Joey DeFrancesco and Ahmir "Questlove" Thompson, who went on to cofound The Roots. Hailed as a prodigy, McBride performed from his teens with important artists, including trumpet players Freddie Hubbard (older guard), Roy Hargrove (a fellow young gun), and saxophonist Joshua Redman. A good window into those growth years is Redman's album *Mood Swing* from 1994, where the musicians—pianist Brad Mehldau and drummer Brian Blade—make a youth brigade supergroup. They've revisited this configuration over the years, on 2020's *Round Again*, and again on 2023's *LongGone*. Those naturalistic, easy-to-enjoy albums are testimony to the value of lifelong collaborative relationships and the way great musicians mature and grow together.

After establishing himself as a national star, McBride organized his own big band around 2010. We hear the bass player's roaring authority and tender support depending on the tunes, and half are McBride originals, so you'll hear how many layers and contrasts he has to master as he corrals more than a dozen musicians with the power of composing. Treat yourself to "The Shade of the Cedar Tree" from 2011's *The Good Feeling*. Play it loud. That's how big bands are.

McBride made the exciting album *Camp Meeting* in 2007 with the great drummer Jack DeJohnette and none other than Bruce Hornsby, who proves himself to be a stupendous jazz pianist with a signature chordal language. I love Bruce, and I love that record. They open with a furiously fun Ornette Coleman tune and then play music by Miles Davis, Keith Jarrett, Bud Powell, and Hornsby himself. In other collaborations with the pop world, McBride has backed Angelique Kidjo and Dianna Krall on numerous albums.

McBride grew up on hip-hop, and he lets it show more explicitly from time to time, as on a 2001 album with Questlove playing drums called *The Philadelphia Experiment*. This kind of funky improvisational instrumental music gets tagged "modern creative" in my digital streaming system, and that's appropriately if incompletely descriptive. If you dig deep, long jams, the best example is a 2006 hip-hop/funk session with drummer Terreon Gully and record scratching from DJ Logic captured on *Live At Tonic* on the excellent Ropeadope Records label. This one isn't on the streamers but is an easy to find CD.

At the risk of throwing too much out there, I leave you with a personal favorite, a long-term series titled *Trilogy*, documenting best takes from shows around the world by a very special trio of McBride with (again) Brian Blade on drums and the late great pianist Chick Corea. Their releases in 2013, 2018, and 2025 are a banquet of expertise, elegance, passion, and rhythmic perfection—jazz for the insider and the newcomer alike, jazz that's transparent and welcoming, in keeping with McBride's outlook.

"It's always been my M.O. to purposefully bring the audience together in terms of how I communicate with them," he told me once. "Because I understand what the image of a jazz musician is, (that) we're all dogmatic and we all like nothing else but jazz. So there's a certain indignance that I think can come off from a jazz artist onstage, you know? Not, 'I'm happy to see you,' (but) 'you should be happy to see me.' You know? And so I always try to make sure that I'm never like that with my audiences. And I find that if you can bring an audience to meet you halfway, just doing that, they will go with you anywhere you go."

PART V

♪

CONCERT

15

KNOWING THE SCORE
The parts and the whole

We've considered sound, tone, melody, harmony, timbre, and the multifaceted role of time in music. All play different roles, and they don't work in isolation. In a process that's wondrous and complex, we fuse these elements together in a harmonious experience. That may sound obvious, but I want to share in this chapter some breakthroughs from my apprentice years that brought this home in a way I might never have fully appreciated without a teacher. I've long considered it the most important insight I was gifted as a listener.

My junior high garage band had two electric guitars, a keyboard, and me on drums, but no bass player, and this deficit began to seem important. Rock and roll needs a low end, and I could be replaced behind the kit. Mom was, as ever, pragmatic and encouraging. I should take up the bass, she said. Perhaps implicit in this suggestion was that she'd lived for years with a teenager practicing drums in her house, so perhaps the bass sounded like sweet relief. Whatever the reason, it was a wise idea that would pay dividends for life. I found a used black electric bass, some kind of starter model from Fender, and an amplifier by Peavey, that icon of the 1970s. I'd need instruction, and I found Alan, a fellow who posted a flyer in a music store.

Alan was a Beatles guy, down to his retro, mop-top haircut. He played the Rickenbacker bass model favored by Paul McCartney in the late '60s. The instrument (whose tone can be heard clearly on "Rain" and "Taxman") was one of the coolest things I'd ever seen up close. So was Alan's home studio and music lair where I went for weekly lessons. He could make recordings there, and this was no small thing in the '80s before personal computers. I found the whole setup captivating, and my time with Alan was revelatory. I mentioned in Chapter 8 that he taught me how to read and write chord charts and chord progressions. The other thing he showed me was more subtle but more impactful.

Having entered the realm of songs played by a band without written-out parts, I as the bass player would be responsible for crafting a line that supported and emphasized the chord changes, while also securing a song's rhythmic foundation. The best way to learn how to do that on your own is to learn bass lines recorded by great players on great records and imitate them. This learning is really only possible by ear, so Alan asked me to listen to bass lines in Beatles songs. I tried to train my attention on Paul.

While I knew the songs pretty well, I'd never singled out the bass or any other instrument to listen to specifically. Except of course for the singing, which jumped right out. But what about listening past the vocal and into the web of instrumentation backing up the singer? This was tricky. The sound of the band was like fabric, or a forest, and before this, individual threads or trees hadn't been a pressing concern. The simultaneity of music is part of its essence. It arrives all at once. But deconstructing it is possible. I was being asked to train my ears for something new, to discern where each instrument's timbre started and stopped.

To walk through the method the way I thought about it, let's start with the low-hanging fruit. Drums are easy. The bass drum thumps, while the hi-hat ticks and the snare smacks in a predictable pattern. Cymbal crashes are easy to hear, but it's important to notice when it's one cymbal or another, because they have specific notes and textures. Then listen for the standout melodic instruments and their timbre. If you hear a horn, what kind? Note whether it's a trumpet or a French horn or a saxophone or a trombone. If you hear a lead instrument whose sound you don't know, dig a little. You might discover the rarified timbres of the baritone sax, the English horn, or the oboe.

The middle of the frequency spectrum, neither very low nor very high, is generally where the chord changes are defined, and that's mostly the role of the keyboards and/or guitars. Note the role of the keyboard—and what kind of keyboard it is, whether electric, acoustic, digital or analog (if you can tell). Can you pick out and count the guitar parts? A lot of pop music uses three or more guitars, making a wash of harmony rather than a picture of specific instruments. At times like this, the ear's ability to clarify parts breaks down, just like you'll never hear any specific violinist in an orchestra.

But what of the bass? It's a bit elusive, because low tones, besides being weak or nonexistent in small speakers or earbuds, require more focused attention. It also takes some noticing to home in on a really important part of the bass line, at the leading edge of each note. Because you're not just listening for the pitch. You want to hear the distinct character of the bass in the music, which is mostly defined by the leading edge, the instant that the finger actually lets go of the string. A soft fingertip sounds different than a pick, a calloused hand, or a thumb slap. An acoustic upright bass has the distinct timbre we talked about earlier. But to guide your ears, you're listening for the lowest note in the band. That is by definition, the bass line.

The lesson that stands out in my memory from working with Alan is Paul's playing on "A Little Help From My Friends" from *Sgt. Pepper's Lonely Hearts Club Band.* To help me hear the line clearly, Alan played along with the record, matching Paul note for note. There it was, a clear and distinct part that was so much more interesting than if he had simply played the root and fifth of each chord, a common strategy for lesser bass players in rock or country. Paul drew a vector through the music that held it together harmonically, structurally and rhythmically, like a savvy classical composer from 200 years before. It had a patient flow where that was needed on the verses, but in the chorus it offered a clean pop pulse, which amped up the energy. Then in the turnaround, where the chorus returns to the verse, Paul lays out and lets the lead guitar carry the song back in its cycle. With Alan's orientation, I could now easily hear Paul's brilliant part when listening to the recording on my own. Likewise I was more alert to the bass line in other Beatles songs and, incredibly, all songs. We studied John Entwistle of The Who, an especially innovative player, and the very different styles of Sting in The Police and Bootsy Collins in Parliament-Funkadelic. Through merely paying attention to these and other bass players, I could discern how bass parts weave in and support music generally.

To make this way of listening more tangible, I want to take you into the world of recording studios and live concert sound, because the technology there offers a powerful metaphor for this mode of careful listening. Here we find mixing boards or mixing consoles, ingenious (and expensive) devices, developed in the 1950s and '60s, that are essential to nearly all commercial music making. They usually look like large desks with many knobs, buttons and sliders arranged in tidy rows. Each vertical row of controls handles the signal from one microphone or "input." The knobs control all aspects of the sound of each input, especially tone (bass, midrange or treble), while the sliders control the all-important *level* or volume of each instrument. The engineer, listening to all the accumulated signals, adjusts each slider to make an optimal mix, a tiny term so central to music-making that the professional trade magazine for recording engineers is called *Mix*.

The mix determines how loud the bass guitar is against the bass drum and then how much keyboard and rhythm guitar are perceptible. Engineers mix the lead instruments or lead vocal in a way that it's neither buried by the band nor obnoxiously "out front" as we say. Enhancements like harmony vocals and tambourine are often recorded separately and mixed in with just the right amount of emphasis. This is an esthetic judgement, informed by training in audio perception and the tastes of the producer and the musicians. In the record-making process, artists often share "rough mixes" of songs they're working on for feedback, or to get friends and colleagues interested in what's to come, with the understanding that the final mix will be more refined and true to the artist's vision.

In recorded music, the mix is chiefly about the relative level of the musical parts, but it goes deeper. Mixers tweak the sonic signature of every input. Using micro control over frequencies, so-called *equalization*, they keep the instruments and voices from competing and possibly clashing in the same sonic space. Another important variable is *panning*, which places instruments and singers in a stereo "soundstage" from left to right, while effects like *reverb* (more on that later) seem to move instruments closer or farther from the listener in the mix. Finally, the engineer controls how loud the music feels when it comes out of speakers. This factor, called *compression*, has fascinating history and controversy that's beyond my scope, but it basically controls the density and intensity of a record. Pop and rock records generally overdo it, crushing the dynamics and flooding the ears with signal to sound louder and more intense on the radio. Yet too little compression leaves the music sounding light and lifeless. In between is a sweet spot that results in rich and dynamic sound.

When listening to music, you have influence over the mix too, because of the beautiful human capacity for selective attention. However quiet the bass or the background vocals are, for example, you can essentially zoom in on them and single them out, making them louder in your mind. That's what I was shown how to do with Paul's bass lines, and it was like unlocking a superpower. Before long—and more by virtue of listening than playing I hasten to add—I was able to adjust the mix of a record in my mind's ear. I could follow the bass, or the rhythm guitar, the horn sections, or the background vocals. And I could also zoom out to hear the connections and relationships unifying the many components of the sound. My perception of the music (and it was even easier with instrumentals) became a kind of forest/trees handshake, a dance between the parts and the whole that would never end.

Years later, I found a new use for my mental mixing board when I started playing in bands. On stage, let's say I'm playing guitar, I'm going to feel like the "loudest" instrument to myself. Because I'm next to my own amplifier and because I'm psychologically and physically attached to the part I'm playing. A similar thing happened playing in my youth orchestra, because my violin was right next to my head. So in both cases, I had to make a mental effort to turn "me" down in the mix. I want to hear myself enough to know I'm playing well and that my instrument's in tune, etc., but I have to be able to focus on (and enjoy) the overall blend. I also need to be able to zoom in on other musicians whose parts connect most intimately to my own. During a jazz guitar solo, I want to be dialed in on the bass player as the heart of the rhythm and chord changes that I'm working with. Listeners should be aware that the musician playing for them are thinking this way—zooming in and out—hearing the elements and the entirety at the same time. Every piece of music with mixed parts can reveal itself in new dimensions.

In symphonic music, the conductor is a kind of mixing engineer, in the sense that they follow every instrument and every instrumental section in the orchestra and issue instructions, verbally or with their hands, to balance the parts into a cohesive performance. Their guide to the music is the written score, which they may or may not have on their podium. (Some conductors' ability to memorize all the parts of entire symphonic works is astonishing.) The score is like a sideways mixing console, with each staff line representing a part that must be properly leveled and shaped to blend with the others. A similar representation of multi-part music flowing through time can be seen on the screens of today's digital audio work stations. Each instrument or voice is seen as a graphic waveform, offering a visual guide to the parts that the engineer must balance in the mix.

Most musicians with experience playing in groups develop an intuitive ability to focus on the parts and the whole simultaneously, but for growing listeners, it might take a bit of concentration. I'd suggest finding music with two parts—cello and piano or fiddle and banjo—so that the voices of each are clearly audible. One example I can recommend for its vivid separation is the duo album from 2008 by bassist Edgar Meyer and mandolin player Chris Thile. It presents the higher, shining voice of the mandolin working with the lower, sonorous voice of the bass (both plucked and bowed) to make a fusion that produces improbable amounts of music with just two parts and the commensurate space between them.

After hearing Chris and Edgar, you can scale up the complexity by listening to classical string quartets. I remember my father getting excited about this age-old configuration of cello, viola, and two violins as an especially good way to hear the weaving of parts into a composed design. I have discovered over my lifetime that I'm most excited by music made by midsize ensembles. I turn to solo musicians pretty rarely, and symphonic music is often too dense and busy for me at home (it's more enthralling for me when it's live). What I enjoy most often has bass, drums, a keyboard, a guitar, and a horn or two. This is the size of most bands in popular genres—between three and ten members. It's my sweet spot where the number of parts to follow and feel is neither too spare nor overwhelming. This is a matter of personal taste.

Instrumental parts are but one way of deconstructing music's tapestry in your mind as a listener, and it's worth considering some of the others. Try concentrating on different parts of the frequency spectrum—the bass, midrange and treble components of a piece of music. This is something hi-fi reviewers do in every column about speakers or amplifiers, because good gear should be timbrally accurate across the spectrum. They might find the midrange, with its guitars and vocals exceedingly clear and defined but hear the treble range as harsh in its reproduction of cymbal sounds or sibilants in the voice. We can also try to mentally isolate foreground from mid-ground and background to ask ourselves how the harmonic heart of the music is working, independent of the lead melodic lines, whether from vocals or an instrument. We can dwell on how much silence or space is playing a role in a piece, just to remind ourselves that all music is a contrast to the absence of music. And finally, something we music journalists do all the time is identify what genres are at play and dancing together in a work. What elements reveal a mix of rock, jazz, soul, hip-hop, bluegrass, classical, etc.? I'm more fond of fusion music than some music purists, and I have developed an ear for discerning the ingredients that went into the gumbo.

The best civilian analogy I can think of for the mindset I'm advocating is a hike in the wilderness. We're naturally inclined to take in the grandeur of the scenery, the sweep of a mountainside to the edge of the tree line and the patterns of water flowing from creeks into rivers. But we also pause to notice a single flower, an eagle circling, the color of a leaf or the shape of a river stone. We integrate these elements, along with the sounds around us and the temperature on our skin and the play of light and the smells, into a complete impression and, if we are deliberate about it, a memory. Our brains process all of those sensations and reactions in different regions and with different chemicals and processes, but we re-integrate them into our personal impression of reality itself.

This sensory blend can be disrupted or broken if our brain is abnormal or damaged. In his remarkable book *Musicophilia: Tales of Music and the Brain*, Oliver Sacks describes the case study of a "gifted composer and performer" who suffered brain and spinal injury in a car crash. During her recovery she discovered that listening to music had become quite difficult, in that she experienced it as "discrete, contrapuntal lines," according to her physician. When Sacks meets her, he notes "her inability to integrate different voices and instruments" into a coherent, pleasurable whole. If she followed a score while listening, he notes, it "served to 'frame' a piece, to prevent the music from 'spreading all over the place.'"

Obviously this is an ultra-rare case, though other forms of "amusia"—an inability to neurologically process and appreciate music—are more common. I present the Sacks story mainly to refresh our appreciation for the mental miracle that is musical cognition. Our brains coordinate the perception of music's many elements in a wonderful concert, and the more attention we pay, the more we get back. As I've said before, I'm not suggesting that you put on an analyst's hat every time you listen to music. We aren't trying to reduce music appreciation to an academic exercise. But taking time to listen critically and with discernment will start a process, and before you know it, listening to the parts and the whole will be second nature.

16

OUT OF NOTHING, SOMETHING
The elusive flow state of improvising

For a time in my early teens, I more or less didn't believe that jazz musicians were actually playing spontaneously—that every take was different and created in real time. Listening in awe to Miles Davis, Charlie Parker, or Thelonious Monk, I harbored a suspicion that it was some weird ruse—that they'd worked out and memorized the parts beforehand. The lines felt too fluid and inevitable, with no missteps or sour notes—none that I could detect anyway. To a kid who'd grown up reading music from a printed page, jazz solos seemed like some kind of otherworldly conjuring. Honestly, they still do.

Improvising has a rich history that wends its way from the origins of music-making itself (there were no scores to follow 10,000 years ago after all), through classical music (Bach, Beethoven, and Mozart dazzled friends and clients with extemporaneous composing), to campfires and dances around the world, to early twentieth-century New Orleans brothels and the river boats where jazz was born as a refinement of the blues. I'll touch on that here, but mostly I will try to take you into the musician's mind and share how it feels to make music this way—inventing new music through a practiced mind-body connection and deep listening. Some of us have sounds and melodies and beats surging in our mind's ear that need a release. As a listener, I'm more engaged by what a pianist, guitarist or drummer has to "say" through expressive sound than I am by the words of most songs. That's not the same for everyone of course, but I hope to persuade you that great instrumental soloists and jazz improvisors are not just tossing out notes in the key of the music and avoiding mistakes. Rather, they are telling a story about themselves that can convey profound meaning to the receptive heart and mind.

Some music-making people are more naturally wired and inspired to improvise than others. I've met classical musicians and teachers who say they feel utterly uncomfortable inventing melodies on the spot. That has a lot to do with training in one's formative years, as formal music lessons have historically concentrated on reading notated music and playing established pieces as written. In recent years, we see this opening up, and in my line of work I'm surrounded by musicians who took classical lessons early on but who pursued bluegrass and jazz, where improvising is celebrated and expected. An upbringing that participates in both makes for a nimble and versatile musician.

Stepping back, aren't most of us musical improvisors at some level? We make up little tunes and sing them in the shower or the car. We drum out rhythms with our fingers on counters and dashboards. And above all, we speak extemporaneously all the time. With words, emphasis, cadence, phrasing, and even pitch, we transmute thought and emotion into sound, and it's not a long step from that to inventing music. It's about how far we push it and how closely we tune in to great improvising musicians and try to really hear them speak with sound alone. I found myself naturally leaning into the language of music from an early age. I "cheated" on my violin lessons by making stuff up on the instrument in grade school. I saw the value of notated, composed music, but I certainly didn't see it as superior or the sum total of the art. I remember borrowing a guitar in junior high and trying to pick out notes that fit the harmonic progressions of songs on the radio. I took to drumming and bass playing, both of which require an improvising mindset. To this day, well into my 50s, my favorite music includes a huge amount of improvising, and nothing stimulates me more as a musician than playing into reality musical ideas I hear in my head.

I am not familiar with all the improvised musical traditions of the world, so I want to define the point of view that shapes the observations ahead. The improv-friendly music I know and relate to, as a twentieth-/twenty-first-century American, and I hope a wide-ranging listener, is built on a foundation of the blues. It's the blues-rock of the Allman Brothers, the exploratory rock of the Grateful Dead, the jazz-like virtuosity in western swing and bluegrass. And encompassing all is jazz, the mega-genre that evolved from the blues into a vast and unprecedented universe of musical creativity. Much of the vocabulary of instrumental soloing one hears in popular genres like traditional R&B and even the vocal flow of rap owes much of its existence to jazz innovations. While it was often maligned in its day, jazz/rock "fusion" was a rich movement of the 1970s. Put all that together, and I'll be talking about musical settings where bands work together to create novel performances of musical works in a fluid interchange between ensemble and soloists. Then I'll address solo improvisation, which is a particular challenge.

Relating to the improvisor's way generally begins with a passionate embrace of melody. Whatever the instrument, most successful improv rests on playing melodies with clarity and accuracy. Melody is not essential to all music, but it's universally relatable, and the skills required to play anti-melodically don't come out of nowhere; melodic mastery comes first. It's rather like what you may have heard about Picasso's cubism—only after mastering drawing and form could he blow the rules up with such brilliance. Jazz standards became canonized because their actual tunes, their composed "heads," are sturdy, memorable and vibrant. Listeners who know the melody and form of a jazz tune will be more able to follow the intentions of the soloists. As a player, one has little hope of connecting to the song without knowing its notes completely and confidently. And learning tunes like "Giant Steps" or "Oleo" or "On the Street Where You Live" is no small thing. If I'm preparing to actually play the tune and solo over it, I want to consider carefully how each melodic passage relates to the chord changes that support it.

The first iteration of improvisation is *embellishment*, which means holding true to the melody while altering or decorating it here and there with grace notes and flourishes. Adapting a melody with restraint helps put the musician in a liminal space between structure and freedom. You could think of it as training wheels, but it's a perfectly respectable way to improvise and to improve as a player. Jazz singers routinely embellish songs as part of their interpretation, so listen for how they depart just so from the strict melody, delaying a note, adding a note, etc. One hears great jazz, country, and bluegrass instrumentalists do this all the time, emphasizing the song's inherent strengths while not needing to show off all their inventive powers at once.

Another strategy is *call-and-response*. We see this engage audiences in church or political speeches, because it creates an atmosphere of reciprocity and togetherness. In a band, call-and-response can be explicit and obvious, but more subtle iterations of it happen during improvised music all the time and on the fly. Listen for moments where a musician plays a phrase and another plays it back, either note for note or with an adaptation. For the learning musician, trading short phrases with another player, bouncing ideas back and forth and mimicking the other's riffs, is an essential step on the road to playing whole solos. Professional musicians "trade fours" or "trade eights" (measures we mean) when they're really cooking, and it's a thrill to hear such spontaneous "conversations."

With these preliminary strategies in mind, let's now put ourselves in the shoes of a musician in a jazz ensemble. In fact, let's make that musician me, because I can be most honest and insightful about my lived experience. I signed up for a six-week course at the Nashville Jazz Workshop built around playing in a band. The class was curated by the school to include one musician/student for each seat in the group—piano, bass, drums, sax, trumpet, and me on guitar. Our teacher Roger, the workshop's cofounder and a bass player, assigned us about six tunes to learn and play together. One I remember pointedly was "That Old Feeling," the swinging standard from the late 1930s. It's not the post-'70s groove jazz that I mostly listen to, but it's a sweet song that's been widely covered over the decades, and our interpretation was similar to the one you can find by Louis Armstrong on his 1959 recording with Oscar Peterson. Its chords are neither easy nor terribly hard, and there is a lot of harmonic movement to inhabit as a soloist. It felt like an attainable goal, but I'd have to prepare to play the song with a band, controlling my chordal support of the group and being ready for my solo when the spotlight turned to me.

The first thing I notice is that the tune has a classic 32-measure structure, divided in four parts. Each eight-bar section offers the band and the soloists landmarks to play toward. As for the chords, I'm not just learning rote hand positions for each change but refreshing my knowledge of the many ways to play those chords and their plausible extensions. Em7(flat 5) may look intimidating, but to the player it's not a code or a hand shape but a tonality with intervals that feel like a key in a lock. My inner ear sketches that chord. My hands play tones on the guitar that fit. And I think about how that chord resolves to the A7 that comes after it, and so forth. My point is that while I want to play freely in the show when I'm on, it doesn't happen without a plan.

"It is my firm belief that there has never been anybody who has blown even two bars worth listening to who didn't have some idea about what he was going to play, before he started. If you just ramble through the scales or play around the chords, that's nothing more than musical exercises," wrote Duke Ellington in the early '60s. "Improvisation really consists of picking out a device here and connecting it with a device there, changing the rhythm here and pausing there; there has to be some thought preceding each phrase that is played, otherwise it is meaningless."

Duke offers a great start to the task at hand. Besides elaborating on the melody, I'm internally thinking about—and externally listening to—the chord changes made by the band and the music. The song's harmonic world defines the notes and intervals I want to use, unless I'm prepared to try something pretty advanced and conceptually unorthodox. Because I'm still a student player, my plan is to play diatonically (not chromatically) and lean on the phrasing of the song's original melody as a good suggestion for where to pause and allow in some space.

At the same time, my inner coach is doing his best to channel all the little suggestions and insights I've heard from musicians and teachers through the years. Here's a partial list: Play passages that would work if you sang them out loud and avoid anything that wouldn't sound good when sung. Plan rests and pauses, and work toward them. Use dynamics to modulate your energy and use accented notes to energize the rhythm. Remember to repeat notes (where the temptation can be to play scale after scale). Remember to breathe and let go of tension. Make a pattern or a motif and then repeat it with different notes. Play more thirds and seventh notes than roots, thirds or fifths, because that's where the real harmonic energy lives. Think like a storyteller or preacher, establishing a mood, building the tension and offering a payoff. Play from the middle out, meaning start with small gestures close to the middle of the music's range, then build larger leaps as the solo progresses. Ascending gradually to a climax in higher harmonic territory is a proven formula.

Some improvisational koans come straight from the greats, including the late Chick Corea, one of my all-time favorite pianists and composers. Years ago, he typed up a one-page list to hand out at clinics that he titled *Cheap but Good Advice for Playing Music in a Group.* It's easy to find on the internet, but I'd like to quote a few of my favorite items:

3. Don't let your fingers and limbs wander—place them intentionally.

5. Leave space—create space—intentionally create places where you don't play.

10. Use contrast and balance the elements: high/low, fast/slow, loud/soft, tense/relaxed, dense/sparse.

11. Play to make the other musicians sound good. Play things that will make the overall music sound good.

My final addition to these lists would be to study this intellectual stuff off the bandstand and then in performance, above all else, as best you can, have fun. Play the music and let the music play you. Reach within and make your own ears and heart happy with your sculpted sound. Embody your enthusiasm for music, and that will translate to your audience. And critically, don't think about your mistakes. Keep moving forward. Don't let your audience see that you're dwelling on something you wish you'd done differently. Be in the moment and concentrate on the next four to eight measures.

My performances in my jazz class were basically competent, nothing you need to hear, and that's okay. I was there not to develop a career as a pro player but to participate in the art form I've admired in others. My years of listening to Wes Montgomery, John McLaughlin, Barney Kessel, Pat Metheny, and so many others informed my spirit and helped me love the greats that much more. All that said, I want to emphasize that this same communion, this honor and love, this inner flame does not depend on you being a player. Most lovers of improvised music do not play themselves. But there's a cultivated empathy on the listener's part, a feeling of being involved almost as if one was in the band, lending their voice to the chorus.

It's important to notice that while I improvised my solo, the rest of the band was improvising too. I've already discussed how the bass player and drummer work together to create a canvas on which the soloists can paint. If the music is full and rolling and swinging hard, the drummer and soloist might get into a conversation, answering each other's gestures, which is a good thing to listen for. The pianist has quite an interesting role because (and it took me years to grasp this), the chord changes on the song's chart are a guide, not scripture. This is where comping comes in, the use of chord extensions, colorations, and inversions that I brought up in Chapter 8. The comping player also uses *substitutions*, which are nearby, connected chords that express new colors. It's best for only one harmony instrument—piano or guitar—to comp at any given time, lest the sound field get congested.

A different set of issues faces the solo improvising performer. You can perhaps imagine how challenging it must be to make interesting music alone, especially for those who play a single-note instrument like a saxophone, trumpet, or clarinet. It can be done, but it takes an advanced sense of melody, harmonic motion, and lyrical ideas. The piano and the guitar stand out for allowing musicians to conjure melody, harmony, and bass lines as a coherent whole, challenging though that may be.

Solo piano is a rich tradition that takes advantage of the remarkable invention of the keyboard. With ten fingers and a musician's passion, the piano can do just about anything, so we tend to see them in solo settings more than any other. The piano soloist might play a personalized interpretation of an existing tune. Or, as on the famous 1975 *Köln Concert* by Keith Jarrett, the artist may create new music on the spot. Jarrett, who suffered a stroke in 2018 that effectively ended his legendary career, was famous for his ability to improvise entire shows, an act of supreme concentration, intention, and transcendent musicality. Every great jazz pianist has recorded solo albums amid their band work, and these are a pure and transparent way to hear an artist's essence. The pantheon of great solo guitar performers includes Joe Pass, Lenny Breau, and the rarely recorded Ted Greene. What they do alone, given the limits of the fretboard and the fingers of the right hand, is quite mind-boggling to me.

My examples so far have mostly concentrated on traditional approaches to jazz, because that's how improvised music evolved in America, and I encourage you to ground your understanding of jazz in classic and historic styles because they're so rich with musical insights. But of course the music evolved, including the rise of so-called *modal improvising* after the seminal Miles Davis album *Kind of Blue* showed the way in 1959. Here, Davis de-emphasized chord changes and instead conjured what I'd call zones of tonality, where simple scales let the ensemble make consistent moods and colors with a minimum of direction or scoring. It's hard to explain in words, but it was a revolution, prompting Chick Corea to call it "a new language of music." Modal improvising became the template for major movements to follow, including soul jazz and funk fusion (also pioneered by Miles in yet another of his re-inventions). I can tell you that as a player it feels much freer to play modally over simple changes than traditional jazz over chord-heavy standards. Trad jazz never died out, but most jazz and improv rock since the '70s has integrated modal playing.

The '60s also spawned a more radical branch of "free jazz," which minimized or dispensed with song structure, chord charts, melody and lyricism in favor of pure sonic expression. Aligned with avant-garde music, free jazz became well-known (and feared) for its often far-out, chaotic, and dissonant qualities. Many have made the mistake, after hearing examples of free jazz, of believing that this heady and intellectual school is the entirety of "modern" or "contemporary" jazz, when that's far from the reality. Jazz of the last 60 years spans a vast spectrum from the bizarre to the beautiful, from the disjointed to the groovy, and you don't have to spend a minute with free jazz to be a complete musical citizen, unless you find examples of it that move you.

I have spent much of my life as a fan and musician immersed in the improvisational realm of bluegrass and string band music, in part because it's a popular music genre with many connections to jazz. From the outset, founder Bill Monroe and the Blue Grass Boys balanced instrumental solos with vocal verses and choruses. And with the broad American tradition of fiddle music inspiring them, bluegrass emerged as a genre where something like a quarter of the music is entirely instrumental, a balance that lends shows variety that's rare in other genres. Musical virtuosity and expressiveness on banjo, mandolin, fiddle, dobro, and guitar was highly valued from the beginning, and subsequent generations of musicians enlarged on that vision while borrowing from other genres including jazz, funk, rock, and reggae. By the 1990s, the concept of "newgrass" had a firm footing, and I was there for it. I became a fan, follower, and chronicler of virtuosos Béla Fleck (banjo), Sam Bush (mandolin and fiddle), Jerry Douglas (dobro), Tony Rice (guitar), Stuart Duncan (fiddle), and many others, including the remarkable younger artists they've inspired, notably mandolinist Chris Thile and guitarist Billy Strings.

Rock and roll spawned plenty of long guitar solos, but nobody developed a spirit of collective improvisation like the Grateful Dead, and their impact can't be overstated. They drew on deep traditions, including tribal music and drum circles, blues, jug band, and, explicitly according to Jerry Garcia, bluegrass. After sparking up in late 1965, they owned psychedelic experiential rock for decades. Anchored by remarkable songwriting, their repertoire extended to country rock, blues, and some totally original forms, but their *method* was paramount and highly influential—weaving in and out of one another and building energy waves that crescendo and climax. Songs were always up for re-interpretation, and no set list was the same. The Dead also kept outside and avant-garde playing relevant through their mid-show sonic excursions called "Drums" and "Space." A few other bands of the '70s like Santana and the Allman Brothers Band stretched out in similar ways, but the Dead had the improv space largely to itself until the 1990s, with the rise of Widespread Panic, the sublimely experimental Medeski, Martin & Wood, Béla Fleck and the Flecktones (a funk/jazz band, not a bluegrass band), the Aquarium Rescue Unit, and the most successful modern expression of creative improv rock, in my eyes, Phish. I think of the common thread here as conjuring of community through *musical time,* an atmosphere of escape and ecstasy, something that ties ecstatic ritual dance to house and trance music. I've seen it genuinely foster peace and togetherness, and I know of no other secular experience quite like it. Somebody called it *jam band* music, and the term stuck for what it's worth. As with any genre, there is good and weak jam band music, often within the space of a single show, but those who dismiss such a rich field of spontaneous creativity as "noodling for stoners" are just being jerks.

I've been focusing on the player's point of view in order to help you understand what they're doing in an improvisatory state. What about the listener? What are we listening for, whether crowded together in a live space or at home between the speakers in a private setting? I hope we're focused on more than merely the groove and whatever flashy technique the soloist shows off. Yet it's hard to put into words what makes a soloist truly great. So allow me to return to *Kind of Blue* for one of the most beautiful things ever written about this art form. The liner notes, which captivated me as much as the music when I was in high school, are by one of the album's pianists, the great Bill Evans. To talk about this band's approach and about improvisation as an art form, he evokes a Japanese form of painting in which the artist paints in black ink on "a thin stretched parchment" with a flowing brush that can't pause, lest it break through the paper.

"Erasures or changes are impossible," he writes. "These artists must practice a particular discipline, that of allowing the idea to express itself in communication with their hands in such a direct way that deliberation cannot interfere. The resulting pictures lack the complex composition and textures of ordinary painting, but it is said that those who see will find something captured that escapes explanation."

I take a few things from this zen metaphor. The soloist should exhibit a balance of confidence and humility. They should be aware and respectful of the band, the song, the audience, and the flow of the music. We want to sense a line in their sound, like the line of a fine artist, from Japan or anywhere. We listen with bated breath, on a ride, mindful of the music's pauses and transitions. Great solos sound inevitable and effortless, when they are anything but. At the top tiers of improvisational music, the players aren't following charts and changes or applying any rules or theory. They've learned all that and forgotten it. The musicians know each other intimately and guide one another into a unified creative flow state. They groove and swing as one, rock out when called for, and turn together like a murmuration of starlings.

My favorite jazz writer Whitney Balliett called the music he loved so much "the sound of surprise," and for me, surprise is one of the most emphatic and eternal musical values. Balancing the grounded feeling of the familiar with novelty and question marks is one hallmark of great musicality. It's not a great leap for fans of song-based popular music. It's like paying attention to a good storyteller. Orators and radio announcers give us a path to follow, a feeling of inclusion and an aura that commands attention. They modulate and cajole and decry and whisper and invite. Let musicians do this to you with sound instead of words (which are, after all, sounds). It's liberating, and you'll find no less impact in the statements and narratives of those who speak to us through tone, time, and timbre.

17

CONDUCTIVITY
Who's in charge and how?

Music is a team sport. I love certain solo musicians and solo works, and there's an audience for them. But the vast majority of music is made by ensembles, from duos to symphony orchestras, and what captivates me—as you've probably gleaned in this book so far—is the *interaction* of musicians playing together. That coordination doesn't just take care of itself. As with anything involving groups of people working toward a goal, there's usually a plan and a leader. Sometimes in music the leader is obvious, and sometimes they're hard to spot. A fan in the audience at a pop or country show may think that the singer in the spotlight is the band leader, but that's often not the case. It may well be the bass player or the lead guitarist, which you'd only recognize if you were to attend rehearsal. It's not always necessary, but the role of music director or producer is woven into most of the music you hear in the world. This chapter is about such leadership, starting with that highly conspicuous yet mysterious species, the symphonic conductor.

"Somebody has to be the controlling force," wrote *The New York Times* music critic Harold Schonberg in his sweeping and incredibly sexist 1967 book *The Great Conductors*. "He has but to stretch out his hand and he is obeyed. He tolerates no opposition. His will, his word, his very glance, are law." To be clear, this is the old Eurocentric, patriarchal concept of the conductor that dominated the way classical music was seen in the twentieth century. Schonberg, perhaps fantasizing how *he'd* rule an orchestra, is exaggerating the autocratic tendencies of most conductors, because many of the greats have achieved results with a lighter touch, with rapport, charm, and trust. But in his defense, he was an impressive writer and listener, and he's right that complicated music made with 60 to 100 musicians needs somebody in charge.

As a child of the '70s, I grew up with the influence of Leonard Bernstein, who guided several generations into the wonders of composed western music. In his book *The Joy of Music*, he compares a conductor to "a sculptor whose element is time instead of marble." In the sculpting, "he must have a superior sense of proportion and relationship. He must judge the largest rhythms, the whole phraseology of a work." Bernstein also talks about how conductors should manage tension and release, communicating with the orchestra through their hands, which "must be a living thing, charged with a kind of electricity." I think he's really onto something here with this metaphor. Think about the term *conductor* in the sense that we learned in science class. A good conductor, like copper or gold, transmits electricity with ease and efficiency. A poor conductor, like steel, inhibits energy flow and kicks off a lot of waste heat. If the job of an orchestra conductor isn't to focus and transfer energy from musicians to audience, I don't know what else it could be.

Conductors influence this energy in ways both visible and invisible. For one thing, symphonic conductors are also musical directors who decide (in consultation with management) what will and won't be performed for the public. These decisions reach beyond the concert hall to shape the community as a whole, because so much of what's seen as exclusionary or elitist about classical/composed music comes down to whose art is being presented. Conductors in the twentieth century decided, by acts of commission and omission, that symphonic music represented a limited canon of white male European composers. In more recent years, a more diverse group of leading conductors has changed that, and none too soon, because the monoculture of classical music was suffocating and off-putting to many. A good orchestra, like the one we enjoy in Nashville, leans into premiering new works and showcasing authorship from different backgrounds. The old classical treasures are still part of the program, as they should be, but in balance with music that feels progressive and revelatory. Only this way can symphonic music expand, evolve, and be heard as welcoming to all—including those of us who crave new ideas.

Once a work is selected, the conductor studies the score, integrating a fresh look at the work with the interpretations they've heard and analyzed in the past. If it's a new piece, the conductor will make a plan. You have to understand that conductors can read a score with its many parts like you or I would read a book or an instruction manual. They hear the music in their mind's ear. They will go over the piece section by section, phrase by phrase, imagining the feeling and presentation they wish to achieve. Then they'll bring their vision to rehearsal, where they impart it implicitly and explicitly. Oral directions and verbal descriptions are common, but as Anne Midgette wrote in the *Washington Post*, "In rehearsal, some conductors try to explain in words what they want before starting to play, but in general, orchestra musicians vastly prefer less talk and more action. Thus, conductors develop repertoires of gestures that are as specific to them as their tone of voice."

If you've never experienced a symphonic rehearsal before, I can't recommend enough that you ask about access for a session or two. I grew up around this culture, both as a participant in youth orchestras and through my harpist mother, who sometimes took me to rehearsals. Once, I even got to see the Vienna Symphony Orchestra in rehearsal because I was traveling alone and they had an open house. In all those cases, hearing passages played before and after the direction of the conductor gave me insight into what interpretation meant at that scale. I heard the music become more cohesive, more emotional and more connecting. Rehearsal makes composed music more transparent and meaningful. Conductors determine how productive those scarce sessions are.

Once in performance, conductors can't use their voices any more than soccer players can use their hands on the pitch. Yet conductors' options for physical communication are many, and boy do they get to use their hands. Typically, the conductor's right hand emphasizes time keeping, often with the familiar slender baton. I learned early on to see the baton sweep through measures of 4/4 time. The downbeat—the ONE—is literally a downward stroke, implying perhaps the source of that term. Then it's TWO with a sweep up and to the left, the THREE with a sweep straight to the right, and the FOUR with a sweep up and back to center, where it's poised to start the cycle again. (We call this the *upbeat*, for similarly literal reasons.) Bear in mind that this is a radically simplified picture of right hand technique, one you'd see more at a youth orchestra than a professional ensemble, which doesn't need the conductor to be a metronome. What you'll see when you watch a high level conductor is the right hand signaling change or flux in tempo, either stretching out or pushing the beat for interpretative emphasis, which is something crucial in classical music that doesn't happen nearly as much in popular genres. The baton will also be used to flick out the tempo for a passage that's *about* to start, so watch for cases when the orchestra, or a section of it, shifts gears under such subtle guidance.

Then there's the left hand, whose role is largely about coaxing expression and directing attention. Often, the left hand will beat time in symmetry with the right, along for the ride as it were. But when it's necessary, the conductor's left hand breaks free and makes any number of gestures—a lowering palm for less volume, flickering fingers to ask for a lighter touch, a pinched thumb and forefinger to indicate staccato beats, or a sweeping flowing full hand to ask for legato feeling. The hand will point to a specific section—the brass or the percussion for example—to make sure they're alert to an imminent entrance. Emotive conductors might place their left hand on their heart to indicate solemnity or rapture, or they might shake a fist to coax more furious passion from the symphony.

And there's more, because a conductor has his or her full body to work with, and while some have been criticized for being too wild on the podium, audiences and orchestras do tend to respond to a conductor using physicality as leverage for expression. Our friend Mr. Bernstein became a massive celebrity for many reasons—his charisma, his rapport with the public, his staggering grasp of the music, and for a gestural vocabulary that would have been welcomed in a modern dance ensemble. He'd bounce on his toes, swivel his hips, thrust his pelvis, loft his shoulders, cock his elbows, shake his outstretched arms like he was caught in a tractor beam from a flying saucer. His face was an encyclopedia of emotions, from impish humor to joyful rapture to orgasmic grimaces.

Big gestures cut both ways though. Orchestral musicians will tell you that if a conductor is really good and displays mastery of the music and technique, then big physicality is motivating and appropriate. But if they're weak on technique and knowledge (which is more common than you might think), it's profoundly annoying, and the musicians will keep their eyes more on the score so as not to be distracted. Of course for nearly all concert goers, the conductor's gestures and facial expressions are directed away from them and toward the orchestra, but if you can attend a concert in seats behind or beside the stage, as is possible in many halls, pay attention to the conductor's full-body music direction.

***

In other genres of music, the director/leader takes a wider variety of forms. Big bands from the early decades of jazz sometimes had actual conductors like Cab Calloway with his ostentatiously long baton, but more often it was a band leader with his name on the marquee and his fingers on an instrument. Duke Ellington and Count Basie directed from the piano. Benny Goodman and Artie Shaw lightly conducted and played the clarinet. Chick Webb and later Buddy Rich set the tempo of their big bands from the drum set, a particularly good instrument for a leader to play. After WWII, jazz became more of a small group affair, and while the genre's ethos gives everybody in the band freedom to be themselves, any given group generally had a leader. If you were lucky enough to see Thelonious Monk, John Coltrane, or Miles Davis, the other musicians were always jazz giants, but one understood that the repertoire and certain aspects of the presentation were set by the artist with his name on the show poster or the album cover.

One of the most important roles played by jazz bandleaders is the recruitment and development of emerging musicians. Every jazz artist's biography is shaped by those who gave them gigs and tours and recording opportunities when they were young. Miles brought on board drummer Tony Williams when he was 17 years old, jump-starting one of the great careers. Art Blakey built his Jazz Messengers band around an ethos of mentorship and growth, and as a result, he graduated future leaders Freddie Hubbard, Donald Byrd, Kenny Garrett, Lee Morgan and dozens of others. And yet even with these examples of authority in mind, we should think on and appreciate the parity in jazz ensembles, the aspects of mutual respect and shared leadership, because this balance is integral to the music's vast history and meaning. In his book *Higher Ground*, Wynton Marsalis nicely ties the jazz way with a call to "engage with our national identity." He writes that jazz "gives expression to the beauty of democracy and of personal freedom and of choosing to embrace the humanity of *all* types of people. It really is what American democracy is *supposed* to be like." This needs saying now more than ever.

In rock and roll and pop music, there are no formulas or rules for who leads, but no band becomes great without leadership, whether savvy or authoritarian, while some bands have been torn apart by competing interests and egos. The Beatles presented to the world as a group of equals, but we get to see firsthand in the 2021 documentary *Let It Be* that Paul and John largely ran the creative process. Ringo waited patiently while songs came together, conjuring his final part only once the song was almost fully formed, while George felt so marginalized that he nearly quit the band before the final two albums were complete. In The Who, Roger Daltry was the conspicuous lead singer and bassist John Entwhistle the most musically advanced member, but it was guitarist Pete Townsend who wrote and arranged the songs. Similarly, historians point to the musical depth of Jimmy Page (a former session guitarist of note) as the locus of musicality in Led Zeppelin. Besides the Beatles, other "co-captains" of great bands include Bono and The Edge in U2, Mick Jagger and Keith Richards in the Rolling Stones, and Tom Petty and Mike Campbell in the iconic Heartbreakers. Frank Zappa, as I've noted before, occupied a special place between contemporary classical music and rock and roll, and his band members followed his lead rigorously, because without the direction of the composer/conductor/guitarist, nobody would have had much idea what was going on.

Another hugely influential form of musical leadership comes from record producers. Even for many who are involved in the music business, it can take some time to grasp what producers do and how they do it. The method and spirit of the job is highly personalized and varied, but the job description is clear enough—the producer is responsible for making sure a recording is made, that it's as good as it can be, and that it is delivered to the entity paying for it, hopefully on time and on budget. That makes the producer sound like a mere project manager, but it's so much more. Producers are creative artists who shape, subtly or decisively, the esthetic of the recordings they make. Most often they work in a peer-like relationship with the recording act. Sometimes they're very much in charge, making key decisions and creating a distinct sound that never would have occurred to the artists.

At the extreme end, some producers are control freaks out to make a personal brand, like Phil Spector, a tragically insane person who in his heyday conjured the famous and saturated "wall of sound" for the Righteous Brothers and the Ronettes. Some, like Quincy Jones, are consummate professionals who know how to blend timeless musical skillsets with enough contemporary touches to make hits. We could point to distinctive visionaries like Brian Eno, who are creative artists in their own right with a distinct, pioneering esthetic that others—in his case Talking Heads and U2 among others—seek out for a collaborative posture. And other producers, like Mutt Lange, develop sonic approaches so novel and compelling that they can hop from one genre to another, in his case from the radio rock of Def Leppard to his former pop-country star wife Shania Twain.

In the early days of recording, the producer's job was defined by the title Artists & Repertoire—the job of scouting for talent and selecting the material to be recorded, whether original work by the artist or songs written by others that made a good match. Actually recording the music—setting up microphones and capturing the sounds on tape—fell to *recording engineers* whose role was more functional than esthetic. And during the first half of the twentieth century, there was a pretty strict division of labor. In the 1960s though, as the creative options for recording increased with the growth of multi-track tape, the roles of A&R and engineer began to blur together. Some continued to specialize in one or the other, but more and more, producers put their hands on the recording consoles and the audio gear to shape the sonics directly, even as they kept an eye on the big picture.

Some producers became famous for their ability to discover talent and build careers, such as John Hammond who helped launch Billie Holiday, Duke Ellington, Bob Dylan, Leonard Cohen, and Bruce Springsteen. Others shaped sounds connected with certain eras, regions or genres. I think about Owen Bradley's pop and big band influence on the so-called Nashville Sound of the 1960s and '70s, through work with Brenda Lee, Patsy Cline, Loretta Lynn, and Jim Reeves. Jerry Wexler, after coining the term "rhythm and blues" as a young journalist, became one of that genre's leading architects in the 1960s and '70s with his work for Atlantic Records, including classics by Ray Charles, Aretha Franklin, Wilson Pickett, and Dusty Springfield. Profoundly influential hip-hop producers include Dr. Dre and DJ Premier.

Whatever the style of popular music, we can find producers without whom the stars we all know wouldn't have found their voice and ultimately successful sound. The process is as variable as the creative people themselves. Many respected producers in the genres I follow—Americana and bluegrass—have told me their method is to gather the talent, set a mood of positive support, and "get out of the way," trusting that the musicians know what they want to play. That's also the model of most jazz recordings, where the playing is live and the band isn't seeking assistance in finding a novel sound, merely to record the event as honestly as possible and be an objective set of ears watching out for issues the band might not hear.

Most recording artists are seeking more involvement and creative engagement than that. In the stage known as "pre-production," artists send a batch of demo recordings to the producer—or they'll play the songs solo on a guitar or piano in person—to get feedback on which songs to keep or drop from a planned album. They'll talk about arrangement ideas, including form, instrumentation, possible guest musicians, instrumental motifs, intros and endings, etc. Some producers discourage overthinking at this stage and find they get the most vivid and honest results when a group has *just* learned a song and has to play it through using intuition and listening.

The producer and artists have to decide whether a recording will be made with all of the musicians in the studio at once capturing a performance or, as is more common in pop, building a record in discrete layers, recording each instrument separately—a drum/rhythm track first, then the bass line, then the keys and harmony instruments, and so forth. Most records are somewhere in between these poles, including a very common format in Americana where the band plays together while the lead singer tracks his or her part in an isolated booth during the first performance. This "scratch vocal" is then replaced with a more focused vocal session, when the singer can try many versions and takes. Sometimes the producer picks a full version of the vocal to mix into the final record, but quite often they will take the best line or verse or chorus from here or there and "comp" them together into one master take. In the same spirit are "overdubs," when extra parts are added (harmony parts, a horn section, more cowbell, etc.), and the producer will oversee the mixing of these parts into a coherent whole.

Before we move on, I'll offer a few words about executive leadership. Recording artists of any genre have to start their careers tracking their income and expenses, and the process quickly gets complicated as other partners enter the picture. They hire managers to oversee sensitive matters and outsource work to accountants and lawyers. That doesn't necessarily make the problem of how to divide the money any easier. Business concerns can be fraught and stressful throughout any professional music career. Bands have tried every manner of arrangement for splitting responsibilities and revenue. Some go proudly democratic, with voting and equal shares, while some great bands have been torn apart by lawsuits over who got what and who stole from whom over the years.

This could get pretty boring, so I'd only urge you to bear two things in mind. First, know that songwriters—of all the creative roles in music—are the ones positioned to make the most money from successful songs, because of the way our copyright and royalty systems work. Band members and sidemen don't tend to get much "mailbox money" from royalties unless the band has created a corporation with rules about sharing the creative revenue.

Second is to keep in mind that money constrains the size of ensembles rather mercilessly. Adding another band member—on a horn or a percussion kit or a background vocal—will divide the band's revenue pie into smaller slices while not growing the pie without a lot of other hard work. That's why we see folk and roots artists gravitate toward duos and trios, even if they'd often prefer to make their music with five, six or seven musicians on stage. They yearn to graduate from DIY touring in vans to a bus with support vehicles and crew, but the revenue has to be there. The era of the big bands—the 1920s to '50s—ended largely because transporting and housing 15 to 25 musicians cost so much. Today's largest ensembles are symphony orchestras, which require raising large amounts of money from philanthropists and donors and a human resources apparatus that usually includes negotiating with a musicians union.

Does all this affect the sound that all of these groups make? Not obviously, but as you grow to love certain musical groups, it can be interesting to know where the big ideas and key decisions are coming from.

Highly Musical Humans

Christian Sedelmyer/Brittany Haas/John Showman

As a youth violinist who became a professional fan of bluegrass, country, and old-time in Nashville, I take the fiddle very seriously, and I seem to be magnetized to the instrument in my social world. Not to brag, but I have more world-class fiddle-playing friends and colleagues than I ever expected to. In this special edition of HMH, I'm pointing you to some of them in the bluegrass/string band corner of Americana music. Because no individual can stand in for "fiddling" in the 2020s, and because I couldn't possibly pick one, I offer you a group of three, with the understanding that I could have picked five or six such lists from our blazing fiddle scenes. This cohort spans old-time to bluegrass to progressive string band to neo-classical music. They are all astonishing to me, and I live in joy hearing them play live, on records, and sometimes in private picking party environments, where the music often cooks the hardest.

Christian Sedelmyer is a Pennsylvania native who sidestepped into the top tiers of fiddling after quitting a corporate consulting job. His uninhibited sense of possibilities in bluegrass settings or with singer-songwriters like Molly Tuttle helped him stand out. And when the legendary resophonic guitar player Jerry Douglas wanted to start a band inspired by 1970s jazz fusion, soul, and country rock, he called Christian. I associate Sedelmyer with late, great Vassar Clements, Nashville's quirky country/bluegrass sideman and hillbilly jazz innovator from the '60s and '70s. He's got a fresh idea every few bars it seems, and he plays wickedly hard figures with ease. Listen to the 2024 Jerry Douglas album *The Set*, starting with Christian's composing and his melodic side on "Deacon Waltz," followed immediately by the more energetic journey in "The Fifth Season," a Douglas/Sedelmyer co-write. Christian's pulsing groove halfway in is simple but so grounding, while his solos show his range and speed.

Check out Christian's own solo album *Ravine Palace* (2021) and its grand opening track "Table Mountain."

***

Brittany Haas is emblematic of the huge impact summer fiddle camps had on recent generations of musicians. The California native, along with her cello-playing sister Natalie, came of age at camps across the nation, where she found a lifetime of connections and mentorship from old-time master Bruce Molsky and progressive jazz-grasser Darol Anger. After graduating from Princeton, Haas signed on with the virtuosic modern folk ensemble Crooked Still, with whom she toured extensively and recorded four albums. The duet album *Haas*, made with her sister and released in 2023, makes a good introduction to her traditional side, with her lines clearly discernible against the cello. She's done her most wide-ranging work and composing with the Nashville-based modern string quartet Hawktail. On the 2022 album *Place of Growth*, the song "Antilopen" foregrounds the fiddler's many skills, including the rhythmic "chop-ping" technique I talked about in the chapter on timbre. That tune was composed by the Swedish fiddle star Lena Jonsson, and Brittany's love of Scandinavian fiddling led her to a duo album with Jonsson called *The Snake*. It's hard to tell who's who on the driving, coursing song "Ten Days of Isolation," but it's fiddling at its finest.

***

John Showman is Canadian like a maple leaf, having grown up in Ottawa, earned his musician chops in Montreal, and launched his key projects in Toronto, where he's lived since 2001. Classically trained, he branched into traditional styles from Ireland, Canada, and the US, ultimately becoming one of the finest old-time and bluegrass fiddlers in the business. His bands have been wonderfully named—the Foggy Hogtown Boys (bluegrass), New Country Rehab (Americana), and his recent old-time trio, the Lonesome Ace Stringband. Despite John's surname, his fiddling isn't about show; it's about flow. Listen for his pulse, his shading, his micro-ornaments, and the way he connects notes with his bow. Start with the self-titled supergroup album *Adeline* (the one with the orange owl), because it's state-of-the-art old-time, recorded live in a cabin in a frigid winter wilderness. Opener "Evening Prayer Blues" is a special tune, with a deep, inter-racial bluegrass history, that captures Showman's grace and focus. "Hills of Mexico" is a classic folk song on the Lonesome Ace album *Old Time*, backed on banjo by Chris Coole and sung by bass player Max Malone, with a stunning, subtle fiddle solo. John's a fine singer too, and his version of John Hartford's "Steamboat Whistle Blues" on the Showman/Coole album *Much Further Out Than Inevitable* is a tip of the bowler hat to an iconic musician who deeply influenced all three of the fiddlers here.

18

REFINEMENT

Interpretation, expression, and connection

first heard about pianist Seymour Bernstein (no relation to Leonard) through a documentary made by the actor Ethan Hawke. Bernstein, 98 years old as of this writing, was a young star in the 1960s and '70s when classical music still had a prominent role in mainstream culture, so the music world was shocked when he abruptly retired in 1977 to become a full-time teacher. Hawke regards Bernstein as a guru and a mentor whose sage advice about performing and art is readily transferable to his own field.

The film, *Seymour: An Introduction*, offers a window into what actually makes some classical music better than others. After all, most of us might hear two versions of the same string quartet or symphony played by high-level groups and have no critical faculties to assess the strengths or weaknesses of each, for this understanding is a lifetime's pursuit. Hawke's film can't bring us up to that level, but as we see Bernstein guide numerous students through passages and pieces, his notes inspire his acolytes to sound more communicative and alive. The differences are subtle but unmistakable to the attentive listener. Watching the players grow in confidence and command is quite thrilling.

More recently, Bernstein has made appearances on YouTube, including a video that struck me, featuring much younger pianist Ben Laude for the channel Tonebase Piano. They sit side by side, Laude at the keyboard, working on the first measure of Beethoven's Piano Sonata No. 14, popularly known as the *Moonlight Sonata*. Just one measure. They spend 40 minutes dissecting four beats with fourteen notes in it. It's one of the most famous—and apparently simple—passages in the world. A three-note D flat minor arpeggio repeats slowly four times, while the left hand plays two D flats an octave apart—whole notes that last the full measure. What could there possibly be to talk about? I watched so you don't have to, and a partial answer includes: how to apply leverage to your finger pad from your shoulder, and why you should never let your fingers leave the keys when playing pianissimo, and what is pianissimo anyway?, and how the keys don't need to be pressed all the way down to get the best tone, and how to discern and convey the music's pulse, and the importance of returning the arms and fingers to a state of "neutrality" between every muscle gesture, and how to play the escapement point of every piano key, and how to use a subtle rotation of the forearm to lift keys without a wooden sound and allow the note "to fade away into the ether waves." That's most of it anyway.

The professor calls the session "an MRI" on the first measure of the sonata. "We went inside of it to conclude everything that's really going on," he tells his pupil with the gravitas of Gandalf and the puckishness of a Hobbit. When I told my wife about this video, she said that it sounds tedious to watch. And I get that, so I'm not urging you to sit through classical master classes to be a complete listener. My point is that musical citizens should respect just how granular and relentless certain artists are in maximizing the expressive potential of every moment. The high-level musician is called to pay micro-attention to pitch, tempo, structure, and feeling in order to fuse the composer's vision with their own for a unique interpretation of a piece. I'm calling this terrain *refinement*, the deep-tissue analysis and final polish that's called for when preparing certain kinds of music for a concert or a recording session.

Appreciating classical music's inner game is another subject that has filled many books and videos, but one indispensable concept is *phrasing*. I've mentioned it before by way of imagining a compelling improvised instrumental solo, but classical players live and breathe phrasing as an organizing principle and vehicle for expression. You'll notice that phrasing is a musical metaphor borrowed from speech and writing. We can imagine music as divided into passages analogous to paragraphs, sentences, and yes, phrases, distinguished and connected by audible punctuation. Phrases aren't as formally defined in music as in language, in that we can identify any group of notes we wish as a phrase. They can be short or long. But they imply a kind of breath at the end of each. Such moments of closure are like mini-cadences, and players will guide their listeners toward them, through phrases, micro and macro, with emphasis on anticipation, arrival, reflection, and transition.

Musicians have a tool kit to shape those phrase-based journeys in ways that can make the difference between a lifeless or a moving presentation of the same notes. Perhaps more than any other, classical artists depend on *dynamics*, which we've talked about in the context of good drumming. Our brains are tuned in to minute differences in volume, and classical pieces, especially symphonies, deliver a huge dynamic range from whispering winds to jet-engine brass climaxes. Still more dynamic action works at small scale, within phrases. In the video mentioned earlier, Bernstein coaxes Laude through a painstaking examination of how loud each note of each arpeggio is relative to the note before it. There are a couple of times when Laude plays this simple triad with a dynamic articulation and precision that's strikingly different and moving.

We can also speak about dynamic refinement in terms of *shading* or *inflection*, through which the sculpting of dynamics gives every phrase an arc and a role in the larger story. These nuances may be most audible and effective during slow and intimate works and passages, and a slow-growing crescendo from a symphony is like some magic mind hack on us listeners. I remember a performance of Samuel Barber's *Adagio for Strings* by the Chicago Symphony. This patiently flowing masterwork swelled gradually and relentlessly to an ocean of harmony that flooded my system and brought me to tears.

Now about that flow. Controlling the pacing of a work, passage by passage, is the other super weapon of the devoted phrase-shaper. I've noted before that tempo is more flexible and malleable in classical music than pop. I told you about jazz and bluegrass musicians who play deliberately ahead of or behind the beat for a sense of motion, and we talked about conductors pushing and relaxing the tempo of a symphony, where the challenge is to get everyone on the stage to ebb and flow together. But I think you can listen for this effect most clearly in solo works, like the *Moonlight Sonata* or Chopin's Preludes, where we mostly hear departures from rather than strict adherence to metronomic beats. The technique is called *tempo rubato*, Italian for "stolen time," and classical music would be a plodding bore without it.

"The art of rubato lies in making imperceptible modifications of the tempo while maintaining a connection to it, an inner pulse," wrote the pianist Daniel Barenboim in his book *Music Quickens Time*. "These modifications should be an exaggeration, but not an alteration, of certain elements in the rhythm. Furthermore, care should be taken that rubato is used only for a limited time, so as not to lose touch with the objective time that keeps ticking all along." In other words, deploying tempo rubato requires taste and discretion, lest the music become melodramatic or schmaltzy. Some authorities maintain that the player ought to be mindful to "return" any time they "steal" with a net zero of acceleration and deceleration, while for others, that's overthinking.

Both Barenboim and Bernstein dwell on the concept of music's "pulse," which is a different way of thinking about time than a beat or a groove. It sounds more subjective, and in some ways it is, because classical/composed music traditionally does not strictly define the tempo of pieces or expect the tempo to remain static throughout. The pulse idea suggests a body's heart rate, which after all adjusts to external change while hovering around a resting average. In this approach to music, the composer writes in general guidance (and apparently it must be in Italian for anyone to take it seriously).

Even the word *tempo* is Italian (for time itself). But it's a weirdly elaborate and kind of adorable taxonomy. *Adagio* means slowly, but so does *largo*, which feels the same BPM (60-70) more *broadly*, so they say. *Lento* means even slower, while *Grave* means slower still (a death-like 40-60 BPM), and *larghissimo* means: we'll all be here for a while, so watch the conductor for every single beat. Speeding up at last we find *andante*, a nice word for 75-110 BPM that translates as "walking pace." Then we get into danceable territory with *moderato, allegro* and *vivace* (which is fun to say in your best Italian accent). You get the idea, and there are many more gradations, plus modifiers that guide the music's vibe and feel—*con brio* means with vigor and spirit, *con moto* with extra motion. Instructions pop up through the score for the various players on horns, strings, etc: *poco a poco*—little by little, *non tanto*—not so much!, and truly bewildering edicts like *allegro ma non troppo*—fast, but not too fast! Sure, that's clear as can be.

I share these terms with you because it's fascinating field research into the lexicon and tool kit of our devoted conservatory-trained musicians. And because it shows us a system with a healthy balance of instruction and interpretation. Possibly a more relatable edict we see in composed scores indicates the preferred approach to *articulation*, with *legato* meaning flowing and connected, while *staccato* means tight and separated. Bowed instruments almost always play staccato with up and down bows and legato with long bow strokes and fingerings that "slur" notes together. Piano requires a ton of practice to develop the touch to achieve these effects. Wind instruments, being made for breath, are naturally suited to legato passages, and musicians learn careful lip and tongue techniques to play staccato. When you listen to concert music of any description, be aware of these articulations alongside dynamic changes and tempo choices. They speak to a collaboration between composer and artist that's tailored to each moment.

Phrasing then is accomplished through adjustment of tempo, dynamics, and articulation, but there's one more vital dimension, and that's our friend *timbre*. As we covered, timbre is the color or texture of every note, chiefly determined by which instruments are in play but then also at the micro level by the individual instrumentalists, who have more timbral options than we tend to understand. Notes have three components or stages—the attack, the sustain, and the decay—which classical musicians think about at a Talmudic level. In the *Moonlight Sonata* class, Bernstein shows Laude that he's been playing a certain note in such a way that the inner machinery of the piano attacks with a subtle "tic" and that it's possible to engage the key without it. The note is thus born with a different purpose and sound. Piano attack can be velvety or springy or hard. A violinist can launch a note with a dry crispness or a lubricated glide. Percussionists determine their attack with their choice of stick or mallet, because the material at its tip (wood, vinyl, yarn) makes an obvious difference.

Remember that the attack phase is where our brains begin to recognize the instrument that's playing, while the sustain phase is where we perceive the note's pitch and overtones. The sustain phase can be shaped too, though some instrumentalists have more control than others. Pianos and plucked instruments like the guitar start to decay just after the strings are played and thus can't be made to crescendo during the note. Whereas the bowed instruments can ride the sustain phase in many ways, with a light breathy touch, a rough rasp, or an increase in volume through accelerating bow speed. Strings and winds have advantages as well in controlling decay. Guitarists like myself use our fingers and palms to shorten the natural decaying vibration of our strings, but we're basically bound by physics. That said, we can turn to electricity, effects, and synthesizer interfaces to achieve as much sustain as we want.

These variables of control, especially articulation and tone, depend on *technique*, the practiced mastery of playing evenly and cleanly at every tempo. Other techniques involve making large melodic leaps with accuracy, executing dynamic shifts with authority and good timing, playing fast without tension, or getting a range of sounds out of one's instrument or voice. By the time you hear professionals on stage or record, they will have devoted vast amounts of their time to developing their technique, and most would tell you it's a foundation of their musicianship and musicality. Of course they also strive to be effective at an emotional level, but there's a shorter distance between emotional intent and execution with a lot of practice and muscle memory.

If it sounds like I'm implying that nonclassical musicians don't make use of these tools and concepts, nothing could be further from the truth. Nor does music have to be complex to benefit from refinement. On the contrary, in simple music, refinement stands out that much more. You should listen for phrasing, dynamics, timing, and timbre in *all* music. But I will say that the world of formal *concert* musicians, call it classical if you like, is more devoted to parsing and rehearsing these variables than other genres. Jazz and bluegrass musicians are extremely aware of and devoted to phrasing, though their vocabulary and methods of communicating tend to be more intuitive and informal than they are in classical. In rock and pop, my experience is that those on the more progressive and experimental edges are more likely to make timbre, inflection, and sonic subtlety a bigger part of their art than the lyrics or the vibe and presentation. I'm only urging you to bring attention and respect that's commensurate with the efforts being made to give music its nuance and its living beauty.

19

WHERE AM I?
How music's forms guide us

When people don't enjoy a certain piece of music (or a whole genre), many factors are in play. It's easy to see how someone would be put off by harsh and dissonant harmony or by textures or voices they regard as odd, eccentric, or ugly. And we've explored how a listener can grow over time to accept and even crave weirder harmonic or rhythmic material. But there's another dimension to think about. I've come to believe that to be engaged, a listener has to feel oriented. Complex or abstract music can lose us if we feel lost in it and if it upsets our craving for a sense of place and direction. It takes a determined frame of mind to ride along with music that feels disconnected to time or landmarks, so this chapter talks about the critical dimension of *form* across some key genres, because form often determines what genre a work is, and our openness to new genres may depend on some basic awareness of that form.

Aaron Copland tells us that "one of the principal things to listen for, when listening more consciously, is the planned design that binds an entire composition together." While composer and educator Rob Kapilow reassures us in his book *All You Have to Do Is Listen* that while this aspect of music can be dry in theory, "learning to define a form is much less important than learning how to experience it."

Most of what we hear day to day is popular music, so let's start there, where forms reveal themselves to the listener with ease. In many ways, that's the point of pop music—to be self-contained and formulaic (in the nonjudgmental, descriptive sense). Pop, rock, country, and folk songs are traditionally organized around *verses* (with basically the same music and structure but different lyrics) and a *chorus* (a repeated lyrical and musical statement that provides the anchor, hook, and usually title of the song). Some schools of songwriting make use of a *bridge*, which is a contrasting section that arrives about two thirds of the way through a song to shift the energy and to set up a climactic chorus or possibly an instrumental solo. Songwriters and producers also write intros and outros, and with that, a song can be organized in a few minutes and taught to musicians through a chart with chords, sections, repeats, and so forth. There are endless variations on the verse-chorus-bridge method. Songs may have just two verses and one chorus (like the bluegrass standard "Dark Hollow") or, as Bob Dylan showed us in the cinematic 1974 song "Isis," 13 verses and no chorus. There are no rules, but there *are* ingrained or shared expectations, which we learn by osmosis listening to popular songs. Songs, I like to say, come with their own instruction manual and road map.

In earlier decades, pop songwriting followed a different form, an influential American invention called the 32-bar (or 32-measure) song. From the 1920s to the '60s, thousands of songs became hits with a structure we talk about as AABA. Not to be confused with ABBA the band, this scheme features an A section taking up 8 measures, establishing the melody. The next 8 bars restate the A section with a similar or modified melody (and likely new lyrics). Then, just when things could get repetitive, along comes the 8-bar B section (the bridge), which introduces new melody with a contrasting feeling and chords. And finally the A section returns, recalling the original melody with a slight variation for a sense of closure.

Each pass through these 32 bars is called a "chorus," and a performance can last for just a few choruses or dozens, depending on the setting. A singer/piano player in a cocktail bar offering "Blue Skies" by Irving Berlin may well play an intro, kick into the 32-bar form with lyrics, play a chorus instrumentally, then repeat the song in full before an outro and ending. (32-bar classic songs seem to rarely have second "verses" with all new lyrics for a second chorus. As with sonnets, it seems to be a one-and-done thing.) In the twentieth century, jazz musicians adopted and adapted popular 32-bar songs as a basis for improvising. When they play instrumentally without lyrics, they stay true to the melody of the song for the first chorus. Then the 32-bar cycles of chord changes become the canvas on which they paint. Each soloist is likely to play several choruses before passing off the solo role to the next musician as they feel it. It's like a train. Every car has the same length and shape, but each has a different cargo, and there can be as many cars as the situation calls for. It's nicely modular while allowing for immense creative interpretation.

The easiest 32-bar song for most people to call to mind—one that's commonly held up as a model of the form—is "I've Got Rhythm" by George and Ira Gershwin. Not only is it an American classic that most adults can hum, but its chord changes are so compelling and foundational that they were dubbed "the rhythm changes" by the music community. Students of jazz all learn to be fluent improvisors over these changes in just about every key. Infinite melodies may be played over the rhythm changes, and musicians use chord substitution and different voicings to give the changes some freshness and variety, but the form is consistent. Besides the songs borrowed from the Broadway canon or popular songs, jazz artists have composed loads of original tunes in the 32-bar rhythm changes form, such as Charlie Parker's "Dexterity," "Oleo" by Sonny Rollins, and Miles Davis's "The Serpent's Tooth." Listen to recordings of these tunes and try to count out the 8-measure A sections (two of them), the contrasting B section, and the recapitulation of the A section. Jazz listeners tend to have an intuitive awareness of each phrase and section ending (our friend, the *cadence*). Your attention will be rewarded if you make an effort to feel this structure.

Recapitulation, the calling back of an already established theme, is a central pillar of composed or classical music, but before we go there, I just want to remind you of the foundational popular music form I first raised in Chapter 8—the blues. With the stipulation that many performances don't strictly follow the form (measures may be added or dropped with artistic intent), the 12-bar blues is everywhere and almost everybody has a feel for it. The idealized model of the 12-bar blues hews to a kind of AABA form, with four measures for the first line ("Well I'm rollin' and I'm tumblin', Cried the whole night long"). That A section repeats with the same lyrics and a slight variation in the melody, again taking up four bars. Then the B section, moving to the V chord, delivers the line "Well I woke up this morning, Couldn't tell right from wrong," which takes just over two measures. The final two measures return to the home chord and fill out the 12 bars, and the cycle starts over. While there are abundant ways to stretch and invert and play with the classic blues form, this robust and predictable flow of chords and sections has given all of us musicians a common language for improvising. It's yet another African American invention that made twentieth-century popular music possible.

While form in classical music is more complex and more challenging to hear and feel as the music plays, it's still full of As and Bs—sections that either repeat explicitly or repeat with modifications. When I was a kid learning the violin, I was exposed to a lot of music by Antonio Vivaldi, one of the big deals of the Baroque era. I found the music grounding and easy to follow for the same reason that pieces like Vivaldi's *Four Seasons* have been popular and widely performed for audiences of all ages for centuries. The form is symmetrical and easy to understand. There are plenty of repeating sections to really drive home the core themes and to make the contrasting sections stand out. Vivaldi remains an easy onramp to listeners trying to take active listening to composed music to a new level. I must say this as a caveat however. I realized in adulthood that all that symmetry—themes packed into bars of 4, 8, 16, and 32 measures—made it harder for me later to listen to or conceive music of my own that didn't come in such clean and predictable groupings. The brain learns these forms at a deep level, and I had to shake myself up when coming to love twentieth-century composed work, where forms were more mysterious or novel.

Our pal Aaron Copland devoted 81 of 230 total pages in his *What to Listen for in Music* book to form and structure, suggesting just how central it is to following and appreciating western classical music.

It's a big subject that even most classical music fans have only a basic 10,000 foot view on, so let's approach it that way by focusing on the most influential and formal concept in the genre—the sonata and sonata form (which, I regret to inform you, are not the same thing). A sonata is a work comprised of multiple movements, usually three or four. Like a good album in popular music, the movements are meant to be heard in order and in their entirety to create an arc and tell a story. This is behind the old convention in the classical concert hall that audiences are asked not to applaud between movements but to wait until the piece is finished. While this strikes pop fans as odd and some as elitist, it's one way that we listeners are encouraged to absorb and reflect on each movement as building blocks in a larger musical edifice.

Certainly there are many one-movement works in composed music, and I'll just mention a few of the most common. "Theme and variations" is just what it sounds like, and I remember as a child being impressed by Mozart's variations on a French folk song that gave us the melody for "Twinkle, Twinkle Little Star." The melody was second nature, so it was fun to hear it decorated, enhanced, sped up, slowed down in such a playful way. It tuned my ears for more complex stuff, such as the essential *Goldberg Variations* by J.S. Bach, composed around 1740. Its aria theme and 30 variations are not focused on the melody but on the aria's harmonic sequence and bass line, and almost every concert pianist takes it on at some point. Then there's Maurice Ravel's famous *Bolero*, which adapts its theme to 18 different textural and dynamic iterations. It plays us by balancing the familiar with small doses of change, while building to a climax. Another one-movement form is the rondo, which alternates a core theme with contrasting themes in a way that circles back to the A section, such as ABACADA. A tone poem is a free-form work, associated with the romantic era, that leans on tonal colors and textures to paint an impressionistic sonic picture evoking a scene or story, such as Debussy's *Prelude to the Afternoon of a Faun* or Jean Sibelius's *Finlandia*.

Most major classical works are however multi-movement, and each movement is typically described in the title by its tempo and feeling and sometimes its key. We went over many of the terms in Chapter 18. Vivaldi's *Spring* has three movements: 1. Allegro (in E major) / 2. Largo e pianissimo sempre (in C# minor) / 3. Allegro pastorale (in E major). You see this all the time. We've got a quick first movement (allegro) followed by one that's slower and quieter in a contrasting but complementary key. (C# minor has a natural relationship with E major, a chord change you hear all the time in popular music.) Then comes the final movement, one that's quick but "pastoral," offering some guidance for how the orchestra might phrase this movement to build on the first.

Now at the risk of some confusion, there's another meaning of sonata that has to do with the structure *within* a movement of music. Sonata *form* dominated music from the Classical era until well into the nineteenth century, so most of the works you hear by Beethoven, Mozart, and the other big names will follow sonata form in their first movements, with selective allusion to the form across the rest of the works. Composer and music educator Oscar Osicki calls the form "a great model for building dramatically engaging pieces of music." If you learn just one formal concept from classical music, let it be this, because it can help you follow the composer's design, and it will illuminate concepts and techniques that are employed throughout many other genres. Sonata form leans on one great source of musicality's power—the careful manipulation of pattern, variation, and repetition.

Sonata form, simmered down to one paragraph, divides a movement into three sections—*exposition, development,* and *recapitulation.* The exposition has two sub-sections, which "expose" the theme or themes in two different keys. Listen for the moment the key first shifts in a movement and you'll be hearing part two of the exposition. The composer is likely to alter the theme or offer up a complementary theme here, but the important part is the contrast of keys, which is meant to establish an aural conflict—a tension seeking a resolution. The development section is more free form, but what generally happens is the composer takes the theme and plays with it, breaking it into fragments and running it through many keys. This is the show-off section, a bit like theme-and-variations but not as explicit, with journeys here and there. Think of it as the themes from the exposition being, as it were, remixed. As the movement comes to a close, it transitions to the recapitulation. Here, the core theme returns, not as a strict repeat, but as Osicki describes it, "a retelling." Critically, the contrasting keys laid out in the exposition are resolved to the opening home key, which some have compared to the reconciliation of a thesis and anti-thesis in expository writing.

As concert music approached and crossed into the twentieth century, the sonata form faded, largely because composers moved beyond the traditional western tonal language and expectations on which the form was built. Vestiges of exposition, development, and recapitulation survived as composers made use of "themes" that weren't melodic but might have been other forms of expression, like certain tone clusters, or dynamic and rhythmic motifs. I've seen musicologists say that the age-old ABA structure is more common in very modern and abstract sounding works than one might think. Older forms like the canon and fugue of the baroque era were revived in the atonal era and used in highly conceptual ways.

All that said, I've found that experiencing a lot of modern composed music depends on analyzing less and just surrendering to the sound. The conceptual pioneer Karlheinz Stockhausen conceived the idea of "moment form," meaning pure flow and lack of traditional development—music that sounds like it had no beginning and will have no end. For sure, most Stockhausen or Schoenberg or Elliot Carter is going to sound rough on the ears of most people. But there's no musicality merit badge for enduring difficult modern music you don't like, and I'm far more interested in stimulating you to enjoy traditional classical enough that the new waves of the twentieth century—especially Stravinsky, Bartok, Barber, and Bernstein—sound like a natural, progressive extension. I also encourage you to engage with the school called *minimalism*, led by Steve Reich, Terry Riley, and Philip Glass, whose structures are based on cycles and patterns that shift to make mesmerizing, kaleidoscopic effects. I heard Reich's famous *Music for 18 Musicians* when I was a teenager, and it blew my mind with its pulsing sound fields. It remains a favorite today.

Knowing musical forms is not essential to enjoying great music, but it can help enhance your feeling for how movements and works have unity and a sense of direction and design. And we have to end with this point. As with any art form, rule-breaking is at least as important as rule-making, and forms can be thought of as prototypes that rarely survive contact with the creative impulse. How sad it would have been if Billy Strayhorn had hewed to a formula when he composed "Lush Life," one of the masterpieces of twentieth-century song? It has no real path and no repeated sections or chorus, and its tonal center keeps shifting, yet it brings me to tears. Queen did something similar in the '70s with "Bohemian Rhapsody," with a half dozen wildly divergent sections tied together with sheer imagination and charisma. Honestly, if it sounds good, and you're not feeling lost, that's what matters.

Highly Musical Humans

Madison Cunningham

In 2018, I got a twinge of professional shame when an artist I couldn't place was nominated for Best Americana Album at the Grammy Awards. This was my journalism beat after all, so who was this interloper with an album called *Who Are You Now?* Soon though, I realized I *had* heard her perform—two or three years before—when she opened for the acoustic supergroup Punch Brothers at Nashville's Ryman Auditorium. Madison Cunningham. Of course! I had been impressed by that performance, but as soon as I heard the album, I knew I was dealing with a generational talent, one who was then only 23 years old.

Madison grew up in Orange County, CA, making music in church, where her dad was a pastor and musical leader. "I had a lot of friends in the band," she told me in 2020. "It was a wonderful introduction to what it was like to perform in front of people and it was safe too . . . a nice net to kind of fall on." Meanwhile, she was transfixed by the guitar, first acoustic, then electric. "I just did a lot of sitting in my room, making mistakes and calling them chords," she said, a clever line that suggests her gifts as a lyricist. She moved to Los Angeles, encouraged by a producer/mentor who helped her get established and make her debut independent album *Authenticity* in 2014. It shows her boldness with both language and harmony, as well as a lovely and distinctive voice. But she took all that even farther, with more economy and concision, on *Who Are You Now?*, released by the prestigious Verve Forecast label.

What you'll hear in these gem-like songs is pop music as high art—a meticulous arrangement of guitar, voice and lyric. Her riffs and chords, mostly played out of unconventional guitar tunings, are fearlessly offbeat on songs like "Pin It Down," "Trouble Found Me," and "Plain Letters." Her melodies take unusual curves, and her grooves slip around with sharp syncopation and selective use of odd time signatures. She is a brilliant guitarist who does not jam or solo.

Her parts are intricately designed to be in concert with her vocal ideas. Moments of ferocious power are contrasted against passages of gossamer delicacy.

The inspiration continued on *Revealer* of 2022, her third recording in a row to earn a Grammy nomination and the first to win one (for Best Folk Album). Its opener, "All I've Ever Known," builds a world over a 3/4 guitar figure offset with Afropop beats. Her greatest ballad is here too—a song about her late grandmother called "Life According To Raechel" that brings me to tears with its poignant honesty and graceful melodic lines. I also recommend the spectacular album *Cunningham Bird*, a song-for-song cover of the 1973 duo album by Lindsay Buckingham and Stevie Nicks from before they joined Fleetwood Mac. The vocal harmonies and instrumentation are perfect.

Fans of Fiona Apple, Rufus Wainwright, and St. Vincent will hear a complex kinship with the music of Madison Cunningham, but for me, she's the heir apparent to the broad musical mastery and ambition of Joni Mitchell. It's no surprise that the Canadian/Californian is a core influence on Madison. It's in the integration of many sophisticated ideas, thoughtfully sifted and edited into a moving whole. Chris Thile, who spotted Cunningham early and gave her stages to play on, once called her "FRIGHTENINGLY good!" and that's how I feel too.

PART VI

$$\int$$

PRACTICE

20

YOUR MUSICAL DIET
Genres, formats, and algorithms

n his 2007 book *In Defense of Food*, Michael Pollan offered this distilled takeaway from his years of research as a journalist on nutrition, agriculture, and health: *Eat food. Not too much. Mostly plants.*

I like that. Call me a fan of concision, I suppose. So, inspired by Pollan's pithy counsel, I came up with my own for a rewarding and lifelong musical journey. I can't make mine quite as terse, but here goes: *Listen attentively to a variety and abundance of music made by people who put art before commerce.*

I'll spend this chapter unpacking that advice. *Variety* takes us into the world of genres and formats, the oft-contested categories with which we organize our sprawling musical world. I'll talk about music's "gatekeepers," those shadowy figures who influence what's easiest to find on the American music menu. And I'll discuss where musical choices come from and strategies for pursuing a rich and balanced musical diet in the digital age.

As I noted briefly in Chapter 3, most people don't widen their musical window much over time. Studies suggest that, for understandable biological and social reasons, Americans remain devoted throughout their lives to the music that grabbed them when they were teens and young adults. "Fourteen is a sort of magic age for the development of musical tastes," Daniel Levitin told *The New York Times* in 2014. During puberty, "growth hormones make everything we're experiencing, including music, seem very important. We're just reaching a point in our cognitive development when we're developing our own tastes. And musical tastes become a badge of identity." That's a wonderful way to start a habit of music enthusiasm, but it takes effort to not get trapped in a nostalgic loop.

We tend to express our likes and dislikes in terms of genres. You'll hear people say things like: *I loved punk in middle school but got into singer-songwriters in college and now I listen mostly to rock.* Myself, I've had stretches of my life when I was primarily devoted to and excited about classical, alternative rock and power pop, folk, bluegrass, classic country, Americana, and jazz. They're all still with me of course, but my focus seems to shift over time. Yet since you've come this far with me, you'll understand that there are other, possibly more enriching ways to express preferences. For example, we can seek out music for large ensembles versus small groups, or music built on syncopated rhythmic languages, or music made chiefly with atmosphere and slow-moving timbral changes. Taking such a non-genre point of view can break you free of learned biases and comfort zones that tend to be pressed on us in a genre-based musical ecosystem. Still, I want to talk more about genre and some specific genres here, because they carry baggage *and* wisdom. Knowing how genres function empowers any listener.

Genre is "a category of artistic, musical, or literary composition characterized by a particular style, form, or content," says the Merriam-Webster dictionary. We don't tend to learn genre distinctions formally; we socially absorb the differences between country, hip-hop, jazz, etc. as we grow up, and we find those categories helpful in orienting us and talking about music with friends. As I studied music though, I noticed that some passionate and knowledgeable people had low opinions of genre as a concept, calling it an artificial construct imposed on music for cynically commercial interests. In his 2023 book *To Anyone Who Ever Asks: The Life, Music, and Mystery of Connie Converse*, musician/historian Howard Fishman wrote that "grouping artists into oversimplified categories that customers could easily understand turned them into flavors and brands, flattening and sterilizing much of the previously bold, idiosyncratic music that was made and recorded in the United States." His protest was on behalf of a visionary 1950s songwriter named Connie Converse, whom he says was unjustly ignored by a music business that couldn't fit her into any existing category. It's a fair point. Converse was what we'd later call a singer-songwriter who arrived before Bob Dylan and Joni Mitchell, so there was no lane for her. Then, Fishman widens his critique with a story that everyone should know, about when old-time and folk music of the 1920s and '30s was marketed as "hillbilly" music when it was made by White people but "race records" when made by Black Americans. This had the effect of pre-segregating the genres that would become country music and soul, even though country, as well as American pop music generally, is rooted in African American blues.

At its worst then, genre has offered cover for cultural appropriation and erasure. And genre-based thinking in the industry has indeed trapped some visionary artists in a marketing purgatory, "falling between the cracks" as we say. At the same time, for anyone who talks about music, genre is a critical tool that brings some order to an overwhelming body of work. When I tell you that last night I heard a concert of old-time country blues, I'd be telling a very different story about me and my week than if I'd attended the opera. Botanists need to distinguish between reptiles and birds. Museums of natural history shouldn't jumble dinosaur bones, live jellyfish and semiprecious stones in the same gallery. Musicologists—like scientists—add value by categorizing music by time, style, influence, region, and purpose. So I don't see anything wrong when streaming services or record stores carve out genre spaces. In my record library, I don't intermingle all music either. While my primary CD collection blends roots, rock and roll, and pop music, I have separate shelves for jazz and classical, plus a few specialty collections of narrower genres that I study or work with. Fans and supporters are out there being champions for historic subgenres, from acoustic blues to zydeco to sacred Sephardic music, and it would be a sin to wish away those categories and traditions in pursuit of a misguided idea that "it's all just music."

Country music offers a window on an important distinction between *genres* and *formats*. A format is a stylistic grouping of artists programmed for radio or through a music service, i.e., an expressly commercial category. A prime example is Top 40, which emerged as a radio format in the 1960s, defined not based on a sonic signature but as a destination for listeners who wanted to hear the hits of the moment. In recent decades, "country" could be a genre or a format depending on how you used the term. Country music the genre is a lineage of American blues-based, narrative-rich music born in the South with more than a century of history and numerous subgenres and regional styles. Country music the *format* refers to industry-filtered songs promoted on the nation's 2000 country radio stations and celebrated on country music awards shows. Thus, for years, the statement "I love country music" from a stranger has required deeper probing. Do you mean the traditional genre of country or the format of pop country? Some love both, and that's fine. There is some important overlap. But most of my friends and colleagues love country the genre, while we don't find as much heart and soul in country the format.

That's not to say that formats are inherently bad or anti-musical. I work in Americana music, a format that's often mistaken for a genre. It's a format because it was conceived in the 1990s as a radio strategy and marketing category, with a mission to support traditional country music (and related genres) at a time when commercial country radio stations no longer would. Americana has grown to be an eclectic roots music format (or mega-genre) encompassing traditional country, bluegrass, folk, singer-songwriter, soul, blues, and gospel. Some say Americana can't make up its mind and is so diverse as to mean nothing. But I disagree. I don't see why a format should have narrow boundaries if the elements and traditions sound good together and have a common story. Thus I've long supported Americana as a frame of reference and a musical kinship community that does the noble work of amplifying, preserving, and spreading roots music in all its varied expressions and traditions.

The genre that dominated popular culture during my coming of age was "rock," our national default soundtrack and a sprawling galaxy of music from the complex to the obtuse, the sublime to the ridiculous. While I respect a lot of rock music, there are several reasons that it's not the field where I think folks should pay the closest attention as they seek out new insights and rewards in musicality. While there is exceptional, advanced musical thinking to be found in rock history, it's a genre that's more defined by attitude than by ideas. Its appeal is generally more visceral and sexual than intellectual or emotional, though I recognize and honor a lot of the songwriting that the industry has filed under "rock" over the decades. Music that speaks to those needs is awesome and important, but at the same time, rock (including hip-hop) is bound up in fashion, show business, and social movements so much more than other genres that it can be hard to untangle innovations in imagery from innovations in music itself. Clearly David Bowie made amazing music, but would we hear him the same way, or would he have risen to fame, without the costumes, the gender-bending, the staging, and the visual art? So rock on, my brothers and sisters. It's a joyful noise. But be clear that (for the most part) it's a world built on simple chords and beats and on guitar solos more about flash and volume than taste and timing. My hope would be that through deeper listening to other, more sonically-centered genres, your appreciation will grow for genius-level rock by the likes of the Beach Boys or Fleetwood Mac or The Dead, with more appreciation for their harmonies, arrangements, and dynamics.

Then we have the so-called *fine art* genres of jazz and classical, which are on one hand necessary labels for broad approaches to music and on the other ridiculously inadequate at conveying the diversity and history of either lineage. Even "rock" offers some clue about the nature of a given work, in that it will almost certainly use electric instruments and a steady beat. Whereas *classical* and *jazz* don't give us a single clue about the sound we'll hear from any given work or artist. Yet sadly, these vast realms of important music get boiled down to clichés and cartoons—guys with a powdered wig and a violin, or sunglasses and a saxophone. The musical citizen should despise that reductive erasure of individual brilliance and inspiration and work to explore different chapters and eras of the classical and jazz stories. I say that while fully understanding that both fields are daunting in their scope with many subgenres themselves. I hope some of the recommendations in this book offer you starting points or new milestones in your journeys.

My advice for what to listen for in jazz has been covered pretty well in my chapters on rhythm and improvisation. Usually an ensemble music, jazz calls us to follow soloists and a band thinking and breathing together, creating and riding waves of energy. Devoting a few months of attention to a select period of jazz, such as 1965 to 1970, and building out from there is one good strategy. Listen for that balance of democratic creativity among a group of musicians that Wynton Marsalis wrote about and to the rich harmonic language that jazz visionaries built on over more than a century. Feel and enjoy the genre's "fascinating rhythm" per Ira Gershwin.

Classical music can challenge and work on us in even more ways and often asks more of us in terms of attention and contemplation. As I've said, I call it "composed music" because I wish to emphasize and celebrate the creativity and design of the music's authors. And I encourage you to listen as if the *composer* is speaking to you, through interpretive musicians, who are interesting in their own right. It's a different genre because it works with a different operating system than jazz or pop/rock, while sometimes borrowing from them.

Many excellent books have been written about how to appreciate composed music, and as a non-expert I can't offer anything terribly new, but I'll say this. Listen to the icons like Bach, Mozart, and Copeland. Listen to notable contemporary composers like Joan Tower and Michael Daugherty. Browse around. But give each work your full attention. And in that spirit, I will share a cool strategy suggested by Rob Kapilow, the composer we met in the last chapter. He calls it "compared-to-what" listening, which embraces the truth that composed music is largely built on the power of patterns, contrasts and anticipation. Unlike a pop song, where a fourth chorus goes pretty much like the first one, composed music unspools and builds worlds through passages, themes, transitions, and interludes. Composed works are longer, with more variation and non-verbal storytelling and sound-making. Kapilow lets us know that following musical stories calls on our mindfulness and memory. You'll listen for motifs and themes and then listen for how they get revisited and developed over the arc of a piece.

The heart of compared-to-what listening is embracing being disoriented and trusting the process, engaging in it and revising how we understand what's come before, informed by the new material we're hearing. "Remembering, comparing, and reevaluating as a piece of music proceeds is the way a listener participates in its process, and this activity not only allows him to enter the composer's world, but to co-create it," Kapilow writes. "People often talk about the enormous task of teaching people to understand music, when what is really required is to get them to hear it fully. It is not more musical knowledge that is needed, but rather the ability to listen completely. To pay attention, notice, and *remember*."

***

In jazz and classical especially, we run into the concept of the "canon," which is a vaguely defined body of works that are widely held to represent the greatest and most historically significant in the story of a genre. Progressives often deplore and condemn the classical canon over its elitism and its "colonialism," because of the unfortunate ways that centuries of European domination of commerce and culture influenced and overwhelmed music from other parts of the world and the indigenous people of the Americas. All those forces are real and important to an understanding of American music, but as with genre, I'd urge everyone to take a forgiving view of any canon you hear about. Consider their strengths and weaknesses and think of them as imperfect works-in-progress, which we are free to argue over and revise. The canon I grew up on helped guide me as a young person, but with time I realized it's basically a twentieth-century listicle, a distilled grouping of worthy figures but not every worthy figure. Important women and people of color are being added to the canon all the time in a kind of folk process, so I encourage you to contribute to the conversation and nominate artists you cherish for the canon of now and tomorrow. Whereas to throw out the very idea of a canon risks losing touch with the truth that some works and some creators are actually better and more worthy of study than others. Because music costs us time, and time is finite, we owe ourselves and the music to be mindful of the greatest, across all fields.

The question of course is who determines what is regarded as great and who decides what gets exposure and promotion in the competitive music marketplace? We often hear about industry "gatekeepers," and any discussion of music variety and choice has to address the complex dance of record companies, radio, media, promotion, and marketing. Historically, major record companies (or labels) controlled the pipeline of emerging talent and the path to stardom. They decided whom to invest in and then how hard to promote any given artist or act. Despite their allure, a record deal never guaranteed riches or acclaim. And yet label resources have been one key factor in the making of almost any long-term career you've heard of going back to the 1920s.

Labels work with music's other influencers—historically radio, television, and the press—to promote their product in a system that can be noble and rewarding, or exploitive and slimy, and everything in between. The public pays attention to the music marketing game when scandals erupt, but it's a distorting mistake to oversimplify the music business as some kind of smoke-filled room with a few bigwigs deciding who's going to be a star. In truth, the music business is chaotic and sprawling, with thousands of people having endless conversations and sizing up countless acts, in a blend of capitalism and openhearted enthusiasm. For every cynical, money-first move made by some record company or radio chain, there are many more stories of individuals you'll never hear about operating out of hope and faith, often making a good deal of money for whole teams of musicians, stagehands, and crew. Even the major label sector works that way a lot of the time, with the indies always there to keep them honest.

From WWII on, independent record labels brought varying degrees of influence and fresh sounds to the marketplace. We've seen indie labels take more chances on "between the cracks" artists, and they've been more open to genre-blending and experimentation. In the genres I cover, indie labels have done a good job helping the most talented emerging artists get on the career ladder. A similar thing happened in radio, which devolved in the late twentieth century from a diverse and competitive business sector into a consolidated industry that programs most of what America hears via a corporate apparatus seeking maximum profit. Meanwhile, (again generalizing) independently owned radio stations, including non-commercial or public radio stations (non-coms we call them), have served wider variety to musically hungry fans. (We who work in this sector often wonder why there are not many *more* musically hungry fans.)

In the twenty-first century, the ability to move digital files around the internet begat streaming music and blew up a long-standing system. Labels and commercial radio lost power and influence (and, for a time, profits). Social media offered musicians more options for reaching a mass audience while giving fans a web of new ways to discover music. We've seen viral videos bolster not only new pop standouts but artists working in composed, improvised, choral, regional, and boutique genres as well. Streaming services offer access to most any recording ever released, which is not to be taken lightly. In such a new world, some musical citizens plunge into the storm of content, seeking out reliable sources of music news and redesigning their way of collecting music. Others however have shrunk their musical worldview, dumping their CDs or records and plugging into a streaming service's personalized playlists.

So far anyway, music programming and discovery assisted by AI and algorithms has been mostly good for the music ecosystem. I've lost count of the superb artists I learned about with the digital assistance of Pandora, Spotify, Tidal, and others, especially in jazz and experimental music where taste can be especially personal. But there's a dark side too. The data suggests that countless millions of people are using recommendation tools passively rather than actively. Much like social sites that show you more and more content that matches your politics, streamers tend to narrow your pool of possible discoveries to genres and periods of music that you already like. And while mass playlisting by the streamers has helped good artists break out, the streaming model (which provides very little context, history, or connections for records) makes it easy for millions of people to never drive their own musical journey.

Taking an active role in your music discovery space is one of the most important things you can do to grow as a music fan. That means going out of your way to teach your streaming service that you are a curious musical omnivore, because it will assume the opposite. Do this by creating several playlists with a range of artists from musical realms outside your comfort zone. Choose artists and scenes you're curious about, and add artists who are known for blending or "crossing over" genres, because they tend to have a lot to say and they can lead you into new terrain, for example the jazz/bluegrass hybrid of David Grisman or the jazz/rock fusion of Weather Report. The point is to kick-start a process in the software with artists and genres you know only a little bit about. Now here's the most important part. Play those lists on repeat overnight when you're sleeping to rack up impressions in the algorithm that will prompt it to start making associations and recommending new surprises. This approach will serve you some music you don't like so much, and you can thumbs-down that stuff (though not too quickly!) as much as you need to. You'll also be more likely to hear that special something that changes your life.

Another strategy for seeking out new frontiers is to think about how artists approach the marketplace. The entertainment business conditions us to associate commercial success and "hits" with musical quality or importance. The musical citizen knows that's not the whole story. What we want is a mindset that recognizes musicians who bring sincerity, independence, courage, and personal vision to the world. I have no hate in my heart for artists who pursue fame and fortune, even those who adapt their sound to the trends in the marketplace. I just think the results are usually pretty dull and those are the artists you're going to see and hear about in daily life anyway. I identify with underdogs in general, and in music, that mentality can lead you to the musicians who set their work before the world as is and then see what they can do about finding an audience for it. That's what I mean by *Listen to a variety and abundance of music made by humans who put art before commerce.* Make no mistake though. I believe that commerce, if not today's version of capitalism, is good for music. The vast legacy of twentieth-century America proves that. But the ones who put the art first most fascinate and reward me. They need us to listen, even if few others are, and to speak up on their behalf.

If you can chase music going forward with these tactics and points of view in mind, I believe your musical diet will grow more diverse and nourishing. I envision you being part of the growing audience of some artists who are local in your region who are making art in less advantaged styles. I've seen open-hearted, risk-taking music discovery change people at various stages of life, from teens to seniors. We shouldn't want to be dependent on the music we loved at 18 years old when we're 40 or 50 or 90. Thousands of worthy players, composers, singers, and producers are out there vying for your attention, as are great recordings from decades past. Sound is infinite and profound, calling us to heed the many ways our fellow humans can make art with it.

YOUR INSTRUMENT
Musicality embodied

Three guitars rest within easy reach in the studio where I spend most of my time. The arch-top electric has a warm, woody tone that's perfect for traditional jazz when played through an amplifier. The solid-body Fender Telecaster electric guitar, with its limpid, silvery voice, evokes a country twang. My most prized instrument, and the most expensive for what it's worth, is an acoustic "dreadnaught" style guitar perfect for bluegrass and folk music—a 1996 Collings D1-A made in Texas of mahogany and spruce. No electricity required. When I'm holding it in my lap, cradling it so the body can vibrate freely, with my shoulders and arms relaxed and my fingers curled correctly around my pick, this guitar feels alive and eager to move.

These three guitars have different designs producing different timbres for different styles and moods of music. Learning what I have about those styles has helped me grow and hear the world with more insight and clarity. And yet I've never hitched any hopes or dreams to the idea of playing on a big stage or making a living from playing music. I figure if that had been my destiny, a path would have unfolded. For me and millions of others, playing is its own reward.

The benefits of music training, especially for young people, are well-studied and widely understood—better attention, coordination, memory, empathy and more. Plato knew this long before there was science to back him up, arguing that music education instils virtues "because more than anything else rhythm and harmony find their way to the inmost soul and take strongest hold upon it, bringing with them and imparting grace, if one is rightly trained." Giving a kid a musical instrument is a superb lesson in creativity and caretaking, as well as a ticket to social relationships. The paradox is that adults often feel the yearning to pursue an instrument, but we have less flexible time. Young people have time but often have no idea why they're being made to march through scales and pieces when they're 9 and 10 years old and there are other, more exciting things to do. I was that kid once.

You don't have to be a music-maker to develop a deep sense of musicality. But playing an instrument, playing with others, and learning how to read (and maybe even write) will supercharge your engagement and insight. It's not for everyone, but it's wise to take stock and open yourself up to possibilities every few years. Do you play an instrument, or have you in the past? Did you quit, and if so, why? Are those obstacles still part of your life? Have you thought about the role an instrument could be playing in your life that it currently is not? And have you made a real search for the instrument that is best for you? Because that's where it starts, while getting it wrong is too often where it ends.

I didn't love the violin, but I didn't fight it either, because I had social support and reinforcement. I also felt like it was taking me somewhere, even if I wasn't sure where. I had a best friend who played violin too (better than I did), and I got into ensemble playing, including youth orchestra, as soon as possible. That felt connecting and inspiring. But then I saw and heard other worlds, especially that Buddy Rich big band concert. From then on I was mad for the drums, and after much whining, my seventh grade Christmas arrived with a sparkle red drum set from a thrift store. I modded it a bit with a new hi-hat and more cymbals and set up a practice station in the basement with my record player next to me. I'd listen through headphones (resulting in a pretty good mix of music and drums) and play along with the Eagles and the Beatles and Santana. In high school I assembled a garage band, which as I've told you led to bass lessons and a few years playing in a working band. That got me in closer proximity to guitars, and when I heard traditional folk music and bluegrass in and after college, the guitar finally emerged as my instrument, the most self-contained, portable, and versatile of the options I'd tried.

Never once did I worry that I was throwing away my training or experience on the other instruments as I moved to a new one. In fact the skills were almost entirely transferable. Playing violin (a melodic instrument), the drums (a rhythmic instrument), and the bass (a harmony and time-keeping instrument) all helped me dramatically with the guitar.

But what about you? Finding your heart's instrument starts with knowing some things about yourself and about the varied roles of different instruments. Maybe start by thinking about physical bodies—yours and the families of music-making objects. Wind instruments are an extension of your lungs and lips, and speaking musically will mean using your breath for every note. I can't imagine that being comfortable for me, while the fingertip control of a fretted and stringed instrument is deeply appealing. The bowed instruments call on us to coordinate our fingers, wrists, elbows, arms, and shoulders with a holistic concentration on body, poise and breath that rivals yoga. Piano not only conjures luminous tones, it makes scales and harmony visible and tangible with the layout of the keyboard, making for a short mental distance between written notes, note names, and execution. And then there's the full-bodied physicality of drums and percussion, which fill a specific and powerful role in any band or group. Drumming (and bass playing) is also one of the faster paths to making music with others, because the basics come more quickly and because there are usually more groups seeking rhythm section players than there are candidates for the gigs.

Hiding in plain sight is the instrument we're (nearly) all born with—the human voice. "To sing," said Joan Baez, "is to love and affirm, to fly and to soar, to coast into the hearts of the people who listen." Easy for her to say, but it is true that we have a strong human desire to process life, join a chorus, share something we wrote, front a band, or pass idle moments with song. It can feel cathartic and healing. I'm someone who can basically sing in tune but who doesn't enjoy my voice nearly as much as making musical ideas with an instrument. Yet I'd offer this advice, rooted in experience. Whoever you are and whatever your exposure to other musical training, take some professional singing lessons. Spending as few as three or four sessions with a good vocal coach, as I did when I first moved to Nashville, will not only help you find the best version of your voice but will also open your ears to how the human voice resonates and how much refinement is possible with experience and attention. It's a step forward for your harmonic knowledge and ear training. It will get you more in touch with your breath, your posture, and the complex systems in your skull that shape how you hear the world. You'll never listen to other singers quite the same way.

In choosing an instrument, you'll also want to think about the role you'd play in music making. Do you see yourself being more comfortable as a team player, as in the violin section of an orchestra, or as a soloist, revving up an audience with your instrumental prowess? Do you feel like a melody person, a harmony person, or a rhythm person? The bass allows you to be all three at various times, and if you're not intimidated by its size, the acoustic upright bass is a very special sounding instrument with many possibilities. Do you want to be able to enjoy playing by yourself *and* in groups, in which case the piano and guitar stand out. They're versatile, adaptable, and allow us to play lead and harmony together. My only musical regret is that I wasn't able to take piano lessons as a young person, because sitting down and playing jazz standards and improvising on the piano is something I'd dearly love to do. Perhaps in my retirement I'll get one more chance.

Think about unusual instruments that will make you feel more unique and perhaps useful as you seek chances to play with others, as well as the specific sounds and timbres you find most alluring. Because many a career has been launched by that spark of sonic love. Many find themselves mesmerized by the pinging sustain and roll of the banjo, and it's a fantastic instrument to pick up in mid-life. Lower-pitched instruments like the viola or cello are more forgiving with a nice tone, as opposed to the violin, which can squeak and squawk until you have good bow control. The whistle or pipe can be a ticket into the world of Celtic music, which is especially participatory and melody driven. I've talked about the allure of the vibraphone and marimba. Dare to be different.

Do you feel drawn to electric or acoustic instruments, and have you pondered the differences? Both worlds are extraordinary and full of brilliant instrument-making and designing, but they evoke different feelings. There is a kind of magic in acoustic instruments—the way they make sound that's louder and clearer than seems possible without amplification. I'll never forget a visit to a music store during my high school years when I got to hold a fine acoustic guitar in my lap for the first time. It was a Taylor, and its resonance and fullness startled me. I actually laughed at how good it felt, with the wood and wire and glue all working together, the sound pouring forth so easily. A similar wonder can be had playing a good quality violin or cello or piano. There seems to be something alive in them, and I believe every person should have chances to play around with high grade instruments, because no words can prepare you for their visceral wonder.

If playing loud is what you crave, electrified instruments can take you there and beyond the threshold of pain. But they have many more virtues. You can control the tone and timbre of electric instruments—subtly with knobs on the instrument itself or dramatically with outboard pedals or effects boxes. Indeed electric and digital instruments offer infinite sonic possibilities. But consider this important trade-off that I've experienced as a guitarist. Electric guitar is more abstract and cybernetic in that the actual sound is produced by a loudspeaker at the other end of some cables. The guitar itself is more rigid and doesn't give much tactile feedback. The instrument is not the guitar but the complete system of guitar and amplifier, plus any gear one might have between the two. The sound arrives at you and surrounds you. But with an acoustic guitar, the sound feels as if it's coming out of you. Both are appealing in their own way.

Learning to read music bogs many people down in their instrumental journey, and I understand it's a grind, like any new language. But here are a few things I took away from my experiences on various instruments. It's a great idea to isolate rhythmic reading from melodic reading; spend time studying patterns of quarter notes, eighth notes, rests, triplets, etc. This aspect comes faster than the pitch information, which requires memorizing where notes are on your instrument's keyboard or fretboard. And crucially, if you can read rhythm, you'll be much more able to follow along on a score for a piece of music while listening to it being played. You'll grow closer to not just the piece itself but to the movement and design behind all pieces of composed music. Second, while I learned to read for the purposes of playing the violin, my reading skills were of little use in learning the guitar, because the strings and note arrangement are different. Fortunately, there are other modes of writing music down that I've spoken of—chord charts for one—that help me understand how a tune goes, whether in country, rock or jazz. Guitar playing—as well as other fretted instruments—can be interpreted through *tablature*, which diagrams what fret is played on which string across the measures of music. Many great musicians do not read or write music, but it's a powerful tool even if you only learn about aspects of it.

Meanwhile, improvising is a gift most people don't give themselves and which some music teachers will (boo) discourage. When I had my violin as a kid, it wasn't long before I started to make stuff up and play freely to satisfy myself. God only knows what I sounded like and what juvenile mess poured forth from my bow and fingers, but it was good for me, influencing how I'd appreciate music years later. When you noodle or hunt-and-peck on an instrument, you'll learn how different intervals sound and feel. Try to improvise in short to medium phrases, repeating them to solidify the connection between your fingers, mind and ears. Play them loud and soft, quickly and slowly. Try to play a phrase forward and backward. Here's another great exercise: sound out familiar melodies, like a TV show theme or pop song you know, from memory. Trust yourself and try to inhabit the intervals. But above all, and this is not as simple as it sounds, listen mindfully and completely to what's coming out. React to what you hear, nudging notes up and down, smoothing your tone, purifying your pitches. Slow down. Dwell on your tone. Listen to yourself.

What about lessons? I'm happy to say that there are many more options than when I was young. There is something special about finding a teacher you spend time with in person on a regular basis, if we stipulate that that's challenging and takes more time than many people have. While I encourage you to get together with other musicians as soon as possible in any context, the internet is a wonder world of beginner and intermediate music instruction. For step-by-step instructions in playing specific songs, or scales and arpeggios, or technique and practice ideas, YouTube is a gold mine. That said, to get serious on an instrument and command it the way you may want to, professional instruction will turbocharge your progress. Virtual instructors abound online as well, through a range of sites with many models for getting you together with teachers who are masters in their field. Some of my favorite bluegrass musicians—guitarist Bryan Sutton, banjo player Alison Brown, mandolinist Sierra Hull—teach through a platform called ArtistWorks.com for example. Most instructors built experience with online lessons during the 2020 pandemic, so now you can reach great teachers from other parts of the world.

I see a sort of spectrum of musical progress and intent that goes like this: Player, Practicer, Performer, Professional. A Player is a dabbler who occasionally likes to touch an instrument and fool around with it for fun. A Practicer sets aside time on a regular basis to focus their mind, set goals, learn pieces of music, and improve their technique and skills. At some point, Players and Practicers may follow a desire, and overcome their nerves, to play music for an audience, at church or in a coffee shop or a local bar. They become a Performer, which is an honored and important role in society. I've been all three of these in my life at various times, depending on how absorbed I was in music making.

I've wavered between Player and Practicer most of my life, and at times I've been a Performer, but I never felt called to be a Professional, someone who makes music for most of their living and who regards themselves as a musician above other vocational identities. They have a hard row to hoe, and they make tremendous sacrifices to do what they love. I have immense respect for them.

Professionals practice and play and teach and gig and collaborate. Some of them write and compose. Some have jobs in orchestras or shows that assign them their work. Others take on the mantle of the performing artist—the headliner and perhaps the star—who spreads their music in the world and asks for attention and compensation.

Most practicing musicians become acutely aware that the musicians who inspire them are far better than they are, and various kinds of psycho-spiritual conflicts can emerge, because seeing the greats play simultaneously excites us and depresses our ambition. I know how great my idols are—Julian Lage, Doc Watson, Wes Montgomery—and with that comes a sinking feeling that nobody needs to hear me play the guitar. And yet I know that we should embrace and love the whole spectrum of talent and be able to truly enjoy local, handmade music among friends too. There should be every kind of audience, every day, everywhere—and performers will take care of the rest.

Practicing itself is a vast subject worthy of monasteries and libraries. The books and methods are uncountable. Practicing will mean something different to the hobbyist musician carving out a few hours a week to keep improving versus the aspiring professional jazz or classical artist crushing it for six or eight or more hours a day. But a few principles seem to be regarded as universal. Mental and physical preparation pays dividends, even if it's just two minutes of stretching, deliberate breathing, and centering your mind. Orient yourself with your instrument and its tone through simple motions. To warm up on my acoustic guitar, I play chromatic scales using even downstrokes at a modest tempo on several parts of the fretboard. Then I move to diatonic scales, major and minor, and chordal arpeggios. This little ritual dials in a pure, rich tone, attunes me to intervals, and forms a sense of where my right hand is for more accurate picking. Then when approaching a piece of music, practice *deliberately* and more slowly than you think is necessary. Repetition of phrases and passages is critical, but don't do it mechanically or with distractions. Focus on training your brain with the right motions and don't teach yourself errors. *Use a metronome* and gradually increase the tempo to performance speed. Pay attention to posture and tension. Drop your shoulders and relax. Take breaks and practice techniques or passages mentally when you're away from your practice space. These widely appreciated tactics apply to learning written pieces, developing an improvisational language, or learning how to back up your singing with guitar or piano. Doing this with your whole mind and body for twenty minutes will carry you farther than running sloppy reps with the TV on. Confession: I cheat on every one of these suggestions much of the time.

Let's leave this discussion with some advice to *anyone* who adopts an instrument, vocal or handmade, from a wise and wizardly bass player from Nashville named Victor Wooten. His book *The Music Lesson* is a dazzling, imaginative story of a frustrated bassist who meets a mysterious teacher, possibly an alter ego, who leads him on an inner quest. Their dialogues about the elements of music—technique, phrasing, tone, etc.—take many insightful and inspiring turns. But they keep coming back to a vital point—that a musician, properly understood, plays music *through* an instrument. Yet people make the mistake of trying to play an instrument in order to play music. "Are you saying you can play *any* instrument?" the disoriented student asks the teacher. "Of course I can, and so can you!" the guru replies.

I love this belief system and wish I'd heard about it when I was a teenager. I was wrapped up in learning notes, scales, chord changes, and technique. I could have done a better job imagining the music and speaking that aloud as if I were using my mother tongue of English. Over the years though, my practice—my guitars in my hands trying new things—has helped me internalize how musicians think, react, listen, and learn. Playing has significantly shaped my feeling for harmony and rhythm. And no small thing, it's led to friendships and community during many chapters of my life, particularly upon moving to a new town. While I had the advantage of having my inner musician sparked at an early age, I'm optimistic that it's never too late to wake up the music maker in you.

22

LISTENING IN REAL LIFE
Spaces, systems, and venues

Everything I've discussed so far in this book is about what can happen inside us when we experience and appreciate music, but it's all just theory until we actually listen. Where, when, and how does that happen for you? Are you prepared to be intentional about it? We happen to hear a lot of music in our media-saturated, ultra-portable age, but setting and sound can make the difference between a throwaway experience and a profound one. So in this chapter I want to get into physical, logistical reality, starting with the story of a day in my life when I realized something perhaps obvious but powerful about this aspect of our lives in music.

This day—June 24, 2016—was memorable, because the live weekly Americana radio show I cohosted at the time—*Music City Roots*—made its annual summer pilgrimage to a venue called the Monteagle Assembly, 90 minutes east of Nashville on the craggy and beautiful Cumberland Plateau. Monteagle is an interdenominational religious community established in 1882 that now acts as a summer retreat for multi-generational families from the region. There, Music City Roots would set up and present four artists over three hours for a live audience and over live radio. It was a thrill to get out of our home venue and put on a road show.

My day started before that though, a few miles down the road, because Monteagle is a nearby neighbor of Sewanee, the University of the South, a private Episcopal school with a classic gothic campus. Housed in the student library is a resource I'd discovered a year or two before—the William Ralston Music Listening Library. Built and run by a faculty couple with student help, it's a beautiful, sound-proof parlor with a custom designed, ultra-high-end audio system. I spent a couple of hours there, while the enormous Wilson Audio loudspeakers took me as far into the sound of music as I've ever been. A small group of us listened to Oliver Nelson, Sarah Jarosz, the music of J.S. Bach, and even Tammy Wynette, all of it producing goosebumps thanks to stunning reproduction of events from faraway studios and concert halls.

Then I had to get back to Monteagle for our show. Amid the stately homes and cottages is a barn-like assembly hall made entirely of timber. It has resonant acoustics, big sliding doors that let in the night air, and a stage with old-fashioned footlights. It's a magical and timeless place to put on live music, and that's what we did, with a mix of bluegrass, vintage folk, and jazz. In typical live show fashion, the music was performed into microphones, routed to a mixing console, then amplified for the audience through loudspeakers.

When that was over and the gear was put away, our show family— the stage and production crew and our guest musicians—stayed up late on a big screened-in porch at our guest house in the woods, where the crickets and frogs mingled with a jam session—professionals and amateurs playing with guitars, fiddles, banjos and voices.

What I realized driving back to Nashville the next morning was that in the space of a day, I'd attended a kind of holy trinity of sonic experiences, the three (and only three) ways to listen: recorded music on sound systems, live music through a PA system, and live music without amplification. Any music you've ever heard was via one of these three modes. I realized that each comes with its own opportunities, costs, benefits and challenges. I'm going to go deeper into each mode with advice and perspective to help you appreciate each one.

Recorded Music

Almost none of us can afford—and no individual or family remotely needs—an audio system like the one in the Ralston Room, with its $400,000 loudspeakers and its exotic amplifiers, cables, turntables, and expertly designed acoustic room treatment. But as rare as they are, such places do serve a valuable purpose, which is to give people, especially young people, the chance to experience something visceral and spiritual. Voices sound like they are in the room. String sections swell with their full complement of overtones, making for a silky illusion. Drums and cymbals are shockingly true to life, blossoming and decaying just as they do in person. Electronic music hits with full, rich low end and no distortion. For a lover of sound, it's extraordinary to hear such systems, but it's far more than one needs to experience music in high fidelity at home. Yet it's easy to be confused as to what that looks like.

Think about that beautiful word *fidelity*. Besides flowing off the tongue, it's a worthy virtue. It makes me think of marriage and friendship, of dogs and patriotism—and of music and sound. Fidelity in reproduction is good. High fidelity is better, and how high for how much investment is a deep question that musical people should dwell on. With a century of innovation behind it, the audio industry is overflowing with affordable options for music lovers who want thrilling, immersive sound. You owe it to yourself to visit a hi-fi store to hear benchmark systems so you know what's possible—as well as affordable systems to see just how close you can get (you'll be surprised). Request to hear music *you* know and love, not what the store wants to play, and I urge you to include in your list one or two artists who record acoustically and naturally (i.e. not highly produced pop music), or some live recordings. Listen via streaming, CDs, and vinyl.

You want to listen for a few key things. Good loudspeakers "disappear," as if they're not the sound sources in the room. Instead, the musicians should seem like they are arrayed in front of you in distinct places, a phenomenon we call *soundstage*. You want to experience an audio illusion of three-dimensionality. Remember that we are binaural, with two ears, and a stereo system's two speakers create a very specific mix in space. We can hear how a piano is oriented to the listener based on where the high and low notes are. The band or orchestra should feel spread out before you, front to back and left to right. Surround or Spatial audio systems (also called multi-channel) have their benefits, but they are much more expensive and tricky, and I see no lasting advantages over traditional stereo.

In that sound field, listen for individual instruments—their personality and clarity. Take turns focusing on the bass, the midrange, and the treble in the music. Can you distinctly hear the bass drum? Are the bass pitches clearly defined, or muddy and indistinct? Do the voices shock you with their presence (they should) and do sibilants (sounds like S or CH) sound natural or harsh? Do cymbals and delicate sounds sparkle? Dwell on just how different the sonic experience is between a proper stereo audio system and listening in a car with road noise or over earbuds from your phone. Let good audio sink into your memory, to make mental benchmarks of quality and your preferences. A friend of mine coined the nice term "threshold of authenticity," meaning a synergy of equipment, music, and room where your brain relaxes and attends to the musicians as if they were there in the room with you. This feeling—and thus a new closeness with your favorite music—is possible with a reasonable investment, and here I want to offer some rapid fire guidance for your audio journey.

Before assembling speakers and amps, you want to identify your listening space. Where in your home are you most comfortable sitting still? Can you find such a spot where you could place two speakers in an equilateral triangle in front of you, anywhere from four to ten feet away? Most folks probably already have an entertainment console of some kind built around a flat panel TV and some electronics. That might be a contender for an audio makeover, but consider all your options. Attic and basement rooms often offer advantages such as privacy or sound-proofing. A room with a concrete or brick floor is excellent because it won't vibrate or transmit sound to another room. What's the noise level in your space, and what can you do about it? Creating a silent background might be the most cost-effective hi-fi technique there is, so take steps to mitigate refrigerators, noisy air vents, fluorescent bulbs, and other electrical devices that hum. A high ceiling can be a boon and a low one can be a challenge. Plan out your listening sanctum with the same thought you'd give a garden or a home office.

An excellent new hi-fi can be had for between $1,500 and $2,000, while savvy shopping for used or vintage gear can cut that significantly. People tend to be put out by that cost, but they're making a mistake of consumer culture, which is to think of an audio system like any other electronics big box purchase, like a PC or video screen. Audio gear isn't disposable though; it lasts decades. Compare your budget to what you'd pay for an acoustic guitar or piano. Nobody tells you this, but *your stereo is a musical instrument,* and you should regard it as such. It's an acoustic device designed and refined to play music accurately, and it's the only one that lets you hear what you want, when you want.

Your essential components are: a streaming source (to receive and decode online music), an integrated amplifier (also called a receiver if it contains a radio tuner), and a pair of speakers. And lately more and more people are (like the '70s when I grew up) building their hi-fi around a turntable for vinyl playback. I can't help you here with brands or models, but watch a few experts on YouTube, and you'll begin to see the consensus choices for top affordable components. Buy components you can return, and don't be afraid to take items back. Spend up to $100 on a good multi-plug outlet that cleans up your power and protects your system from surges. Spend tens of dollars (not pennies) on speaker cables. Ask for "banana plugs" to connect your amp to your speakers, not twisty, hand-stripped wire like in the olden days.

Put your gear on the sturdiest shelf or furniture you can. Your turntable must be level, so use a tool and adjust its feet to make it so. Learn how to handle and clean records, and if you favor new vinyl over used records, you'll have a much easier sonic experience overall, though many relish the surface noise of vinyl if it's not too bad. Assuming you're mostly streaming, my strongest advice is to use a wired connection from your streaming source (phone, laptop, desktop, etc.) to a good quality Digital/Analog Converter. A DAC can be a small separate device, but DACs live inside most modern integrated amplifiers. Do not use the cheap DAC built into your computer or phone by using the headphone output jack to connect to an analog input on your receiver/amp. While Bluetooth and wireless solutions for home audio work fine for kitchen, bedroom or deck, I'd encourage a traditional, all-wired setup for your listening space so that you can have analog sound without digital conversion, which defeats the whole harmonic point of listening to records. Meanwhile, don't get hung up by the long-raging debate pitting analog versus digital music. Both are wonderful technologies with different advantages. I am happy listening to all formats.

Most hi-fi fans find the speakers to be the most exciting and important part of their system. You'll have to decide between floor-standing, tower style speakers and "bookshelf" or stand-mounted speakers. Floor standers have more bass and a taller soundstage, but they take up more space. Either way, one key to getting optimal sound is to place the speakers at least a foot away from the wall. That's why "bookshelf" is considered a misnomer in hi-fi circles; they should be on stands just a bit out in the room, not cocooned on shelves where the sound can't project in all directions. Adjust the placement of your speakers a lot when you first set them up, because mere inches front to back and side to side can make a difference in the reality of the sound, as does toe-in, the angle the speakers are pointing in toward where you sit.

Many people, especially city apartment dwellers, won't have the space and privacy to play a sound system at robust volumes. In such cases, headphone listening can be extraordinary. In fact you'll get much better headphones for loudspeaker money. Look into headphone amplifiers and DACs when you shop for headphones and build a coherent system.

The culture around audiophiles has been complex since hi-fi emerged in the 1960s, and yes, it's a community with some snoots and snobs. But I've found it much wider and more inviting than that. *Audiophile* means nothing more than "love of sound" after all, and there are millions of us who listen with that mindset, not out of some misguided competition over who has the best gear. Home is ultimately where you have the most time and freedom to listen. So experiment. Indulge. Center yourself. Enjoy libations. Get lost in your own private world of sound.

Live Over PA

Records are daily bread for music lovers, but most of our transformative experiences take place at live performances. And in the twenty-first century, with the dawn of piracy and streaming, live music became more of a focus and profit center for the music business, generating well over $10 billion annually in the US. It's wild to reflect on the variety of spaces and places where I've had my heart moved and mind blown by live music, from dive bars to mountain meadows to football stadiums. Each kind of venue presents things to think about to have the best possible musical moment.

While I prefer small to midsize venues, let's start at the top of the market, where convoys of semi-trailers carry the mega-tours from city to city. Stadium and arena shows thrive on star power, spectacle and a communal energy. They're the only viable way to see major hit-making artists, and even with the parking, the crowds, and the eye-watering ticket prices, they *can* deliver overwhelming thrills. While such events are big in scale with exceptional audio/video technology, they can be less rich in musicality, per se. Some artists, particularly jam bands, come to the stage to create in the moment, but honestly, most arena concerts focus on the star and a choreographed show with players in the background making pre-rehearsed music that's sometimes mixed with prerecorded tracks.

The sound systems are better than when I was young, but arena shows often sound muddy, swallowed up by beat and bass, because some buildings are designed for sporting events rather than acoustics. As with any size venue, if you have the ability to position yourself near the front-of-house mixing console, you'll generally find the sound as good as it's going to get. Try to seek out acts that play like *bands* in such settings, as opposed to being backing material for a star's pre-planned show. And I would urge you to weigh any concert ticket above $125 against the five or six musical experiences you could take in at more intimate spaces. Follow your heart and ears, but music nerds often find better values out there than stadium shows.

Music festivals offer rich buffets of artists from headliners to emerging acts, and the best ones live in symbiosis with a city or region's musical culture. While the rock/pop mega-festivals like Coachella or Bonnaroo present some of the same challenges of scale as arena concerts, there are hundreds more that impart a feeling of intimate connection to leading artists in particular genres. I've often said that for me, annual spring visits to Merlefest in western North Carolina during my 20s and 30s felt like getting an advanced degree in roots music, with countless discoveries and ever-deeper knowledge of icons in bluegrass and folk. But music lovers find similar enlightenment and ecstasy at the Newport Folk and Jazz festivals, the New Orleans Jazz and Heritage Festival (and its more accessible cousin French Quarter Fest), Hardly Strictly Bluegrass in San Francisco, and the Telluride Bluegrass Festival amid the peaks of the Colorado Rocky Mountains. Besides the constant flow of sets by artists familiar and unfamiliar, one finds at festivals a camaraderie and family atmosphere that for me attaches to the best music, making an overall lifetime journey truly fulfilling.

The next step down in scale for live music takes us to sheds, amphitheaters, halls, and auditoriums, where the balance of size, sound, and soul can be outstanding. I think of memories I made on the lawn at Wolf Trap near Washington, DC, in the art deco magnificence of the Paramount Theater in Oakland, CA, and the over-the-top 1928 Louisville Palace Theater in Kentucky. Above all others, I love the Ryman Auditorium, the 2,200 seat Mother Church of Country Music here in Nashville. Artists who play venues of this size are by definition successful but usually not so mega popular that you'll have to vie for tickets with big money and ruthless tactics.

Then there are the clubs, with capacity between 200 to 1,500 or so, where so much of America's touring band culture and commerce plays out. I associate this size venue with standing, which some folks like more than others. I'm fond of such venues with a second floor balcony where I can find a stool or at least a spot to lean. Perhaps you're the kind of person who thrives on the energy of being pressed up against the stage, and that's cool, but I'm too claustrophobic for that. The best audio experience is typically near the center of the room, where the sound has had a chance to blend. The sonic experience in clubs varies widely, and I think that most club shows are too loud. When the music is playing at over 100 dB, with peaks well over 110, that's near the threshold of pain for most people, and it's a sign the room is being over-loaded, muddying up the tone and balance of instruments and voices. It's such a shame, because so often the house could sound much better by backing the level off by just 5 percent. In the absence of such good judgment, quality earplugs that filter out glaring highs and tame the overall volume are worth the small investment to protect your hearing from injury.

Another category of venue I love is the supper club, where the audience is seated at tables and served by wait staff. My favorite such venue of all time is the Birchmere in Alexandria, VA, because I lived near it for a number of years and it programs the roots music I love. The City Winery operates such venues around the country with varied, quality programming, good sound systems, and attention to an overall experience.

Then there are bars, where your mileage will vary and where there's no substitute for firsthand research as to the places that are musically intelligent and discerning with good atmosphere and respect for artists. One should try to learn in your town or in a new city where the musicians tend to hang out on nights off and where collaborations by local artists tend to take place. Sometimes a place can seem forbidding or make an awkward first impression if you arrive on a night that's wrong for you, while the same place after a couple of visits can start to feel like a second home. Observe the clientele to see if they respect the bands onstage, lowering their voices and paying attention during performance. Notice if the proprietor has a reputation for being good to musicians, and whether they keep a reliable show calendar at their web site and in the local papers. I also find that bars that present residencies by certain artists (like Nashville's extraordinary country swing band the Time Jumpers playing every Monday night for years) tend to be places where you will find quality musical experiences in any genre. Bars that host jam sessions tend to be good musical neighbors as well. The PA systems in bars are usually bare bones and not ultra-high fidelity, but some places overachieve in this department too. When they're smartly run and programmed, bars are a musical bargain (tip your musicians and servers!). You'll love what you hear, and you can quickly wind up feeling like family.

Live Acoustic Performance

We are, in my experience, more likely to hear acoustic music earlier in our lives—a piano played by a music teacher in grade school, an organ and choir in church, or a brass band at a parade. By *acoustic* I mean hearing the sounds of the instruments and/or voices without the mediation of mics, amplifiers or speakers. Most classical music is presented acoustically, with ensembles assisted only by the design of the performance hall and the quiet of the audience. It's one of life's great sensual pleasures. Chamber music was conceived for smaller rooms where we can appreciate the construction and sound of the instruments and the immediacy of the performers, right down to their breath.

The other place we may likely encounter acoustic music is the house where we live. Once a mainstream form of entertainment before the rise of radio and TV, home-based concerts are pretty rare nowadays, save for a pretty robust network of house concerts held by homeowners with touring singer-songwriters and small folk acts. Still, my life has been full of picking parties and jam sessions, where friends gather to play bluegrass and folk music. Whether just me and a friend on a porch or a large gathering spread out in multiple circles around a house, picking parties were a huge part of my musical foundation and education. And not infrequently because of my professional work in roots music, I've found myself listening to some of the best musicians in the world playing with and for each other in private settings. I count these as possibly the most unguarded and remarkable musical experiences of my life. Hearing Chris Thile's mandolin or Jerry Douglas's dobro over a PA system at a festival is good, but hearing them close up, with every nuance of wood and wire resonating, is sublime.

Seek out live acoustic performances in your community. Notice how the instruments and voices sound coming from the source, as opposed to loudspeakers. Listen for how the room and the audience affect the sound. You may have to lean in and listen harder without that volume boost, but you'll be rewarded for it.

Whether in a public venue, a private space, or your own home, musical experiences mean more when you fully show up for them. When people grow as music lovers, they start making ever-more elaborate plans, traveling to shows at historically significant venues for example. Some invest over time in their stereo systems and record libraries, basking in every step closer to sonic fidelity. Whatever sorts of experiences you're drawn to, approach them with focus and attention. The creators of the music are certainly doing so.

23

THE MEDIA AND THE MESSAGE
The story of music journalism

I found my way into professional music reporting in the late 1990s, and as of this writing, with more devotion than brilliance, I'm still at it. And here, as we near the end of our time together, I want to share my journey as an explainer of and advocate for music, with some background on how I fit into the rich (and challenged) history of music journalism. Because writers, whether in print, radio, or video, have played a huge role in the curation of America's musical choices and tastes. Stories, touching regions, personalities, social forces, and human struggles, offer a more rewarding and personable guide to new music discovery than algorithms. For me, music is rather empty without context, so that's what I try to provide in my essays and interviews. Our role is sometimes misunderstood, and while we still have excellent music writing, it's taken on new forms on new platforms and can be harder to find than it used to be.

From early in high school, I was told that I had a knack for writing (certainly not for math), and the world of journalism called me. I saw a path that rewarded general curiosity (one of my strong suits) along with pursuit of literary expression. Reporters, especially in the years after Watergate, seemed like cool characters who questioned people in power and who sought out and told the stories of everyday people and cultural trends. I also read a lot—including my first music journalism—rock reviews and profiles in *Rolling Stone* and jazz commentary by Nat Hentoff in the *Village Voice*, both of which were in my school library, by the way. I studied English and

American literature in college followed by government, economics, and media studies in grad school. The job market steered me to Washington, DC, where I covered health care policy and business during a dramatic time on Capitol Hill in the early '90s. But after a few years and a move to Nashville, while working as editor of a health business journal, I had time to act on the old advice writers hear—to "write what you know."

By then, I did know something about music as a fan and amateur player/songwriter. Nashville sparked my imagination with its history, its remarkable talent pool, and its welcoming community. Through a friend with a contact, I pitched a 1,000 word reported essay on the emerging Americana music format to the arts page of the *Wall Street Journal*, figuring why not start with a high profile publication that published writers I admired? To my delight, they bought it, and I would write for them every month or two for the next couple of years, exploring what it felt like to tell stories about American roots music. (I also met my wife through that relationship, which is a happy story for another day.) With that exposure and experience, I began writing features and reviews for a handful of magazines, when magazines were still mainly paper and ink. While we were taking advantage of the early internet, I didn't foresee the tsunami that was about to crash on the shore of my chosen profession.

In 2000, I bid health care writing good bye with a new job as a staff writer covering music and the music business for the daily *Tennessean* newspaper in Nashville. I shared a cubicle with the late great writer Peter Cooper who became a historian at the Country Music Hall of Fame before his untimely passing. Our editor was Tim Ghianni, a classic old-school newspaper man with loads of curiosity, high standards, and the proverbial heart of gold. He did his best to shield us from the edicts of management. Our corporate owners, Gannett Inc., rewarded what we thought were the wrong things—celebrity news and hit-driven music coverage that would be recognizable and affirming to the mass audience, whereas we vexed them by working hard to discover and tell the stories of brilliant but lesser-known artists so they might become better known. We thought that's what newspapers were for, what with the word 'new' right in the name.

We also got sideways with corporate Music Row, where some considered us elitists who didn't know our place on the major label hype cycle team. Toby Keith (about whom we had mixed but not entirely negative feelings) wrote a sneering song we understood was inspired by us called "The Critic." And the head of the Country Music Association circulated an email to the label bosses warning them that I was problematic and best avoided because I loved and sometimes played bluegrass. I wish I'd kept a copy of that, but it definitely happened. As for the job, I covered the surprising popular impact of the old-time *O Brother, Where Art Thou?* soundtrack and the canceling of the Dixie Chicks (now The Chicks) when they spoke their minds about the Iraq War. I also wrote about the rise of Napster and file sharing, the history of the pedal steel guitar, and the deaths of Waylon Jennings and Johnny Cash. I got nasty emails from KISS fans when I said their concert was formulaic and worn out, and I wrote that the hot new radio country band Rascal Flatts was "both namby and pamby," to the dismay of some. It was a golden time.

I left the paper in 2004 to seek my way as a freelancer and more importantly to finish work on my first book, which addressed the rise of radio, the great station WSM, and its role in establishing Nashville as Music City USA. That took me deep into the heart of old Music Row, allowing me to interview foundational figures in country music whose memories stretched back to the 1950s, '40s, even the '30s in some cases.

While I waited for the edited manuscript to be published, I found that the writing market was getting tougher. Publishing and the music business were both being clobbered as people discovered how to find, copy and share content at no cost. Advertising budgets for music publications shrank, and freelance writer fees did too. Bloggers began writing about music for little or no pay, flooding the marketplace with more commentary. My survival plan was to diversify my media skills. I'd intended to only write for a living, but I found I really enjoyed telling stories through radio and video too. I wrote for some documentaries and I got trained in developing audio stories for public radio, which led to working regularly for our local affiliate WPLN and the culture desk of NPR News. I started thinking of myself as a producer (quite empowering and clarifying) and began shooting and editing videos for clients, which took me to some exciting locations and situations, including witnessing the final production sessions for Alison Krauss and Robert Plant's *Raising Sand* at a studio in New Orleans with T Bone Burnett.

Then came the biggest surprise of all—one that I adapted to my mission of telling music stories. In the wake of the publication of my book, *Air Castle of the South—WSM and the Making of Music City*, I was approached by some energetic producer/impresarios who were cooking up a retro radio show called Music City Roots. It was a showcase for Americana music based on the early Grand Ole Opry, carried live on the air and on streaming video platforms from a show barn in Nashville and later a hall in Franklin, TN. Each Wednesday evening show featured four artists playing 25-minute sets, and my job was to interview the musicians as the stage was switched out between acts. I also wrote in-depth previews and reviews of every show for our website and, in a sign of how serious the owners were about uplifting every aspect of the show's professionalism, a printed program. This was an interesting experience because it allowed me to explore the fine line between commercial hype and conventional "objective" music writing. My readers knew I was being paid to celebrate, not critique, our musicians. But I never wrote a word I didn't believe, and I have no doubt that the background and enthusiastic insights I offered helped fans bond with the artists. It was high-tempo and a lot of fun; I feel like a lot of my show reviews are among my best work. Cofounder Todd Mayo told me my program notes reminded him of the sportswriters we'd both loved over the years, and I felt that way too. His partner John Walker always called my work "connecting the dots," and I said to anyone who'd listen during these years that for musical citizens trying to find the gold in the straw pile and build a musical world of their own, "context, not content, is king."

Music City Roots had a magical eight year run on radio and public television, and toward the end, we made a broadcasting/ programming partnership with WMOT Roots Radio, a 100,000 watt

FM public radio station owned by Middle Tennessee State University. The station needed a makeover, and we provided the staff and expertise for a new format to get established, one that filled a void for local roots music on the air in Nashville and the area. I signed on to WMOT as music news producer and interviewer, and I've worked very happily there for nine years. It's a dream gig that pulls all my experience and strengths together, and I know how fortunate I am to have a job with benefits in a field of media I love, when most of the rest of the media touching music and culture has been through wrenching change and downsizing.

That's my personal window on music journalism and media. I'm not big time, but I've been of use. I steered my career toward the music I thought had the most heart and soul rather than the music that was at any given time making the most money, and I feel rewarded for that commitment. I've been satisfied by hearing from time to time that a story I wrote or an interview I conducted turned a listener on to some new art and made a new fan. If I sometimes regret I don't have more reach on social media or through our radio station, it's not on my own behalf. It's because I want to elevate more careers and more wide-ranging styles and approaches to music-making. This book represents a next step in that journey.

***

What a journey it's been for music journalism writ large. A quick review will give you some perspective on why writing about music is so much more than "dancing about architecture" as some snarky person once averred. Getting into music takes guides and gurus, and they have an interesting history. I will take a wide view in hopes you will too, because written articles, interviews, books, music documentaries, podcasts, social posts, multi-media web sites and even augmented reality experiences are all means to the same end— education, connection, enthusiasm and discernment to help fans make wise and personal choices.

People have been writing about music for centuries. Plato wrote that it "gives soul to the universe, wings to the mind, flight to the imagination, and charm and gaiety to life and to everything." Every step of music's evolution in the west—chants, polyphony, the tempered scale, Baroque counterpoint, and onward—inspired intellectual and philosophical observations, and we're in their debt, because in the absence of sound recordings, written documentation is the only reason we know much about how music sounded and functioned in the pre-modern age.

The story of my profession starts in Europe in the eighteenth century with the founding of music journals. A number of famous composers wrote for the public about music even as they created their own, including Hector Berlioz, Franz Liszt, and Robert Schumann, who became one of the most influential critics of his time and founder of *The New Journal for Music* in 1834. The only music covered with any depth was art/concert music—what we now call classical—and thus it would remain until well into the twentieth century.

General interest magazines became a thing around the turn of the twentieth century and hit their stride after Henry Luce launched *Time* in 1923. It changed the game in so many ways, including reaching millions with stories about popular music. *Time* put George Gershwin on its cover in 1928, Louis Armstrong in 1949, Dave Brubeck in 1954, and—my favorite—jazz pianist Thelonious Monk in February of 1964. In the story, Barry Farrell, a remarkable writer, told America that Monk's music was a matter of "High Philosophy." He wrote: "Now Monk has arrived at the summit of serious recognition he deserved all along, and his name is spoken with the quiet reverence that jazz itself has come to demand. His music is discussed in composition courses at Juilliard, sophisticates find in it affinities with Webern, and French Critic André Hodeir hails him as the first jazzman to have 'a feeling for specifically modern esthetic values.' The complexity jazz has lately acquired has always been present in Monk's music, and there is hardly a jazz musician playing who is not in some way indebted to him."

I've long held this cover story up as a good example of a great era in journalism that embraced values that have been tossed aside with time. Here we have the biggest magazine in the country not only telling the story of an eccentric Black genius but centering him as worthy of the cover, one of only 52 per year. *Time* used editorial judgment, not focus groups, to confront its mainstream audience living in the last days of Jim Crow segregation with a composer and pianist and American original whom they felt was worth their readers' sustained attention. Another thing—the writing is vivid and sophisticated, engaging the writer's voice as part of the intellectual experience, in keeping with the "new journalism," an era that elevated the dazzling nonfiction of Truman Capote, Tom Wolfe, and Joan Didion.

The same month that Monk was in *Time*, the Beatles appeared on the Ed Sullivan Show, ushering in a new era of music and music coverage. Fans wanted pop music news and commentary, which proliferated through magazines and daily newspapers. A revolution arrived in 1967 with *Rolling Stone*, "a new publication reflecting what we see are the changes in rock and roll and the changes related to rock and roll," according to its cofounder Jann Wenner. There were others—*Creem*, *Trouser Press*, and *Crawdaddy*—but *Rolling Stone* became rock and pop's preeminent tastemaker. Its writers became icons themselves, with their access to artists and their vigorous storytelling. The era produced Lester Bangs, David Fricke, Robert Christgau, Ben Fong-Torres, Sylvie Simmons, Ed Ward, Lisa Robinson, Nick Tosches, and Greil Marcus, among others. Their artist profiles and discourses on albums still leap off the page today. Their work (online or collected in anthologies) is a portal to another time when it was seen as normal and noble for the art forms of literature and music to bolster each other's fortunes and nourish each other's esthetics.

For most of the twentieth century, journalistic and scholarly criticism became a key part of the classical music ecosystem, not entirely for the good. More than any other genre, critics seemed overeager to rip artists limb from limb in their reviews, and even when they were positive, their tone and vocabulary were often impenetrable to newcomers trying to learn about the music. Such critics helped build the edifice of elitism and exclusion that's troubled classical music for half a century. I haven't felt that generally about the jazz criticism I've read. Nat Hentoff, Gary

Giddins, Stanley Crouch, and the remarkable Whitney Balliett to name a few favorites, came across more like intelligent enthusiasts who told stories and illuminated the art, while reserving harshness for rare cases. And in fairness, one of the toughest classical critics made a point that influenced my career when I read his obituary in 2003. We've met him before. He's Harold Schonberg, the fellow who wrote the problematic book about conducting. He made and held to a rule that he would never fraternize in any way with the musicians, conductors, opera singers, or producers he wrote about. "I refuse to believe that if a critic is friendly with a musician he can be impartial," he said. And that was when I decided to step away from critical reviews and focus on explaining and reporting and profiling artists I thought worthy of acclaim. I loved the people in the Nashville community too much to have beers with them one day and then review their records or shows on another. I knew I'd pull my punches, and I decided I'd leave that role to others.

Sadly, criticism was largely abandoned by publishers anyway. In the years after *USA Today* (launched in 1982) became a national paper with snack-sized articles and plenty of what somebody brilliant coined "listicles" (Top 10 lists masquerading as feature articles), popular music writing declined in general interest publications. Daily papers were already paring back on arts coverage when the digital crash came after 2000. Craigslist decimated classified advertising, a key source of newsprint revenue, which fell off a cliff and never recovered. Napster and other file "sharing" sites pulled the rug out from under the music business at the same time. And in a deeply discouraging development, publishers gained visibility into the metrics of how audiences clicked on and spent time with individual stories online, further tilting the balance of coverage away from smaller artists to pre-filtered celebrities. It was a perfect storm. As personal online publishing became easy and cheap, bloggers flooded the zone with opinion, but not much money, and only a few like *Pitchfork* survived to become authoritative voices in music writing. But even that great site was recently absorbed into a bigger media company and relegated to support status under the already declining *GQ* brand. Music blogging now feels like a pale shadow of 2005 to 2015.

The internet provoked an overall decline in print media, and private equity and hedge funds accelerated it, with a business model that hollowed out editorial staff at news organizations by the thousands. Even at legacy publications that stayed in the game, music writing became shallower. In 2017, journalist Ted Gioia wrote a piece for the *Daily Beast* with the following thesis: "One can read through a stack of music magazines and never find any in-depth discussion of music. Technical knowledge of the art form has disappeared from its discourse. In short, music criticism has turned into lifestyle reporting." He noted something I was already familiar with from my years at a Gannett newspaper. I was discouraged at times by my supervisors (not my editors) to back off on the "musicology" in my pieces. We could literally see the sports desk from our pod, and while they were allowed and expected to write about the rules, tactics, lore and history of their games, we were supposed to keep it light and focus on personalities more than the creative process.

Today, there are bright spots to be sure, and if you're determined, you can find solid to excellent music journalism to help you on your way. On one hand it's unfortunate that *Billboard*, *Variety*, *Rolling Stone*, and *Music Business Worldwide* have all been consolidated under one corporate owner, Penske Media Group. On the other, they still do good work and are more consumer facing than in the past. Access to these titles can be found on affordable aggregators like Apple News. Venerable magazines for jazz and classical music like *Downbeat* and *Gramophone* are still out there, independently owned and operated. In my field of roots music, a few print magazines hang on, some under non-profit stewardship. And let us not forget book publishing, which has been a boon for music journalism even through stormy weather for that industry. Every year it seems, a dozen fascinating, important books are published about artists, scenes, record companies, traditions, neuroscience, etc. My experience is that books become a natural part of a personal musical journey. They illuminate how and why specific artists found their sound, the music scenes that gave them a chance, the behind-the-scenes figures who promoted them, and the new frontiers music makers are exploring today. And finally, a lot of "writers" in music today have moved to the dominant medium of our age—online video. Starting about 2015, I began to see really impressive music explainers, advocates and reviewers setting up YouTube channels, and while I'll decline to name names here because that landscape is always changing, searching for music commentary or education can lead you into some smart new directions if you're willing to sift through the weaker content and reward the quality creators with the ever-coveted *Like* and *Subscribe*.

I do not take lightly my freedom in 2025 to interview artists and write traditional feature stories for a respected radio station and to seek out the artists I feel are most interesting without supervisors counting clicks on my posts and second-guessing me. It's a rare and remarkable privilege, and I do my best to live up to it by illuminating and uplifting the Americana musical community and the Nashville music scene, which remains world-class and exciting 25 years after I first encountered it. I get asked sometimes to offer advice to young people interested in music journalism, and I have to be honest and say that it's like writing songs. Don't expect much income unless the stars line up for you and/or you turn out to be so blazingly brilliant and different that the world notices you amid the cacophony of content. Do it because you love it and can't help it. Build as much online reach as you can through consistency. Develop one or more niches of expertise and genre community relationships. Don't get discouraged by your follower counts or your online stats, because nobody really knows what success means anymore. May you get the occasional 'thank you' from a reader or listener who learned something from your work or from an artist or musician who felt seen and heard through your journalism. Serve and love the music, and, to paraphrase Minnie Pearl from the Grand Ole Opry, I've found it will love you back.

24

FINALE
What we bring to music

While I was making the final edits in and final decisions about this book, I made my fourth trip to the Knoxville, TN, festival called Big Ears. It's a perfect name for what many regard as the nation's premiere showcase for progressive music from just about every genre. Conceived and owned by Knoxville native Ashley Capps, the concert promoter who created the rock phenomenon Bonnaroo in the early 2000s, Big Ears has been a focal point for artists from America and the world who live an ethos of unfettered creativity. It is always a thrill to experience music there that ranges so far with thousands of other fans. We musical cosmonauts like to be reminded that we're not alone.

Over my visits, I've enjoyed some of the most rapturous, challenging, and moving musical encounters of my life. A sampler, if you'll indulge me, to give an honest flavor: Jazz trio The Bad Plus, then with their original pianist Ethan Iverson, playing their own audacious arrangement of Stravinsky's *Rite of Spring*; World beat jazz from drummer Antonio Sánchez and his band Bad Hombre, including subsonic synthesized bass parts that shook my bones amid a stellar nursery of harmony; The pulsing, fluxing instrumental rock of Tortoise, a Chicago-born band I've adored on record for years but one I never thought I'd see live; Legendary guitarist Bill Frisell, one of my all-time favorite musicians, in a half dozen different settings, from the serene to the noisy; A quartet of beat-based sound alchemists led by major Los Angeles studio musicians Blake Mills (guitar) and

Pino Palladino (bass) executing complex music I'd fallen for on their recording *Notes With Attachments*; My cross-genre banjo hero Béla Fleck leading his virtuosic My Bluegrass Heart band as they played mesmerizing string band jazz from their Grammy Award-winning album; bass player and composer Meshell Ndegeocello performing profoundly grooving music with spoken word, composed as a tribute to James Baldwin. Whether you know these artists or not, this is the kind of variety, depth and integrity I'm always looking for.

The question at the heart of this book and one that I put to you now as we come to a close, is how big are your ears, and how big could they be? Can we imagine a Big Ears way of life?

Let's start by clarifying what that is not—i.e., some kind of requirement to build your musical world around atonal modern music, or stridently uncommercial music, or the "great masters" of any genre. After all, there are more than a dozen stages at Big Ears, and patrons find their own path among the scores of artists on the lineup. Just because I love Tortoise, Bill Frisell, and Antonio Sánchez doesn't mean you will, but if you chase music, you're going to fall in love—a lot. When I wrote about taste in Chapter 3, I emphasized that it's about cultivating your own unique aural universe, because only you can seek your inner musical self. Taste can't be taught, but it can be practiced and exercised. It evolves through exposure, knowledge, comparison and conversation. Taste leads us to (and is shaped by) social groups and community, whether Deadheads, opera buffs, bluegrass pickers, or metal freaks, and that's a good, healthy part of society. But try not to become monogamous about your scene. Play the field. Taste can be a path *away* from the easy choices served up by market forces and mainstream media toward esthetic and emotional territory that you can stake out as your own.

If our journeys toward richer lives in music are personal, we can find common purpose in looking out for the interests of music and musicality in general. That starts in my mind by honoring and centering musicians and by supporting institutions that support them. When you start noticing, music advocates and champions are everywhere—independent record stores, cultural foundations, advocacy and legal aid groups, music magazines, documentary filmmakers, and the vinyl revival. I think also of the many venues that support original creators in less popular genres, museums that celebrate and protect particular traditions and regions, and audio companies that engineer high quality home stereo gear for low prices. They're all part of overlapping ecosystems whose nourishment comes from fans, entrepreneurs, show promoters, media creators, and educators. Consumers can support any aspect of those symbiotic relationships, from switching to a streaming service that pays artists more, to joining a public or community radio station, to volunteering at a festival in your region.

Of course, "support" is our society's pleasant euphemism for spending, so let's talk about the essential topic of money. In Chapter 20, I described the outlines of a healthy music business, with many labels, supportive media, and a robust live music sector. It's a mixed bag these days. The concert business makes big money, but it's not broadly distributed. Live Nation has overwhelming control of America's stages and arenas, and its ownership of venues, ticketing, and promotion has put independent venues under stress. The company has a case to make for its utility and efficiency, and I know venue owners who work with it voluntarily and without deep anxiety, but this complex issue is beyond my scope.

On the recording and artist development front, I'm more optimistic. I follow several genres closely, and they keep producing more superb artists and recordings in each of them than most fans have bandwidth for. And we have a real-time, online accounting system that pays creators when people listen to them. It's not perfect, but it's kind of amazing when you think about it. You'll hear often that the streaming business isn't as lucrative as the days of record stores selling physical goods, but it's not that simple. The entire world experienced a digital revolution that overthrew an entire empire of music, media, and entertainment. We came out the other side with fewer gatekeepers and more freedom for artists. And it's no small thing that music, unlike newspapers and magazines, has recovered economically. The industry earns more in America annually than it did before the piracy crisis and the crash of the

CD as a unit of commerce. But there is a huge difference that fewer people talk about.

For most of the twentieth century, a devoted person could just about keep up with all of the worthwhile new releases coming from the record companies, and most of it got played on the radio. It was a system that depended on scarcity—a manageable number of artists promoted in broadcast form to a mass audience. That's over. Once people could affordably record at home on personal computers and upload their work to streaming services through distribution platforms, and when generations of young Americans were encouraged to chase their creative dreams (all good things), a historic wave of new players entered the marketplace. Barriers to entry fell, and now we have a kind of supply shock, with tens of thousands of new recorded tracks uploaded to the streaming services every day, crushing our capacity to critically filter out the good stuff. And when supply of a thing grows much faster than demand, you'll recall from economics, the thing is devalued. So when you hear that the streaming companies, especially the market leader Spotify, are ripping artists off, you have to consider that while the overall pie is growing, the number of artists chasing a slice of the pie has grown much faster.

My take on this is out of step with most people I hear from and read in the music business, where the central moral concern is that streaming rates are paltry and unfair. And I sincerely wish streaming paid artists more. But there is a lot to consider here. A third of a cent for a single spin heard by one person—the commonly cited approximation of Spotify's payout—is not far away from what commercial radio used to pay when it broadcast songs to many thousands of people at a time. Back then though, you had to be the fortunate few who got on the radio (and radio royalties then and now pay songwriters only, not artists). Today, any artist can distribute their music to the world, which is a huge step forward from 25 years ago. And while the old music business was often exploitive, the new one is, on balance, more transparent and fair, with more options for building an audience. Of course, artists on major labels get way more promotional investment and more return, as it ever was. But today, independent artists who actually get popular do make good money through streaming, provided they are smart about owning their own songs and masters. According to Spotify, in 2024, more than 70,000 artists received more than $10,000 through the platform. (And the platform pays out a reported 70% of its revenue to rights holders.) That, along with checks from the other streamers, t-shirts, tickets, etc., is the foundation of a middle class income (or better) for more artists than were even in the marketplace in 1980.

So let's keep it real. Piracy was a crisis, and streaming solved it. CDs and LPs are still available to those who love them. The elephant in the room that most don't talk about is that consumers aren't paying enough for these staggering online catalogs of music in the first place. Twelve dollars a month is a paltry subscription fee for all the music ever recorded, but if the streamers charge too much per month, many listeners would return to piracy. How do we encourage our fellow citizens to pay more for the magic of music? As you can tell, I believe broad campaigns of music appreciation would help. Not enough voices are beating the drum for the value of music, so legions of people treat it like fast food. But hey, you pay for food, and for shelter and for clothes, and you should pay for music, even if channels are open for you to obtain it for next to nothing. The options are many. Build digital downloaded music into your listening diet, and buy albums on platforms like Bandcamp, where you can buy CDs and LPs too. Whether physical formats are your thing or not, you can buy merchandise from artist websites, for that is the single biggest boost to the bottom line of artists you believe in, short of a cash grant, which you should consider as well. The value system I pursue and promote is simple: Stream to discover. Buy what you love.

If this sounds like I'm a supporter of Spotify, far from it. It has been a terrible company for music overall, a net loss for musicality, and I would love to see its staggering 260 million subscribers abandon it for the better options out there. Its corporate model and artist pay aside, I dislike Spotify because it treats music like generic audio content, not an art form to be explored. Despite years of promises, it streams only compressed files, so it sounds bad. It has paid staggering retainers to star podcasters, which draw attention away from music. It leverages the power of playlists to coerce artists into accepting a lower royalty rate for privileged positioning. According to a recent book by Liz Pelly, *The Mood Machine: The Rise of Spotify and the Costs of the Perfect Playlist*, it's polluting its playlists with royalty-free generic music. And generally speaking, over 20 years, this market leader has done nothing to build a world of music exploration, education, and discovery for its users. Besides brief artist bios, it doesn't offer musician credits, liner notes, reviews, or linked information that could help a young person "connect the dots" and develop their taste. Tidal and Apple Music have added some credits in recent years, but they're still so far from what they could be.

A few years ago, I discovered an application called Roon that organizes my stored digital music and my streaming collection (from Tidal) with metadata and essays from AllMusic and Wikipedia. Most noteworthy albums have individual reviews, and all names are hyperlinked, so I can search for the work of a given bass player or songwriter or producer. I can tag albums or songs into collections, like I do with my CDs and LPs. It's like having a music museum on my tablet, phone, and computer, controlling my high-fidelity sound system, or piping it into my car. This is what young music fans should grow up with, not Spotify's soporific spreadsheet of artists, albums, and songs. Roon costs extra, and I feel it's worth it. Yet there's nothing in Roon that the streamers couldn't develop as a service for their subscribers and the artists. Instead, the streamers cultivate passive listening and trap people in algorithmic boxes.

While I'm on a rant, I must address possibly the gravest threat to musicality we face—one that wasn't on anybody's radar at all when this book got started. I'm referring to the feverish desire of certain techno utopians and profiteers to foist upon us generative AI music. Artificial Intelligence has its pros and cons, and certain tools for producing, arranging, transcribing, filtering choice, or prompting songs seem harmless enough. But generative AI—"making songs" from a few prompts—is a sinister, anti-musical scam. One leading company says it's "building a future where anyone can make great music." Another says "we are deeply committed to empowering artists." These are lies. Typing words and letting a supercomputer remix millions of dubiously sourced recordings into a series of sounds that resembles music is not *making* music. It's not writing a song or working out how that reflects who you are. It is a simulacrum—a soul-sucking fakery. Most media outlets frame this evolving story around whether AI music is "as good as" human-made music, but that's a morally bankrupt question. If a human doesn't make it, it's not music as far as I'm concerned or as far as this book is concerned. Insta-songs with energy-wasting AI strikes me more like an act of violence, because we are not lacking for great or even mediocre music. Tools to further flood the marketplace with mass-produced plagiarism are not something any real musician I've ever known is excited about. There may be some ethical use cases for AI music—perhaps telephone hold tracks or hotel lobby warbling—but beware of any business promising you can "make music" without effort. I think this is nothing less than where the battle for Team Human is won or lost.

Speaking of battles, I'd also suggest that while music can and should be a source of emotional catharsis and a friend in tough times for all of us personally, it's also a powerful anti-venom for the hateful, coercive, and divisive politics that have sadly roared back in the US and other countries in recent years. Authoritarians, fundamentalists, and religious zealots despise music. They outlaw it. They raise their children to never hear it—or anything beyond manipulative and soulless forms of musical propaganda. Music to my mind can't be honestly made without empathy, dignity, and above all, freedom. Music empowered and reflected America's great Civil Rights struggle because done right, it's an art that thrives in democracy and that calls on society to always do more and better. That doesn't mean you have to hold certain policy views or worship or vote in any certain way to be a deeply musical person. But the creation and reception of music does, in my heart and mind, benefit from what writer David Foster Wallace called a Democratic Spirit, defined as "one that combines rigor and humility, i.e., passionate conviction plus a sedulous respect for the convictions of others."

My natural optimism and my faith in people, even in the face of some nasty dragons out there, is sustained in large part by the humanity and goodwill I witness on a weekly basis coming from today and tomorrow's most compelling musicians. In Americana, jazz, classical, and beyond, I see veterans teaching and young people opening up to new information and new possibilities. I see culture-keepers of all ages representing Appalachia with banjos, and Bay Area jazz with steel pan drums, and Louisiana Cajun music with triangles and accordions. I see emerging talents work together, bolster one another, include outsiders and newcomers, and share trials and troubles in ways that are healthy and ennobling. When I see a 14-year-old mandolin prodigy on the Grand Ole Opry, a media-savvy twentysomething jazz vibraphonist sharing her concert tours and job issues on Instagram, a conductor explaining the purpose and design of a symphony to school kids, or young Black musicians reclaiming and reframing the banjo, I see the future I want to live in.

So music will abide. It's a wonder of the world. It's been my constant companion, my catharsis, my therapist, my community, my livelihood, and virtually my religion at times (in a dance with my passion for cosmology and physics). And yet I know many people who listen more, play more, attend more shows, know more, and die inside over the right song more than I ever will. I wasn't any kind of musical savant—just an American guy born in the 1960s with two ears and a supportive family. I believe sincerely that if I can catch this fever and get as much pleasure out of mere sound as I have, then anyone can. Almost all of us are musical. And I've never seen any downside to embracing and cultivating this particular art form and life force.

Listen attentively to a variety and abundance of music made by people who put art before commerce.

And if it calls you, make music of any genre that you love with any instrument that sounds good to your ears. Practice. Play. Share. Perform. Give and receive applause. You deserve it. I wish you harmony.

SOURCE NOTES AND FURTHER READING

While this book only touches on the neuroscience of listening and the physics of sound, my journey from loving certain kinds of music to my meta-interest in how music shapes people and society started with two books explicitly about those subjects. My late friend and journalism mentor Merit Kimball gave me a book for my birthday in my 20s that changed my outlook. *Measure for Measure: A Musical History of Science* (1994) by Thomas Levenson introduced me to the construction of our western scale, the physics of instrument building, the development of synthesizers, and much more. The other, which I came upon a few years later, was *Music, the Brain, and Ecstasy: How Music Captures Our Imagination* (1997) by Robert Jourdain. It was my first exposure to aural perception and musical cognition, and despite it being early on in the musical neuroscience revolution, it helped me appreciate how and why I was so moved by melody, harmony, and rhythm. I am indebted to this volume as well for much of the ladder structure of this book. Later came the famous *This Is Your Brain On Music: The Science of a Human Obsession* by Daniel Levitin (2006), a key source of information and inspiration as I worked on *Musicality*. I also draw on the best-selling Oliver Sacks book *Musicophilia: Tales of Music and the Brain* (2007), a remarkable compendium of case studies of people's varied musical perception.

I was inspired and guided as well by certain classics of the music appreciation genre. The concept of "listening for" is adapted from Aaron Copland's 1939 book *What to Listen for in Music*. While its chapters addressing musical form will have more minutiae than most are seeking, the first nine chapters are full of timeless insights. More up to date is Rob Kapilow's *All You Have to Do is Listen: Music from the Inside Out* (2008). This one has a companion web site with interactive tools to follow works note by note. Many people know David Byrne's 2012 book *How Music Works*. It's not as comprehensive as its title suggests, but it is a fascinating ramble through different eras and scenes. While I don't quote him directly, I did make frequent use of *Why You Like It: The Science & Culture of Musical Taste* (2019) by Nolan Gasser, the man who developed Pandora's Music Genome Project, the architecture behind one of the best music recommendation algorithms. While I disagree with some of the premises behind his chapters on taste and genre, it's a marvelous reference book for music theory and structure. And a book that came out during my work that reminded me of the spirit of my own is *This Is What It Sounds Like: What the Music You Love Says About You* (2022) by recording engineer and neuroscientist Susan Rogers with Ogi Ogas.

My collection of books about sound and philosophy informed Chapter 2, especially the seminal work *The Soundscape: Our Sonic Environment and the Tuning of the World* (1993) by R. Murray Schafer. The Canadian composer and theorist writes movingly about our aural world, bidding us "to listen, analyze, and make distinctions." Another favorite is *The Listening Book: Discovering Your Own Music* (2011) by composer W.A. Mathieu. This one's more meditative and poetic, and I turn to it regularly for reminders about the rewards of being aurally awake. Also in this vein is *The Third Ear: On Listening to the World (1992)* by Joachim-Ernst Berendt, in which I've made many underlines in over the years. It draws on sociology, anthropology, historiography and other fields to describe what we lose when we privilege the eye over the ear.

While space won't allow me to cite any of the music biographies I've gleaned insights from, I do want to recommend a few broad histories of various kinds of music. General readers may enjoy the works of New Yorker music critic Alex Ross. His 2007 book *The Rest Is Noise: Listening to the 20th Century* is a highly readable history of modern composed music, a grand revolution that is far more accessible than most imagine. While *Listen To This* from 2010 is more broad, with thought-provoking essays on music across time and genre, from the

Renaissance to Radiohead. In my 30s, I found two books that helped me develop a more critical appraisal of pop and rock music than the hype I usually saw in magazines. One was *The Rise and Fall of Popular Music* (1995) by Donald Clarke, which found a through-line from old folk and balladry through big band and popular song to the commercial rock era. I appreciated his courage in calling out weak music and shallow, self-indulgent veins of pop. The other was *Hole in Our Soul: The Loss of Beauty and Meaning in American Popular Music* (1994) by *Wall Street Journal* writer Martha Bayles. It's a polemic that takes a stand for the integrity of the blues and against the degrading commercialization of the post-MTV era. It goes too far and made me want to argue with her. But it demonstrates some clear and passionate thinking on behalf of musical values that suffered in modern culture.

Jazz and its story rooted in the blues has been central to my musical life and learning, and of the books referenced or alluded to in this book, I'd urge everyone to read *Blues People: Negro Music in White America* (1963) by Leroi Jones. I've read no other history or commentary that showed me a more authentic or informed point of view on where our American popular music comes from. I draw a lot of literary and scholarly inspiration from Whitney Balliett, jazz critic for the *New Yorker* for the entire second half of the 20th century. The best single volume is *Collected Works: A Journal of Jazz 1954-2000*, published in 2000. More directly instructive are *What To Listen For In Jazz* (1997) by Barry Kernfeld and *How To Listen To Jazz* (2016) by Ted Gioia, one of my favorite contemporary music writers and cultural critics. In several places, I directly quote Wynton Marsalis, one of the great jazz advocates of my lifetime, and his 2008 book *Moving to Higher Ground: How Jazz Can Change Your Life.* In the course of researching my chapters on rhythm, I came upon *Kick It: A Social History Of The Drum Kit* (2020) by Matt Brennan, an enthralling journey through 20th century drumming.

The chapters on resonance and audio were informed by a long-time favorite book of mine about the evolution of recording and the philosophy of sound reproduction by Greg Milner called *Perfecting Sound Forever: An Aural History of Recorded Music* (2009). A good complement is *Playback: From the Victrola to MP3, 100 Years of Music, Machines, and Money* (2005) by Mark Coleman. Also important to these aspects of the book were *Temperament: How Music Became a Battleground for the Great Minds of Western Civilization* (2001) by Stuart Isacoff and *Piano: The Making Of A Steinway Concert Grand* (2006) by New York Times reporter James Baron. And to the authors of the many wonderful musician biographies I've read and the makers of the many documentaries, concert films and smart YouTube videos that have shown me new ways of thinking about music, I say thank you.

ABOUT THE AUTHOR

Craig Havighurst has been playing music since he was seven and trying to figure out how and why music works for almost as long. For more than twenty-five years, he's been covering the art, tech, and commerce of music from Nashville, TN, as a reporter, author, filmmaker, and broadcaster. Since 2016, he's been Editorial Director for WMOT Roots Radio 89.5 FM, where he hosts the weekly interview show *The String*, covering "culture, media, and American music." He has reported for NPR, WPLN-FM, *The Wall Street Journal*, *Acoustic Guitar*, *No Depression*, and other magazines. As staff music writer at the daily *Tennessean* from 2000-2004, he won the Charlie Lamb Award for Excellence In Country Music Journalism. Craig was the senior producer and co-host for *Music City Roots*, a nationally syndicated weekly live radio show and public TV series that ran from 2009 to 2018. He is also the author of *Air Castle of the South: WSM and the Making of Music City*, which documented for the first time how Nashville was transformed by one of the nation's greatest radio stations. He's the proud husband of Taylor and father of Lu.

ABOUT THE PUBLISHER

The Sager Group was founded in 1984. In 2012 it was chartered as a multimedia content brand, with the intent of empowering those who create art—an umbrella beneath which makers can pursue, and profit from, their craft directly, without gatekeepers. TSG publishes books; ministers to artists and provides modest grants; and produces documentary, feature, and commercial films. By harnessing the means of production, The Sager Group helps artists help themselves. For more information, please see TheSagerGroup.net.

MORE BOOKS FROM THE SAGER GROUP

*Meeting Mozart: A Novel Drawn from
the Secret Diaries of Lorenzo Da Ponte*
by Howard Jay Smith

*The Swamp: Deceit and Corruption in the CIA
An Elizabeth Petrov Thriller (Book 1)*
by Jeff Grant

Chains of Nobility: Brotherhood of the Mamluks (Book 1-3)
by Brad Graft

Death Came Swiftly: Novel About the Tay Bridge Disaster of 1879
by Bill Abrams

A Boy and His Dog in Hell: And Other Stories
by Mike Sager

Eat Wheaties: A Novel
by Michael Kun

Goodbye, Sweetberry Park: A Novel
by Josh Green

Lifeboat No. 8: Surviving the Titanic
by Elizabeth Kaye

Hunting Marlon Brando: A True Story
by Mike Sager

The Sing Sing Follies (A Maximum-Security Comedy): And Other True Stories
by John H. Richardson

Who She Was: My Search for my Mother's Life
By Samuel G. Freedman

See our entire library at TheSagerGroup.net_

THE SAGER GROUP

Artifex Te Adiuva

www.ingramcontent.com/pod-product-compliance
Lightning Source LLC
Chambersburg PA
CBHW021710120626
46545CB00004B/1499